BRIDIE, J.

A 822·91
BR

Colonel Wotherspoon BR1

**This book is to be returned on or before
the last date stamped below.**

2 B 7/93

COLONEL WOTHERSPOON

AND OTHER PLAYS

COLONEL WOTHERSPOON

AND OTHER PLAYS BY

JAMES BRIDIE

With a Preface

LONDON
CONSTABLE & CO LTD

LONDON
PUBLISHED BY
CONSTABLE AND COMPANY LTD.
10-12 ORANGE STREET W.C.2

•

INDIA *and* PAKISTAN
ORIENT LONGMANS LTD.
BOMBAY   CALCUTTA   MADRAS

•

CANADA
LONGMANS, GREEN AND COMPANY
TORONTO

PRINTED IN GREAT BRITAIN BY
LOWE AND BRYDONE PRINTERS LIMITED, LONDON, N.W.10

CONTENTS

PREFACE

At one time I intended to write a preface apologising for this book. I intended to explain how a person whose whole artistic soul delighted in directing the antics of performing fleas might find himself willed by the Forces to be an impresario of elephants. I intended to instance Mr. Drinkwater and Mr. Shaw as proof that even serious dramatists are entitled to their sportive occasions. I intended this and a good deal of other solemn foolishness until I re-read in proof the four domestic comedies that compose the book.

It is now quite clear that I was suffering from ingrowing snobbery of the worst type. I was ashamed of my children because they hadn't been produced in London. Possibly I was ashamed also of their manners and morals. My newspaper cuttings tell me that I am an amateurish but edifying dramatist. I hoped to remedy the first by close study of the best authorities. The second, I felt, invested me with a sacred duty. These little plays, I could not help thinking—and if I could have helped thinking it, the local Press took pains to remind me—were not sound professional pieces of craftmanship; nor was their moral a clear illuminant to the earnest beholder. I must therefore introduce them with a cautious mixture of offensiveness and truckling with the idea of crippling or disarming any criticism that might come their way.

As I have suggested, I am not in the least disposed to write any such nonsense now. As to London, it is a very large place and contains a great many very intelligent people. It is the capital of the civilised world. But, even if one assumes a respect for the civilised world and its capital one does not necessarily feel, the fact that a play has not been produced in London does not mean that it is not fit to be produced there or anywhere else. Plays are produced in London for a great variety of reasons, one of the least of these being that they are good plays. It is true that the only two London managers whom I know really well do, in fact, produce plays for the sole reason that they think them good. These two men have lost a great deal of money because of this eccentricity, and I cannot believe that their example is generally followed. At hazard I should say that the herd instinct, the sex in-stinct and what is called the compulsion psychosis are re-sponsible for the presentation of most London plays and that the intrinsic merit of the works is only incidental.

If these things are true of the plays that are presented, it is equally true that the plays that are not presented have taken a fall from powerful forces over which their author has seldom any control. A little while ago a play had small chance of seeing the West End footlights if it was not about the Brontës. Now, *Hamlet*, *The Misanthrope*, *She Stoops to Conquer* are not about the Brontës and no sane man thinks any the worse of them for that. Please understand that this instance does not contain anything " derogatory " to London managers. It is as much as a playwright's living is worth to maintain a respect for managers, and, besides, the London manager is as fond of a good play as you and I are. What is wrong is that he is under the rule of a number of artistic necessities. One of these is the necessity for reproducing as nearly as possible the play with which another manager has scored a success.

Another is his dignity, which makes it necessary for him to refuse at least one play from an established dramatist every fortnight and forbids him to present a play at a smaller initial cost than £10,000. Another is his economic sense which prevents him from presenting any play not by an established dramatist or costing anything at all to produce.

[viii]

Then the theatre bars, the platonic friendships of the backer, the state of the playreader's digestion, the good-will of the Geoplanistic, or Flat-Earthist, community, the loves and hates of newspaper proprietors have to be considered. Obviously these, and other, higher refinements of the " show business " are outside the playwright's sphere of activity. He may well have composed a neat, well-made, pretty piece of entertainment, capable of interesting and amusing and exciting an intelligent audience for a couple of hours. It is not his fault if, unlike the Snark, it cannot be served with greens and is useless for striking a light.

In my earlier coy and bashful state of mind I wondered what could be said in a preface to withdraw attention from the amateurishness or technical deficiencies of these plays. It is a terrible thing to face the public handicapped by an insufficiency of what is called technique; for, you must know, if the writer of words intended to be spoken on the stage has the gift of prophecy and understands all knowledge and all mysteries and though he has all faith so that he could remove mountains and has not technique, he is nothing.

I find, after careful and prolonged consideration, that these plays are not so technically negligible as I had been led to believe. Indeed, regarded simply as displays of technique they are rather good. I wonder, at times, whether the five million odd lecturers on the Drama, now ravening through the country and using the word " technique " as freely as they use the word " definitely," have any clear idea what it means. At all events, these plays played very smoothly, they gave continuous pleasure to their audiences, they kept bronchitis in the stalls completely in check, they were, I am assured, easy to memorise and speak, the actors were happy in rehearsal and confident in performance. If anyone thinks he can accomplish that without technique, let him try. Technique (forgive me) is the mastery of material and is commonly attained by years of practice. It has nothing to do with the blind adherence to a few arbitrary rules. Which of us hasn't sat yawning in a theatre watching the rules—there are only about twenty of them—being applied like postage stamps on circulars? It is really very dreadful that, at this time of day, such performances should be held up to us as examples of technique. The only sound evidence that an actor or a producer or a playwright possesses technique is his ability to hold an audience. This faculty is seldom found in amateurs and is not easy to attain. It cannot be attained by studying lists of theatrical tricks, old and new.

I do not apologise for these plays on whatever standard of professionalism they are judged. *What it is to be Young*, indeed, shows a stage overcrowded with running hares. *The Dancing Bear* is an unsuccessful experiment in chorus work. The chorus has oozed to the front and swamped the leaders. *The Girl who did not want to go to Kuala Lumpur* is almost unintelligible to anyone unfamiliar with Highland drama and romance. It is a burlesque fore-runner of my equally unintelligible *Marriage is no Joke*. *Colonel Wotherspoon* takes a serious risk in the bare sim-plicity of its plot. But they all, without exception, play well, and that is more than can be said for a good many more pretentious dramas. They have owed, in their theatrical presentation, a great deal to their producers and actors; but a playwright who does not trust his actors and take all the advice he can from his producer is a fool. He is a staff officer who arranges the battle entirely from his office and he is usually beaten.

The other matter is the absence of a moral, and that is difficult for a Scotsman to condone. My West End plays have all had morals and I could not help feeling a little nudist when the publication of these plays was first bruited. I think of each of them, when it was performed in Scot-land, it was said that the first Great Scottish Play had yet to be written. The truth is that Scotland does not yet deserve a great play. She has not yet expiated her scandalous treatment of the Theatre in the past. She is due, however, a little amusement; and the only Scottish dramatist who has reached the very first rank (if we except Ben Jonson) doesn't bother himself much with morals or greatness. Indeed, if we dive for a moral in any one of the plays of Sir James Barrie, we are running the risk of a very horrid surprise. I do not cling to his mantle, but I stand, for once in a way, a cabin boy in his galley and I echo him in the sentiment.

"What's all this ado about edification? Are you pleased or are you not?"

J. B.

Glasgow, 1934.

COLONEL WOTHERSPOON
OR THE FOURTH WAY OF GREATNESS
A COMEDY

" Some are born great; some achieve greatness;
and some have greatness thrust upon them;
while some write Best Sellers."

*The Characters and Incidents in
this play are entirely imaginary.*

DEDICATED TO
MICHAEL SADLEIR

This play was first presented by the Scottish National Players in the Lyric Theatre, Glasgow, on March 23, 1934, with the following Cast:

MRS. KELLOCK	. . . .	Meg Buchanan.
ARCHIE KELLOCK	. . .	James Urquhart.
TOM PERRY	. . . .	Hal Stewart.
EMILY PERRY	. . . .	Jean Taylor Smith.
MRS. KISHMUL	. . . .	Enid Hewit.
DEREK PUTNEY	. . .	Sheridan Aitchison.
REGINALD DEVEREUX	. . .	G. Hervey.
AN ANNOUNCER	. . .	Andrew Stewart.

The Play was produced by Andrew Stewart.

COLONEL WOTHERSPOON

ACT I

The KELLOCKS' *living-room. It is still daylight. Tea has been had and, to it, sausage-rolls.* MRS. KELLOCK *is settling at the fireside to her sewing and a journal called the "British Weekly."*

MRS. KEL. Aye, well. There's the sun at last. Better late than never. It is going to be quite a pleasant evening, after all.

ARCHIE. I don't know what to think.

MRS. KEL. Surely, Archie, it must be obvious even to you that it's going to be a fine evening. Look at it. After all that rain. The sunshine.

ARCHIE. Eh? Oh, yes.

MRS. KEL. There's all nature smiling under the bountiful beams of Providence and you say you don't know what to think. Really, Archie.

ARCHIE. Oh, of course, that, yes. But I didn't mean the weather. (*He begins to clear away.*)

MRS. KEL. Well, dear, what did you mean?

ARCHIE. What we were talking about at tea-time; it keeps running in my head.

MRS. KEL. Archie, dear, you must never, never allow a subject to run in your head after it is closed. What is the good of closing a subject if you allow it to run in your head after it is closed? Put the tea-things on the lobby table. Teeny will take them when she comes home from church.

[ARCHIE *drops a china sugar-bowl. It breaks.* ARCHIE *picks up the pieces of china and sugar.*]

ARCHIE. Oh, bother.

MRS. KEL. Broken?

ARCHIE. Yes. I'm afraid it is.

MRS. KEL. (*sighing*). I thought so.

Archie. I'm sorry, Mother.

> [*A silence, during which* ARCHIE *takes the tray to the lobby and returns.*]

ARCHIE. I'm sorry.

MRS. KEL. What is done cannot be undone. We must bear the most terrible misfortunes as best we may. It's the Lord's will, Archie, the Lord's will. But I wish I could persuade you to be careful.

ARCHIE. I'm sorry, Mother. I was worried. I wasn't thinking what I was doing.

MRS. KEL. You must always think of what you are doing, Archie. Always, always.

ARCHIE. I was a bit upset.

MRS. KEL. I know, Archie. Mother knows. Mother understands.

> [*She holds, over her shoulder, a hand for him to take. He notices it after a bit and takes it.*]

How strong you are, Archie. You forget my rheumatism.

ARCHIE. I'm sorry, Mother.

MRS. KEL. I know. I know. You only meant to be affectionate, but it was agonisingly painful. . . . What was I saying? Oh, yes. Mother understands. You know that, don't you?

ARCHIE. I know, Mother. But at the same time . . .

MRS. KEL. But at the same time I was very much grieved and surprised to hear you speak in that manner about your Uncle Tom. Very, very grieved and very, very surprised.

ARCHIE. I couldn't help it, Mother. I wouldn't mind having Uncle Tom for a sleeping partner if he didn't talk in his sleep. I can't help it.

[6]

MRS. KEL. Oh, but you must help it, Archie, dear. It is a great, great privilege, now your dear father has gone to Heaven, to have a man of Uncle Tom's—hem—mature judgment and—hem—organising ability and—hem—knowledge of the world to guide you in our little business. A great, great privilege.

ARCHIE. I suppose it is.

[*He takes writing materials and a large red dictionary from a shelf and puts them on the table.*]

MRS. KEL. Youth at the prow and wisdom at the helm. What did you say?

ARCHIE. I said I suppose it is.

MRS. KEL. Suppose it is what?

ARCHIE. I suppose it's a privilege.

MRS. KEL. What an extraordinary thing to say. You suppose? You don't suppose it at all. St. Augustine said, I think, " I do not suppose. I know." Or was it Huxley?

ARCHIE. I don't know, Mother.

MRS. KEL. And I should have thought that, considering Uncle Tom is Emily's guardian and considering that you and Emily . . .

ARCHIE. I wasn't discussing that side of it. It was purely the business side of it I was discussing. Emily has nothing to do with it. At least, well, not directly.

MRS. KEL. A-a-a-h. Quite. But indirectly I am afraid my boy thinks a very, very great deal of that side of it. I know. I know. Come and sit by me and we'll just have a weeny little cosy chat about that.

[*She indicates a horrid little footstool.* ARCHIE *recoils.*]

ARCHIE. No, Mother, if you don't mind. Not just now, Mother. I've got some things to do.

MRS. KEL. Things to do? Things? On the Lord's Day?

ARCHIE. It isn't work, Mother. At least, it's the

Novel. I feel to-night somehow as if I could get a move on with chapter thirty-six.

MRS. KEL. Oh, well, I suppose it is only natural that you should prefer chapter thirty-six to your own mother . . .

ARCHIE. No, I don't, Mother. You know quite well I don't. But there are times you feel . . . well . . . that you can *create*. I'll not do it. I'll put the things away if you want me to.

MRS. KEL. Not at all. You are your own master. I am only a poor old lonely woman.

ARCHIE. Mother, please don't take it like that. I feel I'm . . . well . . . I'm . . . I've got hold of something really big at last. I want to. . . . Don't be offended, Mother.

MRS. KEL. I'm not in the least offended. (*She weeps silently.*)

ARCHIE. Mother. Don't. I tell you it's big stuff. I'm writing with my whole soul this time. It's not like these correspondence college exercises. It's like—like Dickens, or Thackeray, or Priestley. It'll make—make our fortune.

MRS. KEL. (*smiling wanly*). Enthusiastic boy. Castles in the air.

ARCHIE. You get £39 for every thousand copies that are sold and often they sell fifty thousand if the book takes. And there's talkie rights, and dramatisation rights and I don't know what. It could easily run into five figures or more. The royalties are on a sliding scale, you know. I know of a fellow they say got £70,000 for one book alone.

MRS. KEL. For a first book, Archie?

ARCHIE. Yes, of course. And then there's lecture tours in the United States.

MRS. KEL. Well, well, darling. If the Lord hadn't wanted you to write on Sunday, He wouldn't have inspired you, would He? Go ahead, my son. Man must work and woman must weep.

ARCHIE.   How do you spell chiaroscuro, Mother?   I can't find it in this Dictionary.

MRS. KEL.   C-h-a . . . no, c-h-i-a- . . .

ARCHIE.   Oh.   I was looking under K.   I suppose that's why I couldn't find it.   Don't bother.   Here it is.

[*He writes and* MRS. KELLOCK *holds her tongue for a minute and a half.*]

MRS. KEL.   We'll all be very proud of you if it's a success.

ARCHIE.   Yes, Mother.

MRS. KEL.   Emily will be a proud girl.

ARCHIE.   Yes, and we'll . . . She won't laugh at me then.

MRS. KEL.   Emily never laughs at my son.

ARCHIE.   Oh, yes, she does.   She can't help it.   I don't know what a brainy girl like Emily sees in a chap like me.

MRS. KEL.   Emily is no doubt a very talented and accomplished girl.   She writes, I know.   I know perfectly well she is an M.A. of St. Andrews.   It is not for me to say anything about that.   It was her own poor mother's business.   I have no objection.   But if a girl begins to give herself airs about that sort of thing she might as well. . . . I don't know what she might as well do.

ARCHIE.   Mother, dear, you know perfectly well that Emily does not give herself . . .

MRS. KEL.   Don't interrupt me, darling, while I'm speaking.   I have never said it to anyone, never breathed it, but I was very, very much your poor father's superior both in education and in social position.   But I knew my duty.   I said to myself, it is my duty to make a home for the poor fellow.   Very well, then, I did my duty.   I think I made him happy.

ARCHIE.   Oh, you did, you did, Mother.

MRS. KEL.   My own boyal loy—I mean, loyal boy. Yes, well.   If Emily is the girl I think her, her only thought will be to make a home for my boy . . .

[9]

ARCHIE. Mother. I know there's something in what you say, but . . .

MRS. KEL. Something, Archie?

ARCHIE. Well, I don't mean. . . . It's hard to express it, really. . . . Mother, I don't think, perhaps, I've been quite honest in all I've said about—about my reasons for writing this book.

MRS. KEL. Oh, Archie! Dishonesty?

ARCHIE. Well, I mean. . . . I do think most people have more motives than one for doing a thing. I felt the impulse to write, all right; but part of it was to try to make a little extra to hurry on the time when Emily and I could settle down; and part of it was—oh, well—to raise myself to her level, if you see what I mean. To make myself worthy of her in a way.

MRS. KEL. But you're quite, quite worthy of her. An honest man's the noblest work of God.

ARCHIE. Yes, but more interesting, don't you think, if He adds a few extras?

MRS. KEL. That is very nearly profane, Archie-boy.

ARCHIE. I'm sorry, Mother. But, Mother, I come all over hot when Emily starts talking about Croce and Gide and people I can't seem to understand somehow. Even if she is so terribly decent about it. You see, she knows I've no time, what with the business and so on to . . . It gives me an inferiority complex. I lost confidence. Well, I thought, dash it, if I become an author myself, dash it, I don't need to wade through Gide.

MRS. KEL. I don't see why you need to anyway. I never heard of him.

ARCHIE. I know, Mother. But Emily and all the nibs think he's great. And . . .

MRS. KEL. It's getting quite dark, dear. Draw the curtains and switch on the light. Unless you'd like just to sit and talk by the firelight.

ARCHIE. No, Mother. Not to-night, if you don't mind. I want to get on.

MRS. KEL.   Oh, well. A wise mother knows she can't keep her children's love for ever.

ARCHIE.   Oh, Mother.

MRS. KEL.   Draw the curtains, dear.

ARCHIE (*at the window*).   Oh, hello, here's Uncle Tom. I'll let him in.

[*He goes out and returns with* UNCLE TOM.]

UNCLE TOM.   Well, well, well, well. How are you, Bethia?

MRS. KEL.   Fairly well, thank you, Tom. Fair-lee well.

UNCLE TOM.   Woof. Good. How's business, Archie? I'm sorry I didn't let you know on Thursday I was buzzing off like that, old man, but I felt I had to have a break or bust. Sea air. Bucked me up wonderfully. Wonderfully. The sea's not the same, though. Even it's changing. Everything's changing. We're all getting damned well Americanised, that's what we're getting. Colonel Wotherspoon said the same thing to me in so many words last time I saw him. Very upset about it. Got a whisky-and-soda?

MRS. KEL.   Yes, Tom. We keep it for you. Archie and I never touch it.

UNCLE TOM.   Quite right, quite right. I seldom touch it myself. But it's a bit chilly these nights, and I find it's good for my kidneys. Thanks. Just a wee, wee drop. A sensation more. Thank you. Don't drown the miller. Aye. I'm quite sure you are perfectly capable of running the business in my absence, Archie.

MRS. KEL.   Oh, for a day or two I'm *sure* he can. He's such a conscientious boy. And it's bad economy to run yourself down, Tom. Things went all right, didn't they, Archie?

ARCHIE.   Yes. A batch of insulators came in, all the wrong sizes. And I couldn't find the specification.

[11]

UNCLE TOM. Eh? That's bad. That's bad. Method, my boy. Method. Now, I just this morning made a cutting from the *Sunday Express*. . . . Where is it? Ah, yes. . . . What's this now? . . . Oh, you'd better attend to that. (*He hands a letter to* ARCHIE.)

ARCHIE. This is the specification. Did you put through the order?

UNCLE TOM. Hey? Oh, very probably, very probably. I had a thousand and one little things to do before I buzzed off. I can't keep every damned thing in my head.

ARCHIE. But, good Heavens!

MRS. KEL. Archie! An oath.

ARCHIE. I'm sorry, Mother, but . . .

MRS. KEL. It's just what one would expect. One thing leads to another. If you will talk business on the Lord's Day, why not go further?

UNCLE TOM. I quite agree. I'm no killjoy Puritan, God knows. But I think we should draw the line somewhere. Sunday is and should be a day of rest.

ARCHIE. Yes. And for some people so are Monday and Tuesday and Wednesday and Thursday . . .

MRS. KEL. Archie, darling, what is the matter with you? Really, I. . . . You haven't brought Emily with you, Uncle Tom?

UNCLE TOM. She's buzzing round later. Popped in to Miss Wilkie's to return a book she borrowed. And you know what these women are. Clack, clack, clack. Blether, blether, blether. Let them get on the chat and a thousand years in their sight is but as yesterday when it is passed or as a watch in the night.

MRS. KEL. You're too hard on us, Uncle Tom.

UNCLE TOM. Not a bit. Mind you, I think women are wonderful. The War and all that. But they will talk. They'll wade in and monopolise the conversation at the least opportunity, and ramble away, talking the most awful platitudes and telling you all sorts of things you haven't the remotest desire to hear, and on it goes with not the jot or a tittle of evidence of the least perception that time is valuable, to some people at any rate; and it's not the least use hinting or yawning or looking bored or at your watch or anything. On they go. And they pride themselves on being sensitive. Sensitive? Woof! Give me a rhinoceros . . .

MRS. KEL. Tom, will you excuse me for a few minutes? We have had—thehe—we have had an interesting family event here since we saw you last. Susan, you know.

UNCLE TOM. Susan? Do I know her?

MRS. KEL. Of course you do. She's had kittens. I must go and see if there is anything she wants. Have some more whisky.

UNCLE TOM. Thanks, Bethia. Yes. I'll help myself.

[*Exit* MRS. KELLOCK. ARCHIE *has begun to write.*]

Tadi-tadiddy-um-tum. Funny experience I had on Thursday. I had only a minute or two to catch the train, so I chucked my suitcase to a porter and ran like the devil to get a ticket, telling him to buzz the thing into a first smoker. I think it's really a bit of true economy to travel first. Good for business, too. You meet influential sort of blokes quite by accident if you travel first. I remember a very funny experience I had some years ago when I was buzzing down to Sheffield or Darlington or one of these places. Immaterial, anyhow. This bloke—quite a decent-looking middle-aged bloke, quietly dressed. You'd never notice him in a crowd. I'd come away without any matches. Imagine that. Five or six hours in the train and no matches. So I said, very civilly, "Excuse me, sir, could you oblige me with a light? I've come away without any matches, most unfortunately." Well, he gave me a match and we got on the chat. Most interesting fellow. I remember I was keen on currency at the time and he was most

interested. Well-informed, educated chap I thought.
He got off, I forget where, and I asked the dining-car
attendant who he was and he told me it was Sir Henry
Campbell Bannerman. Another very funny story. . . .
But, I forgot. I was telling you what happened on
Thursday. Where was I ?

[A bell rings. ARCHIE *gets up and goes out to answer it.*
UNCLE TOM *does not notice and drools on.]*

When I got to the platform, I found that the porter had
simply chucked my suitcase on the seat. So I said, " Put
it on the rack, please." And he said in a most impertinent
voice, I didn't like his tone at all, he said, " You can't put
it there, sir." So I said, " It's beside the point whether
I can or not," I said. " I'm asking you to do it." So he
got as red as a turkey-cock and muttered and mumbled
something about its being too heavy for the rack. So I
said, " Look here, my lad, I've travelled on this line for
the last thirty-five years," I said, " and this suitcase has
travelled with me . . . And what's more," I said, " I'm
an intimate friend of Colonel Wotherspoon, one of your
Directors," I said. Hey ? Where are

*[*ARCHIE *re-enters with* EMILY.]*

you ? That's damned fine manners, I must say! I
never in all my life . . . !

ARCHIE.   I'm sorry, Uncle Tom. Were you speaking
to me ?

UNCLE TOM.   As a matter of fact I was.

*[He helps himself to another drink and begins to sulk in
earnest.]*

ARCHIE.   Won't you take your hat off, Emily ?

EMILY.   No, no. I'm not going to wait.

ARCHIE.   I'm terribly sorry, Uncle Tom. What
were you saying ?

UNCLE TOM.   It doesn't matter.

ARCHIE.   Oh, well. Do take your hat off, Emily.

EMILY.   I believe I will.   I've got a little buzzing beast of a far-off headache.

ARCHIE.   Oh, I'm sorry.   Would you like an aspirin or anything?

EMILY.   It's all right.   It's nothing, really.   It may blow over altogether.

ARCHIE.   I'll put your hat in the hall.

EMILY.   No, no.   Don't bother.   It'll be quite all right there.   Please, Archie.

ARCHIE.   Sit down here.   Would you like a cushion?

EMILY.   Oh, Archie, you do make me feel a female.

ARCHIE.   I'm sorry.

EMILY.   Oh, no.   Don't be.   It's so good for me. Archie, how many times a day do you say you're sorry?

ARCHIE.   I don't know.

EMILY.   Do keep count some time.   I've a passion for statistics.

ARCHIE.   All right.   If you like.

UNCLE TOM.   Woof.   If that's your idea of bright conversation, give me one of those places where the Johnnies there all take vows of silence.   A Trappist Monastery.   That's it.

EMILY.   If I had one, Uncle Tom, I shouldn't dream of giving it to you.   I'd go and keep house for it.

UNCLE TOM.   Woof! (*He sulks again.*)

EMILY.   Oh, look!   We're in the way.   You're busy.

ARCHIE.   Oh, no.   Not at all.   It was only—well, it was only a little thing I was doing.

EMILY.   It looks pretty formidable. . . . May I look?

ARCHIE.   Well, no, I mean . . . I'd rather. . . . Not just yet.

EMILY.   Righto.   I say, what is your mother's objection to the evening sky?

ARCHIE.   I don't understand. . . .

EMILY.   You shut it out rather early, don't you?   I think it's cruel just at the time when the sky becomes so friendly.

[15]

ARCHIE. Mother thought the twilight was bad for my eyes.

EMILY. But so good for your soul, don't you think ?

ARCHIE. Yes. It's the loveliest time of the day, isn't it.

UNCLE TOM. Woof.

EMILY. Uncle Tom, dear, don't make those menagerie sounds. Have your eyes been bothering you ?

ARCHIE. No, no. Not particularly. It was just writing such a lot and . . .

EMILY. What were you writing ? . . . Oh, I beg your pardon. It's a secret, isn't it ?

ARCHIE. In a way it is, yes. I'll tell you soon what it is. That is if . . . Oh, well.

EMILY. It's bad luck to be tied up with work on Sunday. Rain or no rain, I like to be out and about.

ARCHIE. Hiking ?

EMILY. Oh, no. I don't hike. I've got hideous knees.

ARCHIE. I think they're . . . I mean . . . No, I don't think so.   [*He offers a cigarette.*]

EMILY. Thank you. Men never seem to take the large unbiassed view about women's knees. They're horrid objects really.

ARCHIE. Well, I suppose . . .

[*Re-enter* MRS. KELLOCK.]

MRS. KEL. And what are you three talking about ?

UNCLE TOM. Three ? I like that. It's very good that. We've been listening to a blessed monologue.

MRS. KEL. How are you, Milly, dear ?

EMILY. Very well, Auntie, thank you.

[ARCHIE *puts away his manuscript.*]

MRS. KEL. Aren't you going to allow Emily to see your book ? I'm sure she'd love it.

EMILY. Your what ? Don't say you're writing a book.

[16]

MRS. KEL.   Now, if I didn't forget it was to be a great secret.

ARCHIE.   It doesn't matter, really.   I'd be glad of Emily's advice and help, really.

EMILY.   You sweet thing.   Never mind.   You remember I had a mastoid done ten years ago, Aunt Bethia ? I'll turn my deaf ear to what you said just now.   The Nelson touch.

UNCLE TOM.   Hey ?   What's that ?   Archie writing a book ?

EMILY.   Shut up, Uncle Tom.

UNCLE TOM (*truculently*).   What ?

EMILY.   Fermes ta boite.   This is none of your business.

UNCLE TOM.   I'm not altogether so sure of that.   I'm not the sort of man to be perpetually casting it up, but I happen to be Archie's senior partner in the business.   And I fail to see how a young man can give his work that undivided attention that is so necessary in these days of strenuous competition—woof—I say I fail to see it.   If he allows himself to be drawn aside towards—woof—literary composition.   Literature is all very well, but it is apt to become an all too absorbing hobby.   Colonel and I were talking the other day of a mutual friend who . . .

EMILY.   Yes, and he was led astray, wasn't he, darling ? What a pity you didn't warn him.

UNCLE TOM.   I did warn him.   I said . . .

EMILY.   But it was all of no avail. . . . Darling Uncle Tom, don't go on being of no avail.   It's so dreadful for a man with your blood pressure to be continually of no avail.   Don't risk it again, dear.

UNCLE TOM.   See here, Milly, I've stood about enough of your insolence for one night. . . . Please remember who you're speaking to.

EMILY.   Yes.   Isn't it so pedantic to say " whom " and to avoid ending your sentences with a preposition ?

ARCHIE.   Oh, aren't you supposed to end your sentences with a preposition?

EMILY.   No.   Not if you can help it.   Why?

ARCHIE.   Gosh.   I've just done it.

EMILY.   Where?

ARCHIE.   In Chapter Thirty-six.

EMILY.   Oh, do let me see!

ARCHIE.   Wait a minute.   Here it is.   "Was this the pure, fresh innocent girl that in days of yore—how long ago they seemed—he had walked out with?"   Is that wrong?

EMILY.   Well, it depends.   Was it the pure, fresh young person?

ARCHIE.   Yes.   It was, as a matter of fact.   But she had been through a lot since then.   You see, when she was singing in the cabaret at Buenos Aires . . .

EMILY.   What was she singing?

ARCHIE.   It doesn't say.   But I mean, there was that and. . . . Oh, a good lot more.   You see the object of the story—it's a kind of parable—the object is to show that whatever happens to you *externally*, if you see what I mean, your soul may keep all right through it all; I mean it's, well, it's sort of *integrity*, if you understand.

UNCLE TOM.   Sounds like damned drivel to me.

EMILY.   What the devil do you know about it?

MRS. KEL.   Emily, darling.   What a thing to say?

EMILY.   I can't help it, what right has he to . . .?

UNCLE TOM.   Well, what the devil does he know about Buenos Aires?

EMILY.   What the devil does it matter?

ARCHIE.   Emily, please.   It's not worth . . .

EMILY.   Oh, I know, but I can't stand these fat ignorant pigs who can hardly read setting themselves up to judge any work of art.   I don't care what it is.   It infuriates me.   I'm sorry.   I'm behaving badly.   Let's go back to the last remark but one.   Sit down, Uncle Tom.   I've apologised.

UNCLE TOM. I didn't hear you.

EMILY. Didn't you? Well, we'll all sit down round the table—unless Uncle Tom would like me to stand in the corner—and Archie will read us some of his book if he wants to, and not if he doesn't want to. And we'll all keep quiet except Uncle Tom.

MRS. KEL. Yes, yes. We'll do that.

ARCHIE. I don't want to bore you, but there are one or two bits I'd like your advice about, now the cat's out of the bag.

[*All sit round the table except* UNCLE TOM.]

EMILY. What an unexpected boy you are!

ARCHIE. Oh, I don't know. They say everybody writes a book some time.

EMILY. What rot. Think of the manual labour alone. I've written three, but then I'm mad.

MRS. KEL. Oh, no, Emily.

EMILY. Yes. Quite mad. And all the publishers think so too. Go on, Archie.

ARCHIE. Where shall I begin? At the beginning?

EMILY. No. I hate beginnings. Let's turn it round three times and start where it opens. It's better fun that way.

MRS. KEL. Fun, Emily?

EMILY. It is rather fun, isn't it, Archie?

ARCHIE. Yes, in a way it is. . . . Chapter Twenty-seven. Wherein Toby Carteret . . .

EMILY. I wouldn't say " wherein."

ARCHIE. Oh? Why not?

EMILY. I don't know. Books that put wherein in the chapter headings are rather members of the O'Mine Family.

MRS. KEL. What is the O'Mine Family?

EMILY. Oh, Sweetheart o' Mine, Mother o' Mine, Solicitor o' Mine, heaps of them. Never mind. Go ahead, Author o' Mine.

ARCHIE. I'll leave it out if it sounds funny.

EMILY. No, don't. I'll blue pencil it afterwards.

MRS. KEL. I think it sounds beautiful.

ARCHIE. All right. Wherein Toby Carteret . . .

EMILY. Who is — (*she shudders slightly*) Toby Carteret?

ARCHIE. He's the hero. This is where he and One-Eyed Mo' the gipsy escape from Princetown and are lost on Dartmoor.

EMILY. Oh.

ARCHIE. Would daylight never come? It was as though all the fiends of the air had been unleashed and were ravening round them as they stumbled on through the rough marshy via dolorosa of the moor that seemed to clog and impede their every step. The sleet stung their faces as though they were being lashed by a million angry scorpions . . .

EMILY. I like "angry scorpions." Go on.

ARCHIE. Ever and anon a deafening peal of thunder rent the heavens, and from the rent issued forth a ghastly flash of lightning which illuminated the desolate prospect as with a light from some dread bale-fire.

UNCLE TOM. Woof. Stop a bit. Lightning always comes before thunder, you know.

EMILY. Of course he knows. Don't mind him, Archie. It's poetic licence.

UNCLE TOM. Ought to be dam' well endorsed.

EMILY. Shut up.

ARCHIE. The cry of a frightened grouse sounded like some lost soul in torment as it rose weirdly in the midnight air, sending cold shivers down the spines of the fugitives as they stumbled on, on, on. Ever the sleet and hail lashed furiously like a sheet of icy knives cutting through and through their threadbare clothing stamped with the broad arrow, badge of the felon. The roar of a mountain stream was heard on their right like the howl of an infuriated mob athirst for blood.

MRS. KEL. I think that's really very good. I can almost see the storm. That's very good, Archie.

EMILY. Um. Archie. I'll read it afterwards, of course, every word of it, but don't you think we could have a bit with a little less bad weather in it?

ARCHIE. Well, you see, there's a good deal of description of scenery and so on. I want to make the readers really feel they are there—leading the lives of the characters.

EMILY. Yes, yes. That's quite a good idea. But still . . . I say, let's turn it over again.

ARCHIE. Don't you like that passage?

EMILY. Well, it's awfully good in many ways. There's a remarkable lot of colour in it for a first attempt. But we'll have to go over it again, won't we? and deal with some of those clichés and things.

ARCHIE. What's a cleeshy?

EMILY. It's a sort of a word or a phrase or an idea that's gone threadbare like Toby's broad arrow uniform.

ARCHIE. Oh, yes. They said that in the correspondence course. I thought it was pronounced " cleish." I didn't think there were any in that bit.

EMILY. Oh, not *many*, dear. But they're always slipping in. Even in Derek Putney's novels you'll find lots. Go on from there in the new piece.

ARCHIE. Of course I don't pretend to be a Derek Putney . . .

MRS. KEL. I think this is much better than Derek Putney. I simply couldn't read his last book.

EMILY. Couldn't you? Go on.

ARCHIE. This is hardly a . . .

EMILY. Don't funk it.

ARCHIE. Oh, well. . . . She threw him a provocative glance from beneath her veiled lids. A hot wave of passion surged over him.

UNCLE TOM. That's better.

EMILY. Be quiet.

UNCLE TOM. I was only making a remark.

EMILY.   I know. I heard you.

ARCHIE.   Seldom had he imagined even in his wildest dreams anything so utterly, utterly desirable. He felt that just a little more and he would scarcely be answerable for his actions. This would never do, he thought desperately. "Keep a grip of yourself, Toby, old man," he hissed to himself between his clenched teeth, conscious the while of the leaping heart-beats pounding in his brain. He hardly dared look at her. With a swift but graceful gesture she unbound her coils of glorious hair, letting it fall, a nut-brown cascade shot here and there with amber light, round her shoulders, one of which had escaped from the modest covering afforded it by her somewhat shabby black gown. Something seemed to snap in Toby's brain. With a hoarse cry he caught her to him and crushed a rain of kisses on her provocatively parted lips. The sun shone.

That's the end of that chapter. Do you want to hear any more? There's a better bit a little further on.

MRS. KEL.   I'm not sure that I like that bit so well as the first bit you read, Archie. I suppose such things do happen, but I think it's so much nicer to pretend they don't.

ARCHIE.   I think, Mother, if you are writing about life, you ought to show it in all its aspects, pleasant and unpleasant. If you are really sincere, I mean. And if you've a Message, that makes it all right, doesn't it?

UNCLE TOM.   I don't see much wrong with that bit myself. I mean to say, any young fellow who's worth his salt kicks over the traces at times. I've no use for those praying blokes who haven't the guts to look at a girl's ankle. But what's the book all about, anyway?

ARCHIE.   This fellow, you see, lives in the country with his widowed mother in an old sort of tumbledown house, because they're not so well off as they once were and there's a sort of mystery about his father. And he makes up his mind when he is quite a kid that he'll go and find his father somewhere. And he's out riding one day and he meets this girl who lives in the village and there's a sort of mystery about her too, so they are sort of drawn together by that in a way. And she's awfully clever and literary and a good singer and dancer. And a fellow and other four fellows come down and kidnap her, and this fellow, Toby, kills one of the fellows. And then there's a trial and he gets ten years for justifiable homicide, and in the meantime these other fellows have got clean away with the girl. And she's been taken off to Buenos Aires and knocks about the world a bit, and gets a bit hard and bitter. And this fellow meets a gipsy called One-Eyed Mo' in prison—he's rather a fine character, a sort of lovable rascal. And they escape and fetch up in Chicago and join a gang. They're forced to, against their will, you see. And there's a vendetta between the two gangs, and . . .

EMILY. Won't it be rather a long book?

ARCHIE. I don't know. They like 'em long nowadays. All the big sellers are huge lumps of books, like "The Bad Companions" or "The Mad Hatter" or "Fauna of the Lounge."

MRS. KEL. Archie hasn't got a name for it yet. Have you, dearest?

ARCHIE. I thought of calling it "Madonna," that's a topping title, but I think it's been used before. And then I thought of "The Dawn was Grey." It's from a poem I learned from a fellow at school.

EMILY. Why not call it "Madder Music"? That's from the same poem.

ARCHIE. Oh, is it? Oh, yes, rather. That would be a topping title.. By gosh, I think I will call it that. Thanks ever so much, Emily. It describes it in a way, too, don't you think?

UNCLE TOM. It sounds pretty daft all right.

ARCHIE. It doesn't do the story justice, really, telling it straight off like that. There's a lot about what they're thinking; and descriptions of people and places and sea voyages and storms and things. Like that bit I read to you. Funnily enough it's my best, I think.

MRS. KEL.   I think so too, Archie.

ARCHIE.   What do you think of it, Emily, from what you've heard of it?

EMILY.   It's not very easy to judge by one or two extracts. I'd rather you didn't ask me till I've read the book.

ARCHIE.   Oh . . . But you can tell from what I've read and from what I've told you if there's anything in it. I mean, take that love scene with him and the circus girl.

EMILY.   She worked in a circus, did she?

ARCHIE.   Yes. I spent a long time over that scene. You see, I had to make it delicate and yet give the idea of passion, too. I must have rewritten it five times.

EMILY.   It is difficult, isn't it?

ARCHIE.   I can do the descriptive bits straight off in no time. And as for the plot, it just seems to come of itself.

MRS. KEL.   Archie was saying earlier to-night it was Inspiration.

EMILY.   Was he, Aunt Bethia?

UNCLE TOM.   Woof.

MRS. KEL.   Yes. Isn't it a wonderful, wonderful thing?

EMILY.   Yes. Wonderful.

MRS. KEL.   But you haven't said what you think of the novel.

EMILY.   No. I told you why. And besides, it would take rather too long. I've got some things to get ready for to-morrow. We'd better be going, Uncle Tom.

ARCHIE.   No. Don't go yet. Emily, I can see you don't like it. I must know what you think. I was afraid to tell you about it before, but now I've done it, I want to know. I just must know. I—I—I— Oh

well, dash it all, I wrote it for you.   It was all for you.
Every word of it.

EMILY.   Oh, Archie!

ARCHIE.   I've sweated my soul out to make it worthy
of you.   Tell me the truth.

EMILY.   Archie, how can I keep my head and criticise
it after that?   It's more than a book to me now.

MRS. KEL.   I should just think so!

UNCLE TOM.   Woof.

ARCHIE.   No. No. No. You mustn't look at it
like that.   It's either good stuff or it isn't.   If you—if
you're my friend, it's your duty to stop me making a fool
of myself.   If you tell me where I've gone wrong I'll
write the whole blooming thing over again.   A fellow
who's written a book needs a real friend.

EMILY.   That's true, Archie.

ARCHIE.   Very well, then.

EMILY.   Very well, then.   I've never let a pal down
when he's asked me that way.   Archie, it's no good.

ARCHIE.   You mean the book?

EMILY.   You've written one of the world's worst.
Oh, boy, I'm so sorry.

ARCHIE.   I see.

MRS. KEL.   I don't know how you can say that.   It's
a wonderful book.

UNCLE TOM.   I must say it seemed to me to have the
makings of a damn good yarn.

MRS. KEL.   Don't pay any attention to her, sonny.
She's just full up with conceit.

ARCHIE.   Shut up, Mother.   (*To* EMILY.)   Why is it
bad?

EMILY.   Oh, dear, I've said enough for one evening,
haven't I?

ARCHIE.   No, you haven't.   Play the game.   Why is
it bad?

EMILY.   I am playing the game.   I feel as if I'd
thrown a baby's birthday cake out of the window.   Please

let me go, Archie. I'm most frightfully sorry, but you made me say it.

ARCHIE.   In what way is it bad?

EMILY.   I can't tell you in what way it's bad.

MRS. KEL.   Ha. I thought not.

ARCHIE.   Listen. I've not spent seven months writing this book only to be told at the end simply that it's bad and no reason given.   You just chuck the thing back in my face in an offhand manner . . .

EMILY.   That's a damned lie.

MRS. KEL.   Oh!

UNCLE TOM.   Woof. Woof.

EMILY.   Well, it is a damned lie.   I've been sitting all evening listening to the most unutterable bilge because Archie's the dearest chap I know and I would go through Hell for him.   And then he sneaks under my guard and appeals to my friendship and my honour as a professional woman of letters . . .

MRS. KEL.   A lot you make out of your profession.

EMILY.   What the blazes has that got to do with you?

MRS. KEL.   Leave my house.

EMILY.   Not till I've said what I've got to say.

ARCHIE.   Mother!

MRS. KEL.   Don't Mother me.   Either that woman leaves or I do. . . . Very well. Good-night, Tom. Let me pass, Archie.

[*Exit* MRS. KELLOCK.   UNCLE TOM *follows, protesting.*]

EMILY.   Oh, dear.

ARCHIE.   Oh, Gosh, Emily, what must you think of me?

EMILY.   I don't know. What an ill-tempered ugly minded pig I am.

[*He goes to her.   She blows her nose and repulses him.*]

ARCHIE.   Oh, no, no, no.

EMILY.   No, Archie, dear. Don't let's have any more scenes of any sort.

ARCHIE. You're the only girl in the world I care about. You're the only girl . . .

EMILY. No, no, no. Not now.

ARCHIE. What do all the books in the world matter ? You're the only . . .

EMILY. No!!

> [*She rushes out.* ARCHIE, *after a short pause, follows her and bumps into* UNCLE TOM *as he enters.*]

UNCLE TOM. Hi, hi, hi. Look where you're going.

ARCHIE. She's gone.

UNCLE TOM. And a jolly good riddance. Don't you pay any attention to her, my boy. Your mother's gone to bed. Never mind. You'll be another Edgar Wallace yet.

ARCHIE. Oh, Lord, what will she think of me ?

UNCLE TOM. Who cares ? I think perhaps I'll have a wee deoch-an-dorus as you're so pressing. . . . She reminds me—woof—of a barmaid I met in Liverpool. Trixie, her name was. But you're too young for *that* story, my boy. *That* would have made a damn fine novel for you, if you like. I often thought I'd like to write some of my reminiscences. But I never had the time. Too busy. Woof. Well, nighty-night, son. Happy dreams, happy dreams.

> [*He takes himself off. After a pause,* MRS. KELLOCK *enters mousy quiet.*]

MRS. KEL. Mother's boy.

ARCHIE. Go to bed, Mother, please.

MRS. KEL. But, darling . . .

ARCHIE. Please go to bed, Mother. I would rather you did. Honestly.

MRS. KEL. But a mother's place is by her son's side in his hour of need, surely you know that, Archie.

ARCHIE. Yes, yes. It's dear of you, but I'd rather you went to bed. It's all right, really. Don't bother about me. Go to bed, Mother.

MRS. KEL. I'm glad this has happened, in a way.

ARCHIE. I'm not. Please go to bed, Mother. No, don't say anything more.

MRS. KEL. I see. You think I have no feelings. You think of nobody but yourself. Very well, then. I must bear my cross. I never thought my own little boy would speak to his mother like that. It just shows . . .

ARCHIE. Mother. For—God's—sake—go—to bed!

MRS. KEL. Archie!—(*She begins to snivel and turns to the door.*) Remember to put out the light.

ARCHIE. All right, Mother. Good-night.

> [*Exit* MRS. KELLOCK, *closing the door behind her.* ARCHIE *makes an irresolute step towards the door. Halts. Picks up his manuscript. Reads. Puts it down again slowly. Clenches his fists. Goes swiftly to the shelf. Takes down his dictionary, his inkpot and his blotting pad. Pulls his chair into the table with a bang. Begins to write furiously.*]

SLOW CURTAIN

ACT II

Scene : UNCLE TOM'S *Cabin at about quarter past six on a Spring
evening.* EMILY'S *boudoir-study. In the first part of the
scene an attempt should be made to recall, by* EMILY'S *position-
ing and actions, the closing scene of Act I.* EMILY *is in evening dress and is restless and nervy. A bell rings and a letter-
box clatters.* EMILY *darts out and returns with three bulky
envelopes and an evening paper. She looks at the envelopes,
stifles a sob, and turns resolutely to the newspaper. It brings
no balm to her troubled spirit. She withdraws a slip from one
of the returned manuscripts and gives it a wry-mouthed glower.*

A VOICE (*Uncle Tom's*). Milly!

EMILY. My name's Emily. What is it?

UNCLE TOM (*without*). Where's my black necktie?

EMILY. It's on your bed. I laid it out for you.

UNCLE TOM. No you didn't.

[*Enter* UNCLE TOM.]

If you had laid it out for me it would be there still. And
is it there still? No, it isn't.

EMILY. It should be. I'm quite certain I laid it out.
Beside your socks.

UNCLE TOM. No! I suppose I mislaid it on purpose
just to make dressing more difficult. I suppose I have a
little tally-ho after my articles of gent's wear to improve
my figure. Hey?

EMILY. Well, you would dress for dinner. I haven't
the remotest idea why.

UNCLE TOM. It's a thing I've wanted to do for a long
time. After a long day's work, a man starts the evening
fresher if he dresses. Colonel Wotherspoon used to say
to me . . .

[29]

EMILY.   But why this passion for freshness to-night?
I'm perfectly certain Archie doesn't want to dress, and . . .

UNCLE TOM.   My dear, it was partly on Archie's
account that I told him to put on a black tie.   And talking
of black ties . . .

EMILY.   Why on Archie's account?

UNCLE TOM.   Oater tongs, oater mewrs.

EMILY.   What did you say?

UNCLE TOM.   I said "Oater tongs, oater mewrs."
That's French for, Other times, other manners.

EMILY.   No, it isn't.   It isn't French at all.   And
anyhow . . .

UNCLE TOM.   You'll pardon me, I have been repeatedly
complimented on my French accent.   Repeatedly.   A
Madame Dewbwa—whom you've never met, my dear
—told me I spoke it like a native.

EMILY.   Whitstable, I expect.   Why should Archie
change his manners?   He's got jolly good manners.
Oceans better than Colonel Wotherspoon's.

UNCLE TOM.   My dear Emily.   Colonel Wotherspoon
is one of the Wotherspoons of . . .

EMILY.   There's your necktie.   It's hanging out of
your sock.

UNCLE TOM.   So it is.   Extro'ny thing.   As I was
saying, it simply shows how out of it you really are in
spite of having been taken down to dinner once by Derek
What's His Name . . .

EMILY.   Derek Putney.   Here, let me tie it.

UNCLE TOM.   These literary swells are all very well.
I've got a word to say against litercher.   Old Wotherspoon said to me last week, "Tommy, my boy," he
said . . .

EMILY.   Your tie's all right now.   Run along,
Tommy, my boy, and dress up like a Colonel.   Pronto.
Footsack.   Get out.

UNCLE TOM.   Woof.   Thanks.   It's not twenty-past
six, is it?

EMILY.   Yes.   That clock's slow.   Run.

[*He goes.*]

(*Returning dolefully to her rejection slips.*)   O, doux printemps d'autrefois, Comme vous etes fuis . . .

[*Enter* ARCHIE.]

Oh, you startled me!   Well, welcome home.   And my heartiest con . . . my heartiest good wishes.

ARCHIE.   Thank you very much, Emily.   That's very good of you.   I appreciate that.

EMILY.   Oh, my dear chap . . .!   Is Aunt Bethia with you?

ARCHIE.   No.   She'll be along in ten minutes—with Mrs. Kishmul.

EMILY.   Mrs. . . . ?   Oh, that's her name, is it? Uncle Tom got it all wrong.   He gets everything all wrong, poor old thing.   Is she nice?

ARCHIE.   Oh, yes.   In a way, yes.   A bit American, but a good sort.

EMILY.   It doesn't take you long to devastate a continent, Archie, does it?

ARCHIE.   Ha, ha.   Yes. . . . Which continent?

EMILY.   America.   Do sit down.

ARCHIE.   Thank you.

EMILY.   I've just had three such delicious letters from four such famous people.

ARCHIE.   Oh?   Have you?   What about?

EMILY (*reading*).   To E. Perry, Esquire.   Messrs. Hoskins and Brewer are grateful for the opportunity . . . You hear that, Archie?   Grateful, Archie.   Can't you see them with their withered hands clasped and their rheumy eyes turned upwards, thankful to an all-bountiful Providence . . . Och, I'm dithering . . . of reading your essays (on the dotted line); but regret that in the present state of the market . . . Read it yourself.

ARCHIE.   I say.   I am sorry.   I expect your stuff's

above their heads.   Still, it's quite nicely put.   It shows they appreciate you, in a way.

EMILY.   Mr. John Gall of the Saracen's Head has sent me such a nice little woodcut.   And Mr. Duckling says his Reader liked my verses but . . . He doesn't say whether the Reader's a he or a she or anything at all but that.   Just a tender, disembodied wave of sympathy out of the dark.

ARCHIE.   Well, that's a bit more encouraging, isn't it?

EMILY.   Yes, dear, frightfully encouraging.   Did I ever show you my album, full, full, full, to the covers of these kind and helpful little notes?

ARCHIE.   Don't get disheartened.   You've got the goods all right.   Keep pegging away.   You remember what Derek Putney said about your article in *Time and Tide.*

EMILY.   He must have mistaken me for someone else. Oh, nitchevo.   Don't bother about me.   You're a darling for doing it, but I've bumped down so many publishers' doorsteps that I'm tough.   Let's talk about you.   How does it feel?

ARCHIE.   They were awfully nice to me in London. I met Derek Putney, too.

EMILY.   Oh, did you?   Did you?

ARCHIE.   Just for a minute or two—at a party.   We were talking about you.

EMILY.   Not really?

ARCHIE.   Yes.   He remembered you quite well when I described you.

EMILY.   I see.

ARCHIE.   I'm rather looking forward to hearing him again on the wireless this evening.   I'm in a bit of a funk, though.

EMILY.   I should think you must be, poor laddie.

ARCHIE.   He's so down on best sellers as a rule.

EMILY.   Yes, I say, Archie, I've kept the loud-speaker up here. I can say it's not working if you don't want your mother and Uncle Tom to hear.

ARCHIE. Why shouldn't I want them to hear? They'd be frightfully disappointed if they didn't. . . . By Gosh, they won't if they don't hurry up.

EMILY. No. That clock's fast. But, Archie, dear, I thought . . . I thought you might be rather nervous and . . .

ARCHIE. Nervous about what?

EMILY. About what Putney and Devereux might say. These debates on the Book of the Week are sometimes frightfully sarcastic and Oxfordish.

ARCHIE. I don't give a hoot what they say. Oh, I know you don't think much of " Madder Music." And from your point of view you're quite right. It's not beautifully written and difficult like your stuff and Albert Huxley's and Putney's. But it's good honest-to-God stuff, and it's true to Life . . .

EMILY. Oh, Archie, it's not, it's not! Men and women don't go barging from situation to situation like illuminated tramcars, Archie. And they don't talk in old-fashioned movie captions and a good half of them haven't got chronic hysteria.

ARCHIE. I don't recognise my book in your description, Emily. And I don't think the one hundred and twenty thousand people who bought it last week would recognise it either.

EMILY. No. They probably wouldn't. God help them. . . . Archie, I'm being a pig. I'm not jealous, really, dear. I'm as pleased as if you had won the Calcutta Sweep, I am honestly.

ARCHIE. It's hardly the same as winning the Calcutta Sweep, is it?

EMILY. I know. That's just luck and this is solid worth. You wrote it with your heart's blood, didn't you?

ARCHIE. As a matter of fact, I did.

EMILY. Then the hundred and twenty thousand must have seen what I didn't see. I give in. I'm humble. I'm only a pedantic prig and I'll read " Madder Music " all over again and try to understand it. Will you forgive me ?

ARCHIE. There's nothing to forgive. You're so sensitive and delicate and you've such refined tastes that there's no doubt a whole lot of " Madder Music " is rather strong meat for you . . .

EMILY. But it isn't strong anything. It's . . . Oh, shut up, Emily. I'll read it again, dear. Greater love . . . I mean I can say no fairer than that, can I ?

ARCHIE. Indeed, you can't. But don't let's say any more about it. As a matter of fact, I sneaked over early specially to—well, not to talk about books. As a matter of fact, I . . . and then we got talking and wasting time, and it's hard enough to come to the point, anyhow.

EMILY. What's the matter, Archie ? You and I have always been pals in spite of my dreadful cheek. Is anything wrong ?

ARCHIE. No, no. As you say, you and I have always been pals, I mean . . . *good* pals, if you see what I mean. But all the time there's been something so far as I was concerned at least—something a bit, well, deeper. Only, well, what with the business doing badly and one thing and another I never had the heart to ask you straight out, if you see what I mean.

EMILY. Of course I see what you mean.

ARCHIE. Then . . . well . . . Oh, Emily, I love you. You'll marry me, won't you ?

EMILY. Wait. Wait. Wait, dear. Wait for a minute. I've gone all emotional. I hate it. I must give you a sensible answer. Wait.

ARCHIE. I'll wait as long as . . .

EMILY. No, no. It's not that. It's only for a minute. Talk about something else. Tell me about London. Did you have a bully time ?

ARCHIE.   Not bad.   It's all a sort of dream to me.   I met a lot of people.   They gave me drinks and things. I got quite dizzy. . . . I say, are you all right?

EMILY.   Coming all right.   I hate this.   Go on talking.

ARCHIE.   I seemed to meet a lot of women too, with painted wooden necklaces.   I didn't like them, specially. I didn't feel they were sincere.

EMILY.   Weren't they?

ARCHIE.   I like seeing people's faces, and they had faces like circus clowns.   No eyebrows.   I say, Emily . . .

EMILY.   Go on, go on.   Did you get about much?

ARCHIE.   No, not much.   Not so much as I'd like to have—on my first trip to London.   I say, we'll go together some day soon and see Whipsnade and things.

EMILY.   That would be lovely.

ARCHIE.   You could show me about.   All the sights.

EMILY.   I'd love to.

ARCHIE.   It's been a sort of dream of mine.   You and me and London.   It's a great place.   Fine buildings and kind, friendly people and all these historical associations.

EMILY.   I like it too.

[*They are close together now.   He tentatively takes her hand.*]

ARCHIE.   Do you?   Do you?   It'll be jolly, won't it?

EMILY.   Heavenly, dear.

ARCHIE.   And we'll go to Paris and Vienna and all these places.   Dash it, we'll be able to do it, now, with any luck.   My agent says there's no reason why I should worry about money any more. . . . Not that I care.   I want just enough to make a place for you.   And that's all right, Emily.   Isn't it, dear?   I mean . . . I had another reason for not asking you before.   I'd better tell you . . .

EMILY. Archie, I do like your hands. What do you want to tell me, dear?

[ARCHIE *sits on the arm of her chair and hugs her shoulders. She doesn't seem to mind.*]

ARCHIE. Oh, Emily. The point was that I didn't— I didn't think I was worthy of you. I'm not yet, of course.

EMILY. Don't be silly. You're the most angelic creature I ever met. I'm a mean little guttersnipe to you.

ARCHIE. No, no. You see . . . You were so clever and I was such an uneducated mug. I'd never have had the cheek—well, even to touch you, only now . . .

EMILY (*disengaging herself*). Would you be good enough to tell me what you are driving at? ·

ARCHIE. It's different now, isn't it? You see, you were a big noise to me in the literary world then. But now it's me that's the big noise; and you haven't had much luck, so far, anyway. So I thought, well . . .

EMILY. Oh, you blasted FOOL! Go away, will you? Go away!

ARCHIE. Emily, darling . . .

EMILY. Don't darling me.

ARCHIE. Then you won't marry me?

EMILY. No, I certainly won't.

ARCHIE. But why?

EMILY. Never mind why. Go away.

ARCHIE. But, Emily . . . I'll wait as long . . .

EMILY. Go away; go away; go away.

ARCHIE (*after a pause*). Very well.

EMILY. No! . . . Stop. Don't go away. I'm all right now.

ARCHIE. I'd rather, if you don't mind.

EMILY. No. Archie. Don't be so silly. I'm not worth making a fuss over. I'm not really. Listen. Pull yourself together. We must go on with the party and pretend that nothing's happened. If we don't,

Uncle Tom will be facetious, and I couldn't bear that. And Aunt Bethia would weep and try to comfort you and that would be jolly for you, wouldn't it? Truly, dear, it's the best way. It's one sticky evening against weeks of slop and snarl and misery. Please, Archie.

ARCHIE. Very well.

EMILY. You're a darling.

ARCHIE. I suppose it's final, what you said just now?

EMILY. Absolutely final. (*Begins to cry.*) I——

ARCHIE. Emily . . . What have I done? What have I said? Oh . . . Emily!

> [*Yammering is heard in the passage.*]

UNCLE TOM (*without*). Emily!

EMILY. There's your mother now. You go. I'll marry you all right. I don't believe I'm an artist at all. Don't tell anyone, though.

ARCHIE. About——about us.

EMILY. No. Not to-night.

ARCHIE. All right. But don't you think perhaps it would be better if you . . . ?

EMILY. No. You haven't got a face to put right. Run quickly and stall them off, there's a darling.

ARCHIE. Righto. Gosh, I am happy. . . . Gosh!

> [*He goes.* EMILY *repairs the ravages of emotion. Looks at the wireless set—a portable—and seems to be considering whether to throw it out of action. Is about to carry her idea, somewhat irresolutely into effect, when* UNCLE TOM *enters, jovial, effulgent, carrying a tray with cocktails. He is followed by* MRS. KELLOCK *and* MRS. KISHMUL, *a Virginian brunette. Later,* ARCHIE.]

UNCLE TOM. Well, well, well, well. That's where you've got the wireless, is it?

EMILY. Yes. Isn't it? How are you, Aunt Bethia?

MRS. KEL. How are you, Emily dear. Aren't these great days? You've got to admit you were wrong now. Haven't you, dear?

EMILY. Yes. How do you do, Mrs.—Mrs. . . .

MRS. KISHMUL. Glad to know you. My name is Kishmul. It is a vurry peculiar name.

EMILY. Not at all, Mrs. Kishmul. I've heard such a lot about you.

MRS. KISHMUL. Oh, have you? Just what?

EMILY. Well, you can't expect me to repeat it. I don't know yet what your head's like—except that it's very lovely—and I might turn it.

MRS. KISHMUL. Now, I think that's a really beautiful speech. I didn't expect beautiful speeches like that on this side of the Pond. And from one of my own sex, too.

ARCHIE. I didn't tell you that Mrs. Kishmul had sold the serial rights of " Madder Music " in the States for a very hot figure . . .

MRS. KISHMUL. Oh, that was nothing. That's my job.

ARCHIE. Yes, and she's got me first-rate terms for my new book.

EMILY. Oh? I didn't know you'd written one.

ARCHIE. I hadn't. That's what makes it so good. I thought of " Stronger Wine " for a title. What do you think, Emily? It's from the same poem I got " Madder Music " from. " I called for madder music and for stronger wine."

EMILY. Good. I'm sure they'll call for thirty editions.

ARCHIE. No, but really. It's funny, but that's in the poem the fellow taught me at school. " I called for madder music and for stronger wine, and, and . . .

EMILY. " But when the feast is finished and the lamps expire, then falls thy shadow, Cynara, the night is thine; and I am desolate and sick of an old passion. Yea, hungry for the lips of my desire. I have been faithful to thee, Cynara, in my fashion."

MRS. KISHMUL. That is a vurry graceful bit of versification. In what collection is it to be found?

ARCHIE. I don't know. A fellow at school taught it to me.

UNCLE TOM. Never mind about that now. Each take a cocktail and sit down. Sit down. It's just about time for the Book of the Week. Your clock's slow, I think you said, Emily?

EMILY. No. It's right by the church clock.

UNCLE TOM. You haven't got a cocktail, Bethia.

MRS. KEL. I am perfectly well aware of that, Tom. You know my principles.

UNCLE TOM. Let's see if the gadget is working.

EMILY. I think there's something wrong with it, Uncle Tom. Couldn't Archie go round and bring his own? It wouldn't take a minute. And then we could all sit downstairs comfortably and listen.

UNCLE TOM. Upon my Sam, that's a bit thick. After we've all pretty near bust our selves trying to be in time for it.

MRS. KEL. Speak for yourself, Tom.

UNCLE TOM. I am speaking for myself.

ARCHIE. I'm afraid we'd miss half of it if I ran round to Mon Repos. Let me see the set.

[*There is a preliminary howl of the loud-speaker and a voice is heard speaking.*]

THE B.B.C. ... And that concludes the First General News Bulletin. If listeners will wait for a few moments they will hear the National Programme from London. Stand by, please.

UNCLE TOM. There, I told you so. It's working all right. Have another martini, Mrs. Kishmul?

MRS. KISHMUL. Thanks a lot, I will.

[*They settle down, to the accompaniment of some confused chattering, to listen to the debate.*]

THE B.B.C. Good evening, everybody. This is the National Programme from London. You are going to hear a discussion between Mr. Derek Putney and Mr. Reginald Devereux. This is the fourth of a series of discussions on the Book of the Week. Mr. Derek Putney and Mr. Devereux.

1ST VOICE.   Good evening, Devereux.

2ND VOICE.   Good evening, Putney.

1ST VOICE.   Here we are again.   I ought perhaps to tell you that I have been visiting my dentist this afternoon, so perhaps you won't mind if I whistle a little on my sibilants.

2ND VOICE.   Ha, ha.   Not at all.

1ST VOICE.   It's no laughing matter, I assure you.

2ND VOICE.   I beg your pardon, Putney.   Why do we invariably laugh at things like that?

1ST VOICE.   I don't know that we invariably do. Half a minute.   My chair is at an awkward angle for the microphone.

MRS. KEL.   I thought they were going to talk about Archie's book.

UNCLE TOM.   Hush, hush.

MRS. KEL.   Oh, well . . .

1ST VOICE.   That's better.   Well, Devereux, I suppose we are both agreed as to what book we had better discuss to-night.

2ND VOICE.   I think so.   There may be more than one opinion about Kellock's " Madder Music," but I think we must all admit, even the most intransigeant of us . . .

1ST VOICE.   Are you referring to me?

2ND VOICE.   Ha, ha.   No, Putney.   I haven't the remotest idea what your views are.   What I was trying to say was that there is a general consensus of opinion that, whatever its faults, " Madder Music " is at least a very remarkable book.

1ST VOICE.   Agreed.   One of the most remarkable I remember having read.

2ND VOICE.   Yes, but . . . remarkable for what? That's the point.

1ST VOICE.   I should say for its vitality.[1]   [One had read so many books recently by young people who take an

---

[1] Note: *Passages within brackets may be omitted.*

almost corpse-like view of life that one feels—how can one express it ?—as if one were strolling in the catacombs and as if suddenly a large and healthy and Lido-bronzed Mr. Kellock had burst his cerements and asked one to have a drink.   Or is one's image a little far-fetched ?]

2ND VOICE.   Possibly, Putney, possibly.   But you must admit that there is some extraordinarily bad writing in the book.

1ST VOICE.   What do you mean by bad writing ? What we call good writing these days is probably only a temporary convention.   [Personally one considers it intolerably in the Papa-Potato-Prunes and Prism School, coloured infrequently with schoolmasterish bursts of bad temper.   Modern prose, my dear Devereux, is a convention and a convention that may be démodé in a year.]

2ND VOICE.   Oh, come ! . . . But surely this passage —Oh, damn, sorry—Yes.   What about this ? " With a hoarse cry he caught her to him and pressed a rain of kisses on her provocatively parted lips."

1ST VOICE.   Well, that seems to me to describe exactly what happened.   It has been said before, of course, but everything worth while has been said before.   [It is the fashion of the moment to be amused at such passages, but they are really no more amusing than a Scotsman's kilt.   It is simply silly to hoot with laughter because a writer chooses to describe a commonplace happening in the words thousands of his predecessors have found suitable to the situation.] . . . I say, I must speak to my dentist about this.   Shaw says somewhere that what is too silly to be said may be sung, but one hates being compelled to whistle one's sentiments.

2ND VOICE.   Ha, ha.   As much a dental as a mental effort, perhaps.   Hey ? Ha, ha.

1ST VOICE.   Ha.

2ND VOICE.   Hahaha.   Yes, quite.   But we haven't very much more time and we'd better be getting down to brass tacks.   I think I follow your argument.   You suggest that we have a tendency nowadays to lay too much stress on style.

1ST VOICE. Precisely. Damn, they were nearly out there. Exactly. [Dickens wrote shocking blank verse under the impression that he was writing prose, but that does not detract from the merit of his work. On the contrary, it gives his books a characteristic bouquet which is perfectly charming.]

2ND VOICE. Well, there is no doubt that Mr. Kellock has appealed at once to the great heart of the reading public. Do you feel disposed to analyse that appeal?

1ST VOICE. Well . . . Pass that water-jug, will you? . . . Thanks very much.

EMILY (*aside, and the author makes no apology for this; as she has been sitting in ill-concealed torment right up against a pillar of the proscenium and must either have an aside or bust*). O howling spirits of the ether, barge in, barge in and break the transmission. Quickly, quickly, or I'll die.

1ST VOICE. Mr. Kellock's work has that indefinable something which one can only describe as Quality. This is particularly well seen in the almost brutal certainty with which he hurls situation upon situation, climax upon climax, till one holds one's very breath at the prospect of the almost inevitable collapse of the—(*his voice begins to fade*)—whole massively conceived, almost chaotically constructed . . .

> [ARCHIE *dashes to the instrument and twiddles a little button. Derisive howls answer him. Then silence.* EMILY *clasps her hands as if in prayer.*]

UNCLE TOM AND MRS. KEL. What's the matter? What's wrong with the thing?

ARCHIE. I'm afraid the transmission's broken down, somehow.

MRS. KISHMUL AND MRS. KEL. What a pity!

ARCHIE. It does that sometimes on this wave-length. They're trying a new one.

MRS. KISHMUL. Now, isn't that just too bad? Just when the two gentlemen were getting quite hotted up.

MRS. KEL. They said practically nothing about the book.

MRS. KISHMUL. But what they did say was vurry laudatory. Vurry laudatory and appreciative indeed.

MRS. KEL. I can't say I cared much for the other one. Not the one who was speaking last. Who was he?

MRS. KISHMUL. You mean the gentleman with the unsatisfactory dentures? That was the celebrated Mr. Derek Putney. It is generally reckoned that he is the biggest expert on literature on this side of the Atlantic, besides having himself written a number of books which will make a name for him in the history of culture as long as there are cultured men and women to enjoy them.

MRS. KEL. Oh, I know about Derek Putney. Emily used to know him a little. She is a great admirer of his.

MRS. KISHMUL. So is everybody with the smallest pretensions to taste.

UNCLE TOM. A big noise, eh?

MRS. KISHMUL. One of the biggest noises in this or any other continent.

UNCLE TOM. Pity he was cut off like that. He seemed to be pleased with Archie's book, though.

MRS. KISHMUL. Naturally so; Mr. Kellock's book has created a monumental impression in all the best informed circles.

MRS. KEL. I think he was perfectly right when he said that it didn't matter how a book was written so long as it was written from the heart.

UNCLE TOM. Yes, I've often thought that myself. Funny that. I suppose that's genius, really. Saying what we've all thought, only better than you and I could express it.

[43]

MRS. KEL. I suppose so.

MRS. KISHMUL. I consider that a most admirable definition of genius, Mr. Kellock, I should be glad to have you write it in my album.

UNCLE TOM. I'll be very pleased to, I'm sure. Have another cocktail.

MRS. KISHMUL. I am much obliged. My album is a book of some interest. In my work as a literary agent I have opportunities of picking the brains of vurry many distinguished men and women for my little collection. I think you will find my album contains an anthology of great thoughts almost unequalled in the civilised world. Mr. Archibald Kellock has already contributed.

[ARCHIE, *who has been working at the instrument, turns on a burst of military music and at once turns it off again.*]

ARCHIE. That was Berlin. The instrument's all right. It must have been a bust-up in the transmission.

MRS. KEL. Well, it's very disappointing. After we came round early specially to hear it, too. I think it's a piece of disgraceful mismanagement.

UNCLE TOM. They want a business head or two at the B.B.C. Colonel Wotherspoon tells me the place is crowded with a lot of young pups from the Universities who don't know the elements of their job.

MRS. KISHMUL. That is a vurry unfortunate state of affairs in a large and important Corporation like the B.B.C. I have no grouch against college boys in a general way, but they tend to run in vurry stereotyped grooves.

UNCLE TOM. I never had a University education and I don't consider myself a penny the worse for it. Not a penny the worse.

MRS. KEL. Archie never went to a University either, and look at him.

MRS. KISHMUL. Yes, look at him. He has written a masterpiece that has gone thundering across the two hemispheres like a tornado, and you would imagine from his unassuming bearing that he had done nothing but keep a small town store all his life.

MRS. KEL.   Always the same modest, simple boy, Mrs. Kishmul.

ARCHIE.   Oh, well, dash it.   It was only a bit of luck. Like winning a ticket in the Calcutta Sweep.

MRS. KISHMUL.   I told you so.   There he stands, a benefactor to mankind, and you would imagine he had committed a crime.

MRS. KEL.   Miss Perry, there, as good as said he had, once.

ARCHIE.   No, no, mother.

MRS. KEL.   Oh, yes, she did.   Don't you remember ? The very first night she heard anything about it.   She had only heard two or three little bits of it read aloud and she stood up in our house and said it was a thoroughly bad book and advised Archie to put it in the fire.

MRS. KISHMUL.   Well, now, I can hardly believe that of Miss Perry.

UNCLE TOM.   Well, well, well.   Woof.   We all make mistakes sometimes.   I myself have refused to put money on an animal in spite of the straightest of stable tips because I was as sure as God made little apples that the brute hadn't a flea's chance on a red-hot shovel.   And the blinking quadruped cantered home by three lengths at forty to one.   What'd ye make of that, now ?

MRS. KEL.   I think it served you right for betting and gambling.

UNCLE TOM.   As you know perfectly well, I only have a very occasional flutter.   I only used the story to illustrate my argument.   The point is this.   I made a mistake.   I am man enough to admit it.   Very well then.   Why go over it all again ?

MRS. KEL.   I've not once this evening heard Emily admit by thought or word or deed that she was wrong about Archie's book.

[45]

ARCHIE.   Mother, Emily is quite entitled to her opinion.   Quite probably she was right in the first place. But in any case she has promised to read the book again and to give me a considered judgment on it.   And second thoughts are sometimes. . . .

MRS. KEL.   Oh, yes.   Very nice.   After she has heard her great Mr. Derek Putney say it was the most marvellous book he had ever read.   I don't think much of that kind of judgment.

UNCLE TOM.   Isn't it about time dinner was served, Emily?   I'm getting a bit peckish, myself.

EMILY.   I'll go downstairs and see, Uncle Tom.

MRS. KEL.   And a very nice way, too, of getting out of an awkward corner.

ARCHIE.   I say, Mother.   Please.

EMILY.   I'm not trying to get out of any awkward corner.   What do you want me to say, please, Aunt Bethia?

MRS. KEL.   I don't want you to say anything, Emily. I am sure with your University education you don't need to be told what to say by an old body like me.

MRS. KISHMUL.   You will excuse me, but I really think it's quite unfair to Miss Perry to make fun of her because of a . . .

MRS. KEL.   I wasn't making fun of her.

EMILY.   Far from it.

MRS. KISHMUL.   Pardon me . . . because of a hasty and ill-considered opinion she has had every reason to revise.

MRS. KEL.   Every reason, yes.   She'll pretend to read the book again to save her face, and then say she hadn't noticed how splendid it was.   And all because she was jealous and discouraging when she thought the book wasn't going to be a success.   It's a very different story now Archie's made good. . . . Let me alone, Archie. . . . And the great Mr. Putney she thinks such a lot of has said it's all right.   Oh, a very different story.

EMILY.   It isn't a different story.

MRS. KEL.   Oh, isn't it?

EMILY.   No, it isn't.   " Madder Music's " a rotten book.   A thoroughly bad, trashy book.   And it's a tragedy and an insult to human nature that such an enormous number of poor fools, brought up on the language of Milton and Shakespeare and Bunyan, should spend their money on such maudlin drivel.

MRS. KEL.   Oh, do you hear her?

UNCLE TOM.   Woof.   Emily, Emily.

MRS. KISHMUL.   Pardon me, Miss Perry, I cannot sit still and listen to that.   Are we to understand that the entire reading public of Great Britain and the United States are wrong?   Are we to gather that the most superlative experts on English literature, including Mr. Derek Putney himself, do not know what they are talking about?   Is the unanimous voice of the critics in the best dailies and weeklies liable to err?

EMILY.   Of course it is.   Everybody knows that every now and again the critics stampede and rush down a steep place into the sea.   They bob up again all right, but there's no doubt about the stampede.

MRS. KISHMUL.   Ah!   So you reckon yourself to be the one sane individual standing on the levee with a supercilious smile on your face.   Everybody in the West Point Regiment is out of step but our Hank.   That's about the size of it, isn't it?

EMILY.   Mrs. Kishmul, I don't want to discuss Archie's book with you.

MRS. KISHMUL.   Oh, yes?   You prefer to discuss it with folk on the small town standard of dialectics.   I guess you will go over big with them.   But let me tell you, whether you realised the weight you were up against or not, you've come into the ring and we're going to have it out right here and now.

[EMILY *gives a helpless gesture.*]

[47]

Now listen.   You heard Mr. Putney say over the radio that the book had quality.   What you gotta say to that?

EMILY.   I don't know what he meant by quality.

MRS. KISHMUL.   My goodness me.   You don't know what he meant by quality.   And you're a College Graduate.

EMILY.   Oh, I know the catchword all right.   Anybody can say a thing's got quality when he can't think what else to say about it.   It's like saying you like the lines of a car or the points of a horse or the texture of a picture when you don't know the first thing about cars or horses or pictures.

MRS. KISHMUL.   Ah!   Then you wish us to believe that Mr. Derek Putney, who is notorious through two hemispheres for the meticulous care with which he uses words, has employed a catchword to hide his ignorance.

ARCHIE.   Mrs. Kishmul, I really think . . .

MRS. KISHMUL.   Ex-cuse me, I am asking Miss Perry a question purely for my own information and enlightenment.   Well, Miss Perry?

EMILY.   I suppose he knew what he meant by it all right, but . . .

MRS. KISHMUL.   And what do you suppose he meant by it?

EMILY.   I've said I haven't the faintest idea.

MRS. KISHMUL.   Do you think it possible he meant there was something real and vital and enduring about the book?   Something only appreciable by a sixth sense that tells us, " Here is an immortal work of art; I cannot tell why, but it is so?"

EMILY.   Yes.   That's probably what he meant.

MRS. KISHMUL.   A matter of feeling, possibly?

EMILY.   Quite probably.

MRS. KISHMUL.   I gather you don't feel that way about Mr. Kellock's book.

EMILY.   No.   I don't.

MRS. KISHMUL.   Well, if Mr. Putney's honest he feels

something that you can't feel. If you were blind and I told you about the trees and the flowers and the deep blue ocean you wouldn't say there was no such thing because you couldn't see them? Would you, now, Miss Perry? You'd jest have to believe me. If you were deaf you'd have to take the songs of the birds and the noble toons of Brahms and Beethoven and Gershwin on trust. If you'd no sense of smell you'd have to go to someone else for information about the drains. Now, it's a bit more likely, it seems to me, that Mr. Derek Putney, who is one of the greatest experts the world has ever seen, is the possessor of that mysterious sixth sense than you. For he's got away with it, and so far as I can hear, you haven't. Not to any considerable extent. You take up that book again, Miss Perry, and read it through humbly and, yes, prayerfully, and you'll be surprised.

[*A gong sounds.*]

Oh, Glory There's the dinner-gong. Come along. We'll be friends now.

UNCLE TOM. Yes, yes. Dinner, dinner, dinner. Come along, Bethia.

MRS. KEL. And I hope this will be a lesson to you, Milly.

EMILY. No. Stop a minute. I've got something to say. A book should be about real things and real people. A book that does nothing but reflect the silly, sluttish day-dreams of a lot of morons is a crime. It's pandering to the filthiest kind of vanity. It's making them think their rubbishy systems are fit for a decent world. It's bolstering up their conceit by making them thrill with horror at what their imaginary opposites do. And it's making the horror delicious to them by smearing it with smut—smarmy, hypocritical, leering, winking smut. And . . .

UNCLE TOM. And in the meantime the dinner's getting cold. We'll have this all out after dinner. You mustn't mind her, Mrs. Kishmul.   I have to put up with this every day of my life. You'll take Mrs. Kishmul down, Archie.   Come along, come along.

> [UNCLE TOM *and* MRS. KELLOCK *go out. They are followed by* ARCHIE *and* MRS. KISHMUL, *but not before* MRS. KISHMUL *has squeezed* ARCHIE'S *arm in silent sympathy and* ARCHIE *has conveyed to* EMILY *with a look that he is cut to the heart by her all too accurate description of his book.* EMILY, *after a short pause, during which she indicates doubt, despair and baffled fury, strides rapidly to the fireplace and smashes the cocktail glasses one by one against the bars. Then she puts out the lights and runs across the stage to the doorway.*]

CURTAIN

ACT III

SCENE I

A Thames-side garden. It is no more than a patch of grass with a few perennial bushes and garden walls over which other Thames-side houses rear their immoral-looking heads. The house to which the garden is attached is represented by a rather mean glass porch with a wistaria. There are a modern sundial and three deck chairs in the garden. It is an Autumn evening some months after the events of the Act before. EMILY is seated on one of the chairs reading a book. To her MRS. KELLOCK.

MRS. KEL. Now, I wonder where I left my . . . Emily! You're still here?

EMILY. Yes, Aunt Bethia. I'm still here.

MRS. KEL. All by yourself.

EMILY. All by myself, Aunt Bethia.

MRS. KEL. The young gentleman has gone?

EMILY. Some time ago, Aunt Bethia.

MRS. KEL. Aren't you afraid of catching cold?

EMILY. No, darling.

MRS. KEL. Let Auntie bring you a nice warm coat.

EMILY. I don't want a nice warm coat, Auntie.

MRS. KEL. (*sitting down*). We mustn't let you catch cold, dear; but it is rather warm, isn't it?

EMILY. Yes, isn't it.

MRS. KEL. (*with a sigh*). Not like up at home in dear old Bonnie Scotland.

EMILY. No. I expect it's quite cold there, compared to this.

MRS. KEL. I don't think I'll ever get accustomed to

London, or London ways.   Be it ever so humble, there's no place like Home.

EMILY.   No?

MRS. KEL.   No.   It's nice that Archie is a great man now; and it's nice that he is not ashamed of his old mother with all these grand people coming about the house.   It must be a great temptation to look down on his poor old mother and push her into corners.

EMILY.   I don't think so.

MRS. KEL.   I'm glad you don't, Emily.   I know some people who aren't very keen about introducing their fine friends to their poor old aunties.

EMILY.   What do you mean?

MRS. KEL.   That young gentleman you were having such grand jokes with all afternoon.   I think you might have thought that a lonely old woman might like to share the fun.

EMILY.   You kept out of the way.   I didn't see you anywhere.

MRS. KEL.   Auntie always keeps out of the way when she is obviously not wanted.   Always, always.   And you might have seen me.   I was standing at the drawing-room window for hours.

EMILY.   Oh?   Were you?

MRS. KEL.   Yes.   Emily, darling, you don't mind if Auntie talks a little seriously to her girlie?

EMILY.   Girlie is giving Auntie her closest attenshy-wenshion.

MRS. KEL.   There is no need for flippancy, Emily.   No need at all.   Who was that young man?

EMILY.   That was Mr. Derek Putney, Aunt Bethia.

MRS. KEL.   Mr. Putney, the author?

EMILY.   Yes.   He is coming round later to take me out to a cinema.

MRS. KEL.   To a cinema?

EMILY.   Yes.   It is a kind of magic-lantern exhibition, Aunt Bethia.   By a very ingenious mechanism the figures on the screen are made to appear to move and even to talk—with American accents it is true, but . . .

MRS. KEL.   I am well aware what a cinema is, Emily. Only too well aware.

EMILY.   Of course.   You went with Uncle Tom last week.   I forgot.

MRS. KEL.   That is different.   For two persons of opposite sexes to . . .

EMILY.   Uncle Tom and you are of opposite sexes.

MRS. KEL.   Emily, there is no necessity to be coarse. . . . But never mind that.   I have one question to ask. Are you being fair to Archie?

EMILY.   To Archie?

MRS. KEL.   Yes.   To Archie.   My boy's happiness is everything to me.

EMILY.   So it is to me.   What do you mean?

MRS. KEL.   When Mr. Kellock was paying attention to me I never permitted other young gentlemen to call and tell me funny stories in the garden; nor would I have dreamed of going to the cinema . . . in almost total darkness.

EMILY.   Auntie, look here. . . . Oh, this is so very, very stupid.   If you knew what a poor inhibited shy creature I am . . . I'm no use at nameless orgies, really I'm not.

MRS. KEL.   I should hope not.   You are a Perry, just as I am.   I am only asking you to be a little more discreet. I will not have Archie's affection—his deep and true affection—tampered with.   I have never tampered with it myself, and you should be the last to do so.   You are engaged to him.

EMILY.   Of course I wouldn't hurt Archie.   He knows that.   Do please believe that.   Oh, I know it sounds priggish and silly, but I've got to have men friends to—to—to, well, to give my immortal soul an airing and some exercise, if you see what I mean.   Dash it all, Aunt Bethia, we're living in the capital of the world in 1934.

E   [53]

Archie knows that as well as I do. I never see him anyway. He's running about with Mrs. Kishmul from morning till night.

MRS. KEL. That is very, very unworthy of you, Emily. You know quite well that that is entirely a business relationship.

EMILY. So is mine with Mr. Putney . . . in a way.

MRS. KEL. In a very peculiar way. Archie is working with Mrs. Kishmul on the proofs of his new novel. To-day they are seeing a gentleman about the dramatisation of " Madder Music." I suppose your business with Mr. Putney is of similar importance.

EMILY. No, it isn't. I've been a failure as a writer, and a failure as a woman, and a failure as a human being. Derek's taking me round to studio parties, and theatres and night-clubs to give me the illusion of being alive. It's better than nothing. I like it. I'm doing it because I like it, and you and Archie can blooming well lump it.

MRS. KEL. I never thought to hear my future daughter-in-law talk like that. Never, never, never. And my own niece, too, that I bathed my own self in front of the fire in Uncle Walker's house in Nithsdale Road. What would he have thought?

EMILY. I haven't the least idea what he would have thought. And I don't see what my infant ablutions have to do with . . .

MRS. KEL. They were happy days. Happy, happy days. I remember well that awful night you fell out of the bath right into the fireplace. I wouldn't wonder if you've still got the mark on your wee tummy.

EMILY. Yes, I've still got the mark on my wee tummy, but . . .

MRS. KEL. And there with all these happy memories and—and everything to remind you of them you can stand there and tell me . . .

EMILY. Aunt Bethia. Forgive me if I'm stupid, but I can't see what a big burn-scar on my wee tummy has

to do with Archie and Derek and Mrs. Kishmul;
and I . . .

MRS. KEL. There you go again. Making unworthy
suggestions about Mrs. Kishmul.

EMILY. I wasn't.

MRS. KEL. Pardon me, you were. Mrs. Kishmul is
a most cultured woman. A most cultivated, cultured
woman—for an American. And I am quite, quite certain she strongly disapproves of your wild goings-on.

EMILY. They're not goings-on. Oh, dash it all.

MRS. KEL. I'm afraid they are, Emily. And don't
sulk at your old auntie, darling. She knows what's best.
And she's really very, very anxious about you.

EMILY. You needn't be, truly. I've just told you . . .

MRS. KEL. Auntie hasn't finished speaking. It's very,
very easy for a young girl to have her head turned by all
this whirl of gaiety.

EMILY. Oh, look here! I'm not a young girl any more,
and . . .

MRS. KEL. Please let me finish. . . . I make all the
allowances I can; but I can't help feeling that if you
really cared for Archie . . . I mean, for an engaged young
woman . . .

EMILY. If that's what's worrying you, I can easily
settle that. If Archie feels as you do about it he can have
his engagement ring back. And chuck it in the river.
Or give it to Gloria Kishmul—Heavens, what a name!—
and a lot of good *that* 'll do him.

MRS. KEL. Emily!

EMILY. He'd love that. Having the *Ladies' Home
Journal* talked at him morning, noon and night. . . .
Oh, Auntie, I'm a beast and a pig. I'm a jealous beast.
I'll tell Derek I'll have nothing more to do with him.
Honestly, I will.

MRS. KEL. (*weeping*). Oh, dear; oh, dear; oh, dear;
oh, dear.

EMILY. I've been a selfish pig. Only—I wish

Archie . . . No, no.   It's all right.   He's *got* to get on with his new book.   When it's published, perhaps he'll have more time to—I mean . . .

MRS. KEL.   Of course you never had a particle of sympathy with Archie's work.

EMILY.   Oh, I have, I have.   Only he does it so badly. And he's so cocky about it.

MRS. KEL.   Cocky?

EMILY.   No.   I shouldn't say that. . . . I wish he'd never tried to write a book.   I wish we'd settled down and had babies up North. . . . Oh, stop me.   I'm an idiot.   I'll try to be good.   I *will* be good.   Just like Queen Victoria when they told her she was to be Queen.

MRS. KEL.   You couldn't follow a better example, Emily dear.

EMILY.   You can tell Archie, if you like, that I won't see Mr. Putney again.   I'll go and ring up Mr. Putney now.

MRS. KEL.   I think that would be the best plan.   In your own interests, Emily dear. . . .

EMILY.   What the devil do you mean, " In my own interests "?

MRS. KEL.   Emily, don't you dare to speak to me like that.

EMILY.   Well, what do you mean?

UNCLE TOM (*without*).   Milly!

EMILY.   Oh, damn, damn, damn, damn.

[*She rushes out by the river gate.*

UNCLE TOM (*entering from the house*).   I can't get the hang of this crossword at all.   I thought I heard Milly.

MRS. KEL.   You thought you heard Milly, did you? Well, you were quite right.

[*She marches into the house like an infuriated grenadier.*

CURTAIN

ACT III

SCENE II

*The same a week later. It is a hot, sunny day in September.
An enormous parasol lies on its side on the exiguous lawn, and
from behind it come the strains of a Hawaian-Negroid Lullaby-
Spiritual from the Tin Pan Alley Plantations. It is accompanied by a banjo-uke.*

MRS. KISHMUL (*unseen*). Colonel Wotherspoon was
right. I sing Wally Ziggezein abominably.

ARCHIE (*unseen*). I thought you sang that with great
feeling and expression.

MRS. KISHMUL. Oh, feeling; yes.

ARCHIE. I think those Autumn evenings in London
are the loveliest in the whole world. I say, the sun's
gone round and we haven't noticed it. Let's slew round
the parasol.

> [*He slews round the parasol. We now see, to our astonish-
> ment, ARCHIE and MRS. KISHMUL in bathing dresses. A
> bottle of something is beside them in an ice-pail.*]

I say. This is heavenly. Have some more Liebefraumilch?

MRS. KISHMUL. Thanks a lot. I will. It's dry
work being a Honolulu baby.

ARCHIE. Cheerio.

MRS. KISHMUL. Here's mud in your eye.

ARCHIE. Gosh! It's nearly midday. How the time
does fly. The papers will be here any time now.

MRS. KISHMUL. Now, Archie-boy, don't you start
getting nervous. Believe me or believe me not, it's

[57]

going to be another of the same. A big success, do you hear me ?

ARCHIE. I don't think myself it's so good as " Madder Music."

MRS. KISHMUL (*patting his cheek playfully*). You are telling me.

ARCHIE. Well, I didn't take the time to it that I took to " Madder Music." . . . It's funny, too, publishing it at the week-end. It's taking a risk.

MRS. KISHMUL. And where would Napoleon have been if he hadn't taken a chance ? A real daring idea of old Simmy's to go bang for the Sunday papers.

ARCHIE. I wish I could feel certain about it.

MRS. KISHMUL. But sure! All the book-fans read the Sunday papers. It's a cast-iron proposition. You'll rush them off their feet again all right. Gloria knows.

ARCHIE. It was one of your strokes of genius to think of this way of spending the morning. It's made the waiting time pass like lightning.

MRS. KISHMUL. Oh, that's an old spiel of mine. When I was Business Manager to J. J. F. Finkelstein I used to tote him away to Palm Beach, Florida, for a week before his publishing date.

ARCHIE. Oh! Did you ? Like—like this ?

MRS. KISHMUL. Now, Archie, don't tell me you're jealous. It was all in the way of business. Shucks! What's the use of having a figure ?

ARCHIE. It's funny . . . somehow . . . I know there's no harm in it. . . . But . . . somehow . . . I don't like to think of you and . . . well . . .

MRS. KISHMUL. Just what are you getting at ? I am a good Presbyterian like yourself.

ARCHIE. I know. I never thought of suggesting for a moment . . . But you see it's all rather new to me. I mean this ultra-violet business. And you'll have to give me some time to get acclimatised.

MRS. KISHMUL. Sure. Take your time.

ARCHIE. I don't think my mother, for instance, is frightfully keen on this sun-bathing.

MRS. KISHMUL. That's because she's not used to the sun. We'll have her out in a two-piece suit before many weeks. Your Uncle Tom likes it all right. I expect he'll be down in his pyjamas soon.

ARCHIE. Yes.

MRS. KISHMUL. We haven't seen much of that little cousin of yours since we all came to London.

ARCHIE. No. She's staying in a Hostel now.

MRS. KISHMUL. Too bad. A dear little thing, that. I adored her, even on our short acquaintance.

ARCHIE. She's a very brainy sort of girl.

MRS. KISHMUL. Yes, and pretty too, in an undistinguished sort of way. And I should think she has a vurry pleasant personality.

ARCHIE. Yes. Very. She's a bit quick-tempered at times, of course.

MRS. KISHMUL. There's no harm in that. No harm at all. I think a gurl's so insipid without a little irritability, don't you? I love her, Archie. A nice, sensible, bachelor gurl. Of course, she's a woman's woman. You'd scurcely be likely to appreciate her, Archie.

ARCHIE. Oh, I do appreciate her very much. We've always been the greatest pals till—well, till lately. But there's something wanting about her. I don't know what it is.

MRS. KISHMUL. Personality?

ARCHIE. Well, yes. I believe it is. It's funny. I know her awfully well, and you would have thought that, unconsciously, I'd have put some of her characteristics into some of the girls in my novels. But I never have.

MRS. KISHMUL. She wasn't your dream-girl, Archie?

ARCHIE. No. You hear of fellows writing and all the time a girl's face is sort of floating before them. Well, it didn't to me. At least not after the first two chapters of "Madder Music." At least, well, not my cousin's face.

MRS. KISHMUL. Now that is real intriguing. What sort of a face did you see?

ARCHIE. Different kinds. They were mostly dark, I think, and Emily—Miss Perry, is fair. Funny. Dark, with long eyelashes, and tall. Sort of creamy olive complexions with just the faintest touch of dark red showing through. And long graceful arms and legs . . . and . . . Oh, I say, I am talking drivel.

MRS. KISHMUL. Oh yes? It sounds a vurry good sense to me.

ARCHIE. Oh, I say, Gloria, I didn't mean . . . But, yes, by gosh. She *was* like you.

MRS. KISHMUL. Was she? Your dream-gurl? (*She puts her hands on his shoulders.*)

ARCHIE. Yes.

MRS. KISHMUL. Well, I think that's a vurry delicate compliment. (*She kisses him.*) Oh, dear, I shouldn't have done that.

ARCHIE. Gloria. Oh, Gloria. Yes, you should.

[*He embraces* MRS. KISHMUL *with remarkable violence for one of his temperament.*]

MRS. KISHMUL. Oh, Archie. Don't. I never knew. Archie, do you care for me—in that way?

ARCHIE. Of course I do.

[EMILY *appears at the French window.*]

EMILY. In what way, Mrs. Kishmul?

MRS. KISHMUL. What dó you mean?

EMILY. I've heard it so often on the talkies—" Do you care for me—in that way? " I've often wondered what it meant.

MRS. KISHMUL. I think you are absolutely unpardonable.

EMILY. Good morning, Archie. There didn't seem to be anybody about so I came right through. I didn't know you and Mrs. Kishmul were in conference. Where is Aunt Bethia?

ARCHIE. I don't know.   She was having breakfast in bed.

EMILY. I see. I'll run upstairs to her bedroom. It's just facing the stairs, isn't it ?

ARCHIE. Yes. At the top of the stairs. You can't miss it.

EMILY. Righto.

[*Exit* EMILY.]

MRS. KISHMUL. Well, I call that pretty tough.

ARCHIE. Yes. O Lord! What do you think she'll do, Gloria ? What do you think ?

MRS. KISHMUL. Search me.

ARCHIE. D'you—d'you think she's gone to tell my mother ?

MRS. KISHMUL. I don't know. Seems to me that in our conversation a little ago we were seriously under-estimating your little cousin.

ARCHIE. What do you mean ?

MRS. KISHMUL. Well, I'll say this, she made a great come back. I should think she's real glad she waited six months for this.

ARCHIE. Gosh! It must have been a dickens of a shock to her.

MRS. KISHMUL. Oh, yes!

ARCHIE. I don't know what it was. I lost my head somehow.

MRS. KISHMUL. Well ? And are you sorry ?

ARCHIE. No, by gosh, I'm not. Gloria, you're the only girl in the world for me. We'll get married as soon as I can get a licence. There's nothing I won't be able to do when . . .

MRS. KISHMUL. *Just* a minute. There's another gentleman may have something to say to that.

ARCHIE. You're not—you're not married ?

MRS. KISHMUL. Sure. What *does* " Mrs." mean in front of a name on this side of the Atlantic ?

ARCHIE. But I thought you were a widow.

[61]

MRS. KISHMUL. I imagined you might. My husband is Stanford Kishmul, the polo player. Ever heard of him ?

ARCHIE. No.

MRS. KISHMUL. Reach me my wrap, there's a good boy. Thanks. . . . Oh, we're not that fond of each other that something couldn't be arranged. A cable from me and he'd be off to Reno by the first train, poor boy.

ARCHIE. Oh, then that's not so bad. . . . What would you say in the cable ?

MRS. KISHMUL. I've not quite decided to send it yet.

ARCHIE. But you must. You must. There's no time to lose now. It would break my mother's heart if she thought I were in love with a married woman. She thought you were a widow too, or she would never have let me engage you as my business manager. She's most frightfully particular about—about these things.

MRS. KISHMUL. Oh, God, Archie. You make me feel like a cradle snatcher. How did you contrive to run that store of yours up North ?

ARCHIE. I know I sound like an absolute idiot. But in a way it's not me that's making noises like an idiot. It's a poor little kid who's not been allowed to blow his own nose without asking mamma first—and then she's criticised the way he did it. I'm not like that though, really. I don't care, really. Not the part of me that wrote " Stronger Wine." The point is, I want you to marry me and—well—what with one thing and another the sooner the better.

MRS. KISHMUL. You *are* in a hurry.

ARCHIE. Of course I'm in a hurry. Haven't I just told you . . .

MRS. KISHMUL. I don't think you quite realise, Archie, dear, that in America we look on marriage as a vurry serious matter.

ARCHIE. How the dickens do you think I'm looking at it ?

MRS. KISHMUL.   Vurry seriously, no doubt.   But you must remember that, from what I saw of your home town, it must be a vurry unusual experience for you to sit in a garden for two hours listening to an attractive woman in a backless two-piece beach suit playing to you on the banjo-uke.   If you'll allow me to say so, these circumstances conduce to a state of mind highly unsuitable for making big decisions affecting your entire future.

ARCHIE.   Gloria, you don't understand.

MRS. KISHMUL.   You'll pardon me, that is one of those matters I understand vurry well.

ARCHIE.   I don't believe you do.   Of course you're clever and—er—sophisticated and you've knocked about a bit . . .

MRS. KISHMUL.   For thirty-seven years.   How old are you ?

ARCHIE.   Twenty-seven; but, dash it, what does that matter if we—if we love each other ?   And you—well—you care for me, don't you ?

MRS. KISHMUL.   Oh, gee!   I do!   I wish . . . But what does it matter ?

ARCHIE.   It doesn't.   It doesn't.   Nothing matters but . . . Oh, send that wire, Gloria.   Send it right off now.   Please, Gloria.

MRS. KISHMUL.   Oh, well!

[*Enter* UNCLE TOM *in pyjamas.   He carries a huge pile of Sunday papers.*]

ARCHIE.   Oh, gosh.

UNCLE TOM.   Well, here they are.   Here they are.   I haven't looked at one of them.   I've left the—chrm—first bloom of triumph for you, old boy.   I don't need to look at them.   I'm certain you've knocked 'em again. Another winner, eh, Mrs. Kishmul ?   Colonel Wother-spoon told me at luncheon yesterday—did I tell you ?— " Mark my words," he said, " he'll do it again.   That boy's got the stuff in him," he said.   " By Gad, yes," he said. " He'll go on from strength to strength," he said. So I said, " I quite agree with you, Colonel," I said. " The boy's got guts," I said. " Runs in the family," I said.

[*Enter* MRS. KELLOCK, *with* EMILY *behind.*]

They're busy with the press notices, Bethia.

MRS. KEL.   Well, I don't approve of Sunday papers, but perhaps to-day. What do they say about my boy's book this time, Archie boy ?

ARCHIE.   I can't find anything about it in the *Chimes.* Funny; there must have been some mistake . . .

MRS. KEL.   How careless of the Editor. What have you got there, Mrs. Kishmul ?

MRS. KISHMUL.   The *Sunday Scrutator.*

MRS. KEL.   *They've* got a bit about my lamb, haven't they ?

MRS. KISHMUL.   Yes. They have.

ARCHIE.   Let me see ?

UNCLE TOM.   Ah. Hum. Woof. Where are my glasses ? Wotherspoon says the *Scrutator* is the soundest of the whole bunch. Ah. There's the *News Reel.* Let me see.

MRS. KISHMUL.   No. . . . Oh, well. You may as well.

[*She hands the newspaper to* ARCHIE.]

MRS. KEL.   Read it aloud, Archie boy.

ARCHIE.   " Mr. Kellock's ' Stronger Wine ' is pretty considerably under proof; and it is doubtful if the ladies of the scullery to whom it is obviously addressed will get much kick out of it. I dislike having to deal harshly with the work of any young author, but a reviewer has a certain public duty to perform, and the recent cataclysmal sales of the author's first book deprive him of the protection of obscurity's decent veil. In dealing with that book, I drew attention to certain crudities in the hope . . ."

MRS. KISHMUL.   Drew attention to certain crudities !

I know what he said.   It's in print on the dust jacket of
" Stronger Wine." Of all the nerve! He said, " In
spite of certain crudities, this is a book that will live." . . .
Reginald Devereux, in the *Scrutator*. Gee, I wish I had
my knuckles under his green silk collar.

ARCHIE.   " . . . in the hope that he might bombinate
a thought less offensively in his intellectual vacuum."
I'm not sure what that means.

MRS. KISHMUL.   It's a Bloomsbury wise-crack.

MRS. KEL.   You must write to our lawyers at once.

UNCLE TOM.   Woof. This fellow in the *News Reel*
doesn't seem any more enthusiastic.

MRS. KISHMUL.   The Sunday *Sentinel* gives it Hell.

MRS. KEL.   It's all jealousy. It's a conspiracy.

[*A silence.*]

UNCLE TOM.   } Of course I always . . . You've got
MRS. KISHMUL.   } to remember . . . I think it's
MRS. KEL.   } simply . . . I beg your pardon . . .
                     } No, no, please go on.

UNCLE TOM.   You remember I always told you, even
about " Madder Music," that you were a bit weak—
woof—in your thingumbob. Wotherspoon said he liked
it well enough, but he was never quite carried away by it.
Of course. I always stuck up for you, being your uncle
and all that, but you see what I mean ? I mean to say.
And you know perfectly well you wouldn't take a word
of advice about " Stronger Wine "—potty title . . .

MRS. KEL.   Uncle Tom's quite right, dearest, though
it's hard to have to admit it. Very, very hard. Time
and again both Uncle Tom and I have told you what you
ought to put in and what you ought to put out. But no.
You were the great author. You would go your own
way.

UNCLE TOM.   You've got to admit, old boy, you got a
bit above yourself. You recollect my saying to you:
" Go slow, old boy. Wait a bit. You never know," I

said, " how they'll take your next effort." And here we are.

MRS. KEL. And then moving into this very, very expensive house. Will these notions affect the sale of the book, Mrs. Kishmul ?

MRS. KISHMUL. Oh, I don't know. I should think if they're all like Devereux they can't help it. And they seem to be, too. It's all vurry upsetting.

MRS. KEL. It's simply too, too dreadful. Oh, Archie, my son, my son, if you'd only taken Mother's advice.

MRS. KISHMUL. Perhaps I might vurry respectfully suggest that you should write his next book for him.

MRS. KEL. I fail to see, Mrs. Kishmul, that my poor son's misfortune is a matter for making jokes about.

MRS. KISHMUL. Nobody is better informed in that respect than I am, Mrs. Kellock; I'm his business manager.

MRS. KEL. What is a business manager to a mother ? And besides, if you are his business manager, you ought to have warned him.

MRS. KISHMUL. Will you oblige me by telling me of what I ought to have warned him ?

ARCHIE. Mother. It's no use talking about it now. It's no use getting angry now the damage is done.

MRS. KEL. I am not getting angry; only a leetle surprised that after all you have done for Mrs. Kishmul . . .

ARCHIE. Don't speak that way, Mother. All the— all the obligation's on my side.

MRS. KEL. I beg to differ. Mrs. Kishmul has had a very handsome commission, indeed, on everything she has done. I don't know whether that includes lolling about on a Sabbath morning more than half naked . . .

ARCHIE. Mother ! Oh, stop. I can't listen to this.

MRS. KEL. . . . singing American songs to the banjo . . .

ARCHIE. They were negro spirituals, Mother.

MRS. KEL. But I am not accustomed to such behaviour,

and it's high time I said so.   If, even by accident, I had
ever exposed one-twentieth as much of myself to a member
of the opposite sex, I should have died of shame.

ARCHIE.   Mother, you mustn't.   Mother.   I won't
have it.

MRS. KEL.   It is nothing more or less than an incite-
ment to all the baser passions . . .

ARCHIE.   You don't know what you're saying.   Mrs.
Kishmul and I are engaged.

MRS. KEL.   Mrs. Kishmul and you are what?

UNCLE TOM.   Woof.

ARCHIE.   Didn't—didn't Emily tell you?

EMILY.   I didn't know.

ARCHIE.   Oh, dash it, you might have . . . Well,
at least . . .

MRS. KEL.   This is a terrible, terrible shock.

MRS. KISHMUL.   Yes, isn't it?   If you will vurry
kindly excuse me, it has gotten a little cold.   I'll go
inside and put something on.

[*Exit.*]

MRS. KEL.   And high time too.   I might have known.
Oh, Tom, how blind I've been.

UNCLE TOM.   I could have given you a hint all right.
I had a notion how things were shaping.   I did try once
or twice to give you the office, but you wouldn't listen.
Nobody listens to me in this house.   Might as well be
a bit of furniture.   You haven't heard half of it yet
either.   Woof.

MRS. KEL.   I don't want to hear any more.   I forbid
any further mention of the very idea.   Archie, this has
got to stop.   Do you hear?   And at once.

UNCLE TOM.   I should jolly well think so!

ARCHIE.   What the devil has it got to do with you?

UNCLE TOM.   Eh?   It's . . . Eh?   What say?

ARCHIE.   I said, what the devil's it got to do with you,
and I'd very much like to know.

MRS. KEL.   That's no way to speak to your uncle.

UNCLE TOM. Don't mind me. Woof. I don't matter. I'm nobody. I'm only the head of the family. I've got to listen to what everybody's saying and keep my mouth shut. I've got used to sitting like thingummy on a monument. Nobody can say of me I don't know when to hold my tongue. But a time comes when it's criminal to keep silence. Criminal. And I may as well tell you now, Bethia . . .

MRS. KEL. How long has this been going on, Archie?

ARCHIE. Oh, I don't know. There was nothing. At least Gloria gave me no encouragement till . . . At least not even then. . . . But for months I've . . . Oh, Mother, she's a topper. She's . . . I wish you could . . . It's difficult to explain . . .

MRS. KEL. Mother knows, Archie boy. But my lamb knows very, very little of the world. And although it's very, very hard, my lamb must believe what Mother says when she says that this engagement will never, never, never do. There are certain kinds of women, dearest, who . . .

ARCHIE. I know. I'm not a child. But she's not. Honestly, Mother, she's not.

UNCLE TOM. Woof. Ha!

ARCHIE. Uncle Tom, I've had about enough from you. It's natural for Mother to be worried about—about all this and to say things she'll maybe be sorry for afterwards; but if I have another word from you I'll pitch you into the river.

UNCLE TOM. You heard that, Bethia? You heard that, Milly? He threatened me with assault.

ARCHIE. Yes, and I meant it. I'm just desperate.

MRS. KEL. Archie, this is too, too much. You should feel black burning shame of yourself.

ARCHIE. Well, let him be quiet.

EMILY. Archie, don't. He can't help it. It's just a sort of reflex. Don't pay any attention to him. He's an old man.

UNCLE TOM.   An old man!   Ho.

ARCHIE.   I'm sorry, Emily.   This must be dreadful for you.   I forgot myself.   I'm sorry.

MRS. KEL.   I should think so indeed.

UNCLE TOM.   Well, my boy, I accept your apology. I . . .

ARCHIE.   I wasn't apologising to you.

UNCLE TOM.   Oh, you weren't, weren't you?

EMILY.   Shut up, Uncle Tom.   Do sit down, Aunt Bethia.   We're all getting excited about nothing. Archie, you're chittering with cold.   Go in and put something on.

MRS. KEL.   Don't dare, Archie.   And that woman dressing in the house.

EMILY.   Aunt Bethia, what a mind you have.

MRS. KEL.   Will you leave my mind alone, please, Emily?

EMILY.   Joyfully.   Run away in, Archie.

ARCHIE.   It's all right.   I've got a pair of bags and a jumper in the boat house.

[*He goes out by the garden gate.*]

MRS. KEL.   Oh, dear.   I little thought this would happen to me in my old age.   And Archie always such a loving, considerate boy.

UNCLE TOM.   Woof.

EMILY.   Auntie dear, don't you think you are making up your mind a little too quickly?   Mrs. Kishmul is a little old for Archie, but she's a very clever sensible woman, just the sort to keep him on the rails and— and give him that little touch of the practical that he lacks.

MRS. KEL.   Emily, it's no use talking.   Do you call this mixed bathing in the back green practical?   I call it scandalous.   Simply scandalous.

EMILY.   It isn't really, Aunt Bethia.   Lots of decent people do it.   Blake did it.   It's quite usual.   There's no possible harm in it.

MRS. KEL.   There is.   Our first parents made themselves aprons out of fig leaves.

EMILY.   Well, dash it, Archie and his lady friend were over-dressed compared with them.

MRS. KEL.   That is a little irreverent, Emily.

EMILY.   I'm sorry, Aunt.   Would you like this hassock for your feet?

MRS. KEL.   No, thank you, Emily.

EMILY.   I'll take Uncle Tom for a walk.

UNCLE TOM.   Oh, you will, will you?

EMILY.   Yes, I will.   After all, you're not directly concerned in this business, and I don't know that *I* want to be.

UNCLE TOM.   And I suppose I am to have no say in what's going on?

EMILY.   Well, you've said your say, haven't you, dear? And nearly got chucked into the Thames for it.

UNCLE TOM.   Hey?   You think so, do you?   Well, I've not said my say.   Not by a jugful.   Bethia, Colonel Wotherspoon told me a thing you ought to know.   Colonel Wotherspoon said to me . . .

EMILY.   Oh, come along, Uncle Tom.   Aunt Bethia can hear about Colonel Wotherspoon another time.

UNCLE TOM.   No.   Woof.   Let me go, Emily.   How can I go for a walk in my pyjamas?   Don't be a fool. Woof.   Listen, Bethia, this is very important.   Colonel Wotherspoon told me, Bethia . . .

MRS. KEL.   What did he tell you, Tom?   Such a nice man, the Colonel.   Such a thorough gentleman. So refined.

UNCLE TOM.   He's a good fellow, old Wuthers.   A darned good fellow.   My best friend.   Many the laugh we've had together over this and that.   I remember once . . .

EMILY.   Uncle Tom, will you stop remembering things.   Tell Aunt Bethia what you want her to hear and come away and put on your breeks.

UNCLE TOM.   Right.   I'll tell her.   Are you aware, Bethia, that Mrs. Kishmul is a married woman?

EMILY.   Don't be silly, Uncle Tom.   Everybody called " Mrs." is a married woman.

UNCLE TOM.   I hope the Lord preserves your innocence, Emily.

MRS. KEL.   What's this?   What did you say, Tom?

UNCLE TOM.   You thought Mrs. Kishmul was a widow, didn't you, now?

MRS. KEL.   But she is, isn't she?   She always talked about her poor dear husband.

UNCLE TOM.   Woof.   Poor dear husband all right. But he happens to be alive and kicking.   Colonel Wotherspoon knows a fellow who played polo with him last year at Ranelagh.   And they're not divorced either.   Wuthers says he met a lot of fellows who were talking about Archie and Mrs. Kishmul at the Rag.

MRS. KEL.   At the where?

UNCLE TOM.   At the Rag.   Wotherspoon's Club.

MRS. KEL.   And my Archie was a topic of scandalous conversation at a place with a name like that?   Oh, Tom.

UNCLE TOM.   Ask Wotherspoon.

MRS. KEL.   A married woman!   Oh, oh, oh!

EMILY.   Auntie, don't be so silly.   It's . . .   You're a married woman yourself.

MRS. KEL.   But how different!   I think I'm going to faint.   Take me into the house.   Oh, Archie, Archie, Archie, where are you?   Oh, Archie, my boy, that a tragedy like this should have befallen us.

[ARCHIE *enters during this lament.*]

ARCHIE.   But, Mother, it's all right.   She's going to get a divorce at once.

MRS. KEL.   All right!   You can stand before me with a brazen face and tell me it's all right.   I knew it.   I've seen it coming.   I've seen your face hardening, and the lines of vice deepening upon it for years.   I have prayed

for you, Archie, I have even spoken to the minister about
you.   And this is my reward.   An adulterous intrigue
with an abandoned creature whose husband plays ludo at
a Rag.   I am thankful—I say I am thankful your poor
father is safely in his grave this day.

> [MRS. KISHMUL, *fully and even fashionably dressed, appears
> at the french window.*]

MRS. KISHMUL.   What's the matter?

MRS. KEL.   Take me into the house.   Take me into
the house.   I can't bear to look at her.   There she
stands.   Look at her.   There she stands.   Oh, you
wicked, wicked woman.

ARCHIE.   Mother.

EMILY.   Aunt Bethia, don't be an ass.

MRS. KEL.   I am an ass, am I?   Yes, yes.   A poor
blind beast of burden, toiling and moiling all these years,
wearing my fingers to the bone to keep the home
together. . . .

EMILY.   You've done nothing of the sort.   Archie's
done all that.   You've sat on your bottom on a comfortable chair and interfered and criticised and snivelled and
slopped and made his life a living Hell.   Hold your
tongue, you silly old woman.   Let me speak for a change.

UNCLE TOM.   Emily, you forget yourself.

EMILY.   I'll deal with you presently.   I've been away
from the tropical environment of the Kellock Family
Robinson for over six months now, and I've got some
blood back in my veins.   I want to tell your desert island
what I think of it.

UNCLE TOM.   What's the matter with you?   Nobody
did anything to you.

MRS. KEL.   Emily, I won't bear it.

EMILY.   I know.   You won't stand up to anything,
Aunt Bethia.   You're just a cringing old parasite.

UNCLE TOM.   Look here . . .

EMILY.   *You're* worse.   You're a paranoiac's delu-
sion of voices.   Archie, are you going to be a man?

What's the good of trying to conciliate those two? Take a big stick and hit them a crack on the head apiece and take your Gloria along to the boat train.

MRS. KEL.   Is nobody going to take me into the house?

EMILY.   Go into the house yourself. You've got a pair of legs—somewhere.

MRS. KEL.   Tom.

UNCLE TOM.   Come along, Bethia. We can't stand up against hysterics. Woof. Mind the step. I remember a girl I used to know in Bristol—woof—steady does it. Colonel Wotherspoon says . . .

Exeunt UNCLE TOM *and* MRS. KELLOCK.]

MRS. KISHMUL.   Well, I'll say, Miss Perry, you have gotten a faculty for inspired invective that makes you a pleasure to listen to.

EMILY.   Oh, dear. Poor miserable old things. I can't help it. They madden me. Mother, my head, my head!

MRS. KISHMUL.   If I may be permitted to prescribe, I should say a glass of Liebefraumilch and a cigarette would be just right for your complaint. Get a drink for her, Archie. She deserves it.

ARCHIE.   Righto.

MRS. KISHMUL.   Here's a light. And a cushion? That better?

EMILY.   Thanks ever so much. What's that you've got there?

MRS. KISHMUL.   Oh, a cablegram I was drafting.

ARCHIE.   Do you think Mother will be all right?

EMILY.   If you go near your mother or mention her or think about her for the next two hours, this lady and I will walk out of the house and never see you again.

ARCHIE.   But . . .

EMILY.   Put your Œdipus complex in a bag. We've got to talk sense for once in a way. What's going to happen about his book, Mrs. Kishmul?

MRS. KISHMUL. It's not easy to say. I sold a big block of the rights in advance and a complete edition was sold before publication. He's gotten on the wrong side of the critics all right, but then, there's a darn sight more folk read " Madder Music " than ever read all the critics put together. I'd reckon on a fairly large hick public for anything he writes for a good number of years to come.

ARCHIE. I'm not going to write another word. I can't write. Emily told the truth six months ago when she said so. I'm going back to business. I've made a fool of myself.

EMILY. I think you're wise. I think it's the honest thing to do.

MRS. KISHMUL. You'll pardon me, but I disagree *in toto*. I see nothing dishonest in giving innocent enjoyment to a large number of one's fellow-citizens.

EMILY. But don't you think it's dreadful to debauch the public with a false view of life ? Derek—Mr. Putney—was saying to me yesterday . . .

ARCHIE. Mr. Putney ? You've met him again ?

EMILY. Yes. He says he's going to let you down lightly over " Stronger Wine."

ARCHIE. He is, is he ?

EMILY. Yes, he . . . Well, he promised me.

ARCHIE. Look here, Emily. It was very decent of you, and all that. But I can't take favours of that sort.

EMILY. Why not ?

MRS. KISHMUL. Yes, why not ? My dear boy, I'm your agent and I've been exerting every nerve to get a line on Derek Putney for the past year, and he's the sea-green incorruptible. If Miss Perry can vamp him we'll pull the highbrows yet.

ARCHIE. Hold on a minute, Gloria. . . . No. . . . No. . . . I see things clearly now. I've felt for months that it was all moonshine and plain ignorance and . . .

MRS. KISHMUL. Pardon me. I shall be glad to have you give me your personal reactions later. Do I understand that you have definitely decided to abandon the pursuit of literature ?

ARCHIE.   That's what I've been saying. . . . Emily, you've always been a trump, and I've been a beast to you and . . .

EMILY.   Do stop talking like *The Boy's Own Paper*. Mrs. Kishmul has some more remarks to make.

ARCHIE.   No, no. Just a minute, Emily. What are you going to do ?

EMILY.   Me ?

ARCHIE.   Yes, you. And you should say I.

EMILY.   No, I shouldn't. But why do you ask ?

ARCHIE.   Because I must know.

EMILY.   I don't know that it's any of your business—now.

ARCHIE.   It is my business. I must know.

EMILY.   Well, if you must, I'm going to bolt with Derek.

ARCHIE.   You're what ?

EMILY.   You heard what I said, Archie dear. I'm going off with Derek Putney.

ARCHIE.   That lisping, stuttering, gesticulating little tick ! Besides, he's got a wife.

EMILY.   Oh, somewhere or other.

ARCHIE.   But you can't do that. You can't. You, you of all people.

EMILY.   Stop quoting " Madder Music " at me.

ARCHIE.   Stop doing literary sneers at me. You're not going off with that stinking highbrow.

EMILY.   Oh ? Why not ?

ARCHIE.   Because decent girls don't do things like that.

EMILY.   You're away back in Queen Victoria's glorious days.

ARCHIE.   You're away back to the monkeys. Anyway, I won't have it.

EMILY.   You won't have it ?

ARCHIE.   That's what I said.

EMILY.   You dictate to me, you ignorant, illiterate brute.

ARCHIE.   That's a caddish thing to say.   I've as good a mind as you have.

EMILY.   You've got a mind like an accident in a brewery.   Besides—I mean to be caddish.   You're absolutely maddening.

ARCHIE.   And you're a rotten little highbrow.

EMILY.   You liar.

ARCHIE.   You're a liar yourself.   I may be a damned failure but I'm not a heartless intellectual snob.

EMILY.   You're not a failure.   Don't you dare to say that.

ARCHIE.   I am a failure.   You know I am.   Don't lie to me again.

EMILY.   I'm not lying to you.   What are you doing, Mrs. Kishmul?

MRS. KISHMUL.   I'm tearing up a cablegram.   Listen. Archie, I've one word to say to you.   You and Emily have been acting, till now, like a couple of linotypes banging out thousands of words.   Forget it.   You're a man and a woman.   And don't you worry about me. This won't keep me awake.   And another thing.   Just pause a moment and ask yourself, "What would Toby Carteret have done?"

[*She vanishes.*]

ARCHIE.   Now, who the devil was Toby Carteret?

EMILY.   Never mind, you big idiot!

ARCHIE.   Emily . . . Is it all right . . . I mean . . . between us?

EMILY.   Well . . . what about that woman?

ARCHIE.   There's only one woman for me.

[*They sit on adjacent chairs.*]

EMILY.   You're sure?

ARCHIE.   Dead sure.   Emily, will you help me in my

[76]

work? I mean, let's collaborate. I mean, let's do a play. I've an idea for it. It could be about a fellow who writes a book and a dashed clever girl who helps him up when he's down, and . . . I mean, you could put the psychology into it and the style.

EMILY. That would be lovely, darling.

ARCHIE. I know a fellow who said he'd do my first play, and . . .

EMILY. We'll rough out a sort of scenario to-night. . . . Oh, my goodness!

ARCHIE. What, dear?

EMILY. Derek. I was to meet him at Victoria in half-an-hour.

ARCHIE. We can't write a scenario in half-an-hour.

EMILY. No. . . . The river is lovely to-day.

CURTAIN

WHAT IT IS TO BE YOUNG

The Characters and Incidents in
this play are entirely imaginary.

DEDICATED TO
R. L. B. M.

CHARACTERS

A WAITER.
A CHAUFFEUR.
A LANDLADY.
A LADY ARTIST.
AN EX-OFFICER.
A PROFESSOR, *turned Landlord*.
A GENERAL.
A GENERAL'S DAUGHTER.
A GENERAL'S WIFE.

SCENE.—*The Anglers' Arms.   An Inn in wilder Perthshire.*
TIME.—*November, 192–.*

The play was presented by Sir Barry Jackson at the Birmingham Repertory Theatre on Nov. 2nd, 1929, with the following Cast:

KELLY	Norman Claridge.
MACDONALD	Kenneth Fraser.
MRS. GRYCE	Susan Richmond.
MISS PARKER	Cicely Oates.
CAPT. COCHRAN . . .	Harry Wilcoxon.
GRYCE	Reginald Gatty.
GENERAL DIX	William Heilbron.
VIRGINIA DIX	Daphne Heard.
MRS. DIX	Isobel Thornton.

The play was produced by H. K. Ayliff and the scenery designed by Paul Shelving.

WHAT IT IS TO BE YOUNG

1. JOE KELLY: a Waiter. A wiry, acid ex-corporal of the Scottish Rifles. He wears an artificial leg. His manner is sardonic. He is handy-man, chauffeur and general factotum to the Inn. He is obliging if he is taken in the right way. If not, he is very, very disobliging. Mrs. Gryce knows how to take him in the right way. He has three voices—that of waiter, that of a Lanarkshire pitman, and that of a Jock Non-Commissioned Officer.

2. JOHN MACDONALD: a temporary chauffeur. He is twenty-three, handsome, dressy and talkative. He has no misgivings about anything. He talks with a beautiful Inverness-shire accent.

3. MRS. GRYCE: aged forty-five. She has been a barmaid, but the only sign of it, apart from her coiffure, is a profound knowledge of human nature and a capacity for effective action in most circumstances. She is the landlady. Gryce has been her only weakness and she is trying to live him down.

4. MISS PARKER: aged thirty or so. She is good-looking in a vague way, very good-natured and almost an imbecile. She is a painter and reserves any capacity she has for this trade. Her most positive trait is a desire to explain everything very, very clearly.

5. COCHRAN: aged thirty-five. An ex-Army Captain. The Secretary of the local Ex-Service Men's Society. So true to type, in his appearance, as to be almost incredible. An athlete and a lover of blood sports.

6. GRYCE: aged sixty. Husband of Mrs. Gryce and Emeritus Professor of Metaphysics. He weighs

eighteen stone. He is a large, bald, dirty, slovenly, lazy greybeard, with some remnants of cleverness, but he has never been any use to anyone. He is quite happy.

7. VIRGINIA DIX: aged eighteen. A clever, red-haired child, determined to take every ounce out of what she knows as Life. This has entailed learning ALL about EVERYTHING from a strictly theoretical standpoint. At school she has been taught by the muscular virgins, her mistresses, that she should aim at being a sort of a-sexual male. She has forsworn all sentiment. She can jump five feet and run the 100 yards in $11\frac{1}{5}$ sec. She has read critically Freud, Einstein and Marie Stopes. She is quite nice in spite of it all; very pretty in an intense sort of way; and extremely well-dressed. Mrs. Dix has seen to that.

8. MAJOR-GENERAL DIX: aged fifty-six. A sharp, small, blunt-faced, tidy man. He has risen from the ranks. He is a very able, conscientious little fellow who got his commission by eloping with his Colonel's daughter when she was Virginia's age. He wrestles continually with an inferiority complex. His marriage was the only occasion when he really scored a fall against it.

9. MRS. DIX: aged forty-seven. She looks younger; but she has an old-fashioned, stately manner, acquired through keeping subalterns in their places in India. She is so religiously a snob that her snobbery is not offensive in the least. She is so darned superior that she has found it necessary to chatter about all sorts of domestic details to make common people feel at ease. But she is honestly and unaffectedly the Princess who couldn't sleep on the sea. The audience must not be allowed to think her a fool—even a handsome fool—for she comes out strong in the last Act.

PROLOGUE

A hen is heard clacking over her lay.

[FATHER TIME *appears, complete with Scythe, Forelock and Iron-Rimmed Spectacles ; and speaks :*

In " Studies of the Psyche," we are told
A Baby laughs at Seventeen Days old;
But when Experience grows on apace
It laughs upon the other side of its face.
The Caves of Time engulf the silvery din
And Eld approaches with its twisted grin,
Having discovered where the Joke comes in.

A Mr. W. Shakespeare, Dramatist,
Has given Posterity his little list
Of Mankind's Seven Ages; but he missed
(In his account) that interesting state
Between the schoolboy who was always late
And the young man who took to writing Verse—
That half-light age that we could find much worse
Described than where old Wordsworth says (I think)
" The halflin twigs the shadows of the clink."

That age at which, by Nature's primal laws,
The boy stops laughing and becomes the cause
Of laughter in others. And your kind applause
Is confidently awaited for this play,
Epitomising as it does the way
In which Life suddenly becomes intense
For creatures yet untouched by Common Sense
(That mangy, truckling, toadying, avaricious,
Cowardly quality of the old and vicious).

G   [85]

What is it to be young?   It is to feel
Rebuff and glory and the bruising heel
Of brutal, careless Fact.   It is to go
Where dotards fear to tread.   It is to know
Honour and loyalty and the love of friends,
And Eldorados where the rainbow ends. . . .

Well, that is what this drama is about.
The theatre is deodorised throughout
With Jeyes' life-giving Fluid, kindly lent
By an anonymous friend.   The management
Is not responsible for articles
Left in the vestibule, nor any bills
Contracted by unauthorised contractors.
Now, Ladies and Gents, I leave you to the Actors.

ACT I

The Lounge of the Anglers' Arms.   At back a large show-case
with plate, and a big window.   L., a screened door ; R., a
fireplace.
Late afternoon.

> [JOE KELLY *is emptying a scuttle of coal on the Lounge*
> *fire.   He whistles the song " Après la Guerre " as he*
> *makes the fire-place tidy.*
>
> *To him enters* MACDONALD.]

MACDONALD.   Good afternoon.   It is a cold, raw day,
but we must be expecting that at this time of the year.

> [KELLY *grunts.*]

Did the General leave any instructions for me ?

KELLY (*in his Number* 3, *Lanarkshire voice*).   No, he
didnae.

MACDONALD (*picks up the " The Motoring World " and*
turns over pages).

KELLY.   Showfoors is not supposed to use the Lounge.

MACDONALD.   Indeed, now !   Do you tell me ?   They
will be polluting the pure air of this lovely Lounge, the
low fellows that they are.

KELLY.   Funny, aren't you ?

MACDONALD.   It's a wonder, now, I am not struck
dead for being funny in the Holy of Holies.   Dear me,
now, should I have taken off my boots and my leggings
before I crossed the door-mat ?

KELLY.   You've a hell of a lot to say, for a paid servant !

MACDONALD.   If they pay YOU for civility, it is a bad
bargain they make, whatever.

KELLY.   I'm no' paid for being civil to a capitalist's
lap-dog.

MACDONALD.   Well, now, there's lots of answers to
that observation.   You can take your pick of them,

[87]

indeed yes.   But if it is a fight you would like, it is only fair to tell you that I did not so very badly in the Amateur Light Heavyweights last year.

KELLY.   A fight! I've had all the fight I want.   I lost my leg and my right eye fighting.   What do you ken about fighting?   Where was you in 1914?

MACDONALD.   I was in the school in Salen, learning my A B, ab.

KELLY.   Tyach!

MACDONALD.   If I had known you would feel it so badly I would have got myself born ten years earlier. You are a very difficult gentleman to please.   (*He lights a cigarette.*)   Will you be one of these Socialists, now?

KELLY.   No; I'm a Communist.

MACDONALD.   It is a queer, queer political creed to be held by a waiter.

KELLY.   What way that?   You cannae get a living in the Capitalist State without crawling on the belly of your manhood.   What about yoursel'?   You're an educated kind of a block to be a showfoor.

MACDONALD.   It is a job where you need all the education there is.   People trust their lives to you.

KELLY.   Much use their lives are!   Brass-necked, hard-faced, guzzling swine!

MACDONALD.   Dear me, now, you are all wrong, whatever.   No guzzling at all.   The General is on a diet, and so is Mrs. Dix.   And Miss Virginia is in training, forbye.

KELLY.   You don't need to tell me anything about Generals.   I was a General's batman for a twelvemonth.   Damn't, if blackmail was a respectable occupation there'd be no need for a Ministry of Pensions.

MACDONALD.   Oh, my General is not so bad at all. Not so bad at all.   He is almost illiterate, but he is a gentleman—in so far as one who is half English can be a gentleman. . . .   He is what they call a ranker.   He was a bombardier when she married him.   You will, I

[88]

suppose, be taking part in this League of ex-Soldiers' Rally we have all come up for?

KELLY.   Will I Hell!   None of that dope for me.   I went to the War.   I got what I was asking for.   You'll no' get me God-blessing the Prince of Wales to show the next generation the kind of damned fool I was then. . . . Here, what way did your General no' get to Cloy, where the Rally's being held?   This is twenty mile away.

MACDONALD.   Mrs. Dix is not partial to crowds when she stays in an hotel.   There was a little matter last year over the way the people at the next table took their soup.   Och, it was nothing at all, nothing at all.   But she is an Honourable, and very pernickety.

KELLY.   Pernickety!   You do three months' service wi' the landlady here, and you'll ken what's pernickety.

MACDONALD (*sitting down comfortably*).   Now, did I not think the dogs don't bark but there's a tod in the kail-yard!   We will now hear what for you glower at your neighbour like a wild cat in the whin.

KELLY.   No.   Honest, chum, they're no' that bad. But it disna thole tellin'.   And who's she anyway to come the tin man over the likes of me?   A barmaid she was.   In a station hotel, too.   An' jist because she mairrit on one o' the intelligentsia . . .

MACDONALD.   I did not catch the word.   I beg your pardon.

KELLY.   Intelligentsia.   You know whatamean. They bounders that dinna wash theirsel's and speak like they was gargling.   Ye've seen the old runt?

MACDONALD.   No.

KELLY.   He was a Professor in the Edinburgh Coallege. He was touched in his lung—the tuberculosis—thirty years back, so they pensioned him aff.   So then Mary, she hookit him and took this pub to keep him in.   That'll be ten years syne.   A right auld masterpiece he was then, they tell me, and he's no improved wi' keepin'.   But ugh! we just never heed him.

MACDONALD.   It's a queer come-down from a Professor to be a landlord in a pub.

KELLY.   It is a queer come-down for a decent pub to have him doitering about, talking the hoose empty wi' his blethers. . . . What's the joke?

MACDONALD.   I was thinking you flew at my throat when I came in, and here's us two collieshanging about our employers.

KELLY.   Aye.   The bodies have their uses, too, in a way.   I see you're looking at the Angler's Club plate. It has a kin' o' history, yon.

[MRS. GRYCE *comes in.*]

MRS. GRYCE.   Kelly!

KELLY (*in the voice of a waiter*).   Yes, Mrs. Gryce?

MRS. GRYCE.   Tell Mirn to get Number 14 ready. Captain Cochran is staying here to-night.   Who are you?

[KELLY *collects his impedimenta and goes.*]

MACDONALD.   General Dix's driver, madam.

MRS. GRYCE.   Are you aware this is the Lounge?

MACDONALD.   The Lounge, madam?

MRS. GRYCE.   Don't repeat things after me.   You know perfectly well you've no business here.   Kelly!

[*Re-enter* KELLY.]

I'm going to the gathering to-night, so get the Morris ready.

KELLY.   Yes, ma'am.   (*He goes.*)

MRS. GRYCE.   Well?

MACDONALD.   I did not speak, madam.

MRS. GRYCE.   I didn't expect you to.   Take yourself out of here.

MACDONALD.   I was just about to go, madam.

[*Exit* MACDONALD.]

[MRS. GRYCE *bustles about the room, moving objects for the
    sake of moving them, testing the tops of furniture for
    dust, preening herself at the mirror—a restless woman.*

    To her MISS PARKER.]

[90]

MISS PARKER. Oh, hello, Mrs. Gryce.

MRS. GRYCE. Good afternoon, Miss Parker. Have you been out painting?

MISS PAR. No. Just walking. It was too cold to sit down. Have you—er—have your new guests arrived?

MRS. GRYCE. The General's party? Oh, yes. An hour or more. They are upstairs in their rooms. Captain Cochran's coming too. The hotel will be quite cheery.

MISS PAR. Who is Captain Cochran?

MRS. GRYCE. Haven't you seen him? Oh, he's the Secretary of this Ex-Service Men's League. He's got a wee shooting-box over by Cloy. It was him got the General down. Fine young fellow he is. Just your type, Miss Parker.

MISS PAR. Oh, I haven't got a type. At least—I mean—I don't mean just ANYBODY would do. But my ideal is not very clearly defined, if you know what I mean. It's so difficult to explain. And it's all rot, anyhow.

MRS. GRYCE. I'm not so sure of that, Miss Parker.

MISS PAR. Not so sure of what? I mean, of course it doesn't matter, but, as I say, the point is . . . Will they all be dining in the coffee-room?

MRS. GRYCE. Yes, I expect so.

[GRYCE *is heard booming " The Mariners of England " in
a very flat boom. He enters ; sees his wife, and stops.*]

GRYCE. I beg your pardon, my dear. I didn't know you were here. I was looking for my . . . [*He withdraws abruptly.*]

MRS. GRYCE. Hi, you! Come back here.

[GRYCE *comes back.*]

GRYCE. Did you call?

MRS. GRYCE. Yes. Andrew, are you going to try to help me, or aren't you?

GRYCE. My dearest, as you know, I have no weaknesses; but if I had one, it would be over-anxiety to help. In what way, exactly, can I assist you?

MRS. GRYCE.   I found Kelly in here a minute ago, gossiping with the General's chauffeur.   Here.   In the Lounge.

GRYCE.   Tut, tut!   But what is my function in this *contretemps*?

MRS. GRYCE.   Well, I can't be in ten places at the same time.   Why can't you speak to Kelly?

GRYCE.   But I do, my love, I do.   I say "Good morning" and "Do you think it will rain?" or "Do you think it will go on raining?" and all sorts of pretty civilities.   There is no response, ever.   I will say that for Kelly.   He never answers back.   He doesn't think it worth while.

MRS. GRYCE.   It's not everyone likes the sound of your voice so well as you do yourself.   The servants think they can do what they like.   The General's lady 'll think we never had company before.   I don't know what Miss Parker thinks of us.

MISS PAR.   Oh, I think the world of you, Mrs. Gryce. And you, too, Professor.   And the Hotel.   And the scenery.

MRS. GRYCE.   It's very kind of you to say so, Miss Parker.   I don't like to be too hard on people, but I do not like chauffeurs in the Lounge.   Such a look as he gave me, too!   That's all, Andrew.   Away you go.

[GRYCE *goes*.]

How would you like to be married to a man like that?

MISS PAR.   Well, it's so difficult to imagine what it must be like to be married at all, I hardly . . .

MRS. GRYCE.   It's not that he isn't frightfully clever. He is.   All brains and no energy, he is.   Bone-lazy. Not that I don't admire him, really, in my heart of hearts. But I don't think you can be married to a man for ten years, even if he is a famous professor, and really respect him.   Do you?   Well, I must be getting things straight. You won't mind my rushing off?

MISS PAR.   Oh, no, Mrs. Gryce.   Not at all.   You've got such heaps and heaps of things to do, and I am just an idler.   In the meantime, anyway, at least.

[*While she is talking* MRS. GRYCE *hurries out.*

MISS PARKER *sits down at fire,* R., *and looks at last summer's* "*Tatler.*"

To her CAPTAIN COCHRAN.   *He carries a portfolio, which he lays on table at the opposite side of the stage from* MISS PARKER.   *He pauses.   They cough alternately.*]

COCHRAN.   I say, it's cold in here.   Would you like the window shut?

MISS PAR.   Oh, no, please.   I like it.   At least, if it's not bothering you.   Blowing your papers about and so forth.

COCHRAN.   No.   Not at all.   I like it too.   I thought you might not like it.

MISS PAR.   Oh, no.   I like it.   I mean, I like fresh air.   It's so—fresh, if you know what I mean.

COCHRAN.   I can't understand how some people can sit with the window shut.   Fugging.

MISS PAR.   Yes.   It seems so silly.   When they might be sitting with the windows open.   So much more —well—healthy.

COCHRAN.   Yes.   Isn't it?   Sitting with the window shut is like missing one's morning tub.

MISS PAR.   Or not brushing one's teeth.   At least, not exactly that.   I hardly mean—but it's so unhealthy, isn't it?

COCHRAN.   Yes, isn't it?   Are you staying here?

MISS PAR.   Oh, yes.   At least—well, for a bit, anyway.   I like coming here.   It's so—quiet, if you see what I mean.   At this time of year there's nobody.   Except, of course, Mrs. Gryce and Professor Gryce— and then there are the servants, of course.

COCHRAN.   Yes.   It is peaceful.   Nothing doing. I've got a place not far off.

MISS PAR. Oh, really. Have you ? What sort of a place ? A house, or anything ?

COCHRAN. Yes. A sort of a house. A little box of a place. It does quite nicely.

MISS PAR. Yes. That must be quite nice. I'd like a house here—not yours, of course. Any house. It's so—well—quiet.

[*Enter* GRYCE.]

GRYCE. I beg your pardon. I didn't know there was anybody here. I trust I do not intrude ?

MISS PAR. Oh, not a bit. At least, I mean—unless Captain Cochran wants to work. And I'm afraid I've been—You *are* Captain Cochran, aren't you ?

COCHRAN. Yes. Cochran. Oh, no, Professor. It's quite all right.

GRYCE. I was looking for—now, what was I looking for ? Truth. " What is Truth ? " said Jesting Pilate, and did not wait for a reply. Truth. Truth.

MISS PAR. I believe I'm sitting on it. No. This is " The Light Car."

GRYCE. It doesn't matter. I forget what I wanted it for. I say, let me shut the window, Miss Parker. The wind is blowing on your naked neck.

MISS PAR. But I like it, Professor. Please don't.

GRYCE. But if you sit in front of an open window you'll get like that perverse generation in the Bible— stiffnecked. Or don't you read your Bible ?

MISS PAR. Oh, often. At least, fairly often. Bits of it. Well, not very often, I'm afraid.

GRYCE. Good book, the Bible. Pas pour les jeunes filles, perhaps. What's the matter with Kelly ?

KELLY (*without*). Hey, miss ! (*He is speaking in an agitated fashion, but in his No. 2 or N.C.O. voice.*) Look out there ! Stop it, now ! Go in at once. It's not safe. Mrs. Gryce ! Hey ! You showfoor fellow ! General ! For God's sake !

GENERAL DIX (*without*). Virginia! Get in by that window at once. At once, do you hear? Wait a bit. I'll come down.

MACDONALD (*without*). Keep you a hold of that rhone pipe, Miss Virginia. I'll get a blanket.

KELLY (*without*). That's right. Jump to it. Hold on tight, miss.

VIRGINIA (*above*). Oh, shut up, everybody. You only rattle me.

MISS PAR. Whatever is the matter?

VIRGINIA (*above*). Heads below!

> [*A confused rumour from below the window.*
> VIRGINIA, *who has climbed out of a window on the second floor, swings herself into the room and falls on all-fours.*]

That's that.

GRYCE. What's what? Where have you come from?

VIRGINIA. Up topsides. It looked easier than it was. You see, I'm Vice-President of our Architectural Alpine Club at College. The men call us the Cat Burglars. Only we're not burglars, of course. And I don't think we're cats. We always try to be sporting.

COCHRAN. By Jove! Sporting all right! Did you come out at the second-storey window?

VIRGINIA. Yes, and along the roof. Tore my frock doing a glissade. Oh, there was nothing in it. Are you the Professor?

COCHRAN. No. This is Professor Gryce.

VIRGINIA. I thought he looked too like a Professor to be one. I say, it was splendid of you to marry Mrs. Gryce.

GRYCE. I—well, I felt greatly honoured when Mrs. Gryce accepted me.

VIRGINIA. Oh, I don't mean that. She's all right. I meant chucking the frowsy old University and doing what you liked. I admire that.

GRYCE. It is a long time ago. A definitive action

rather loses its momentum in ten years.   Even less time
is sufficient for poor benighted *homo sapiens*. . . .

VIRGINIA.   Yes.   Are you the lady-artist?

MISS PAR.   Well.   Yes.   In a way.

VIRGINIA.   In what way?

MISS PAR.   Oh, one way and another.

[*Enter the* GENERAL, *followed by his* WIFE *and by* MRS.
GRYCE.]

DIX.   Virginia, my darling!   What on earth do you
mean by doing a thing like that?   You might have
killed yourself!

MRS. DIX.   You might have killed me.   Don't you
ever give a thought, up in your roof-tops, to my rheu-
matic heart?   It feels simply dreadful.

[MACDONALD *and* KELLY *appear at the door.*]

VIRGINIA.   Oh, well!

MACDONALD.   I beg your pardon, ma'am.   Is Miss
Virginia all right?

MRS. DIX.   I really don't know, Macdonald.

VIRGINIA.   All right, thank you, John.   Thank you
very much for asking.

MACDONALD.   Not at all, Miss Virginia.   Not at all.
(*To* KELLY) She's all right.

[*They withdraw.*]

MRS. GRYCE.   You're sure you don't want a drop of
something?

VIRGINIA.   No, thanks, Mrs. Gryce.   I'm T.T.
Mother, I wish you'd go upstairs and lie down, if you
don't feel well.   It's bad form to be ill in a Lounge.

MRS. DIX.   I'm a little better now, thanks.   No thanks
to you.

VIRGINIA.   Well, I'm very sorry.

MRS. DIX.   A lot of good that is, and my heart going
like a sack of live hens!

VIRGINIA.   Well, I've apologised.   I can do no more.
Do sit down, everybody, and go on with your crossword

puzzles or whatever you were doing before I—before I came in.

MISS PAR.   We weren't doing anything, really.   Just talking and so on.

DIX.   Julia, perhaps you'd better . . . I mean, you are a little *négligée* for a public room in an inn.

MRS. DIX.   Thank heaven it's all right, anyway. I just hurried on anything and came down expecting to find my only daughter all over bits of bone sticking out. And she's always doing things like that, Mrs. Prowse. She was bathing off Mull when she was only ten, and she caught a cormorant and tried to drown it.   She was pecked and scratched all over.   She has the marks still. My husband and I were in India . . .

DIX.   Good heavens, they don't want to hear your autobiography, Julia.   Let's get upstairs.   It's all right.

MRS. DIX (*to* MRS. GRYCE).   What an old bully he is! Does your husband bully you?

MRS. GRYCE.   No, he certainly does not.

MRS. DIX.   You lucky creature!   But then he's not a soldier, is he?

MRS. GRYCE.   No, ma'am; he's not.

MRS. DIX.   I've got used to "all orders promptly and cheerfully obeyed."   I'm a soldier's daughter, you see, and all my men-folk were in the Service.   I feel such a worm when I meet all you fine, free, civilian women.

MRS. GRYCE.   Oh, I'm sure you're joking, ma'am.

MRS. DIX.   Oh, no joke.   No joke at all, I assure you. But it's an advantage, in a way, to be sair haudden doon. One doesn't have to think for oneself, does one?

DIX.   Julia, I wish you'd . . .

VIRGINIA.   Mumsie, please go!

MRS. DIX.   What did I tell you?   Sure you're all right, Virgie?

VIRGINIA.   Oh, yes.

MRS. DIX.   Well, there's no need for me to stand here drivelling any longer.   Coming, Georgie?

[She goes out, DIX and MRS. GRYCE following.]

VIRGINIA. And now, what were you talking about when I came in by the window?

COCHRAN. Oh, nothing in particular. Just general conversation.

VIRGINIA. But what was the subject? How can you talk at all without a subject? If you haven't got a subject it's just beast's jargon.

COCHRAN. There may have been a subject, but I've forgotten what it was.

VIRGINIA. Let's talk about the Unconscious. By the way, what's your name?

COCHRAN. Cochran's my name.

VIRGINIA. I know all about you. I'm glad I've met you. What's yours?

MISS PAR. Parker. Miss Parker.

VIRGINIA. What's your Christian name—or, rather, your first name? One has to be so careful these days.

MISS PAR. Well, it sounds rather silly, but it's Charity. Charity Pennycook Parker. One can't help having a funny-sounding name, can one? I mean, it's so early one gets one's name. And it's sort of disrespectful to change it.

VIRGINIA. Charity Pennycook Parker. It doesn't sound a bit funny to me. It's two dactyls and a trochee. Do you read Freud, Miss Parker?

MISS PAR. No. I can't say that I . . .

VIRGINIA. Yes. I think he's beastly, too. And I wouldn't mind it being beastly if it weren't such rot. Don't you think so, Professor?

GRYCE. Well, you imply rather a sweeping condemnation of a theory I have not had the leisure to examine so thoroughly as I could have wished. It is an interesting fact that . . .

[Enter the GENERAL.]

We were on the point of discussing Freud, General.

DIX. Who?

VIRGINIA. Freud, Daddy.

[98]

DIX. H'm. Met him at Simla. In 10th Lancers, wasn't he? Well, Cochran. Everything ready for the tamasha to-night?

COCHRAN. Everything's ready, sir.

DIX. But what about my speech, eh? What about my speech?

COCHRAN. I should think you'd manage that all right.

DIX. They'll expect me to say something about the financial position of the Branch.

COCHRAN. Oh, I don't think so, sir. It's a social gathering.

VIRGINIA. They won't want to hear a long string of figures, Daddy.

DIX. It isn't what they want to hear; it's what's customary. I don't expect they want to hear me at all.

MISS PAR. Oh, I'm sure they do. At least, I don't know exactly, but I've a sort of feeling they must. Old comrades, you know, and that sort of thing.

DIX. They like a few words, I know, but it's not because they enjoy it. Not at all. Don't make noises, Cochran. You know they don't. It's like those old monk-fellows putting peas in their boots. Plenty of peas, plenty of figures. What about the figures, eh?

VIRGINIA. Let's go for a walk, Miss Parker.

MISS PAR. But I've just come in from a walk.

VIRGINIA. Come for another, then. I want you to tell me what's pretty in the walk, and then I'll go over it again for myself and try to work out why it's pretty. Please come.

MISS PAR. Oh, very well. There's plenty of time before dinner. After you.

VIRGINIA. No. After you. You are much older than I am.

> [*Exeunt* MISS PARKER *and* VIRGINIA. COCHRAN *falls into a reverie.*
>
> *The* PROFESSOR *sits down by the window and lights a foul pipe.*]

DIX.   Now then, Cochran.

COCHRAN.   Yes, General ?

DIX.   Let's have a dekko at these books.

COCHRAN.   I really don't think there's any need, sir. Flourishing financial state and all that.

DIX.   I like always to speak by the book.   It's more business-like.

COCHRAN.   We have a fair balance, sir.

DIX.   How much ?

COCHRAN.   It's in three figures.   I can't give you the odd shillings and pennies.   And you might say the membership has gone up by seventeen since last year.

DIX.   Yes, yes.   I got all that before I came down. Where's your financial statement ?

COCHRAN.   I've got it upstairs, sir.   I'll let you have it after dinner.

DIX.   Damnation, man ! let me have it now.   One would think you were an infernal defaulting babu pay-clerk !

COCHRAN.   General Dix !

DIX.   Well ?

COCHRAN.   I am not accustomed to be spoken to in that fashion.

DIX.   Then don't hedge and wriggle and jolly me as if I was a harmless old imbecile and you were my keeper. What have you got in that leather thing over there ?

COCHRAN.   Some papers.

DIX.   What papers ?

COCHRAN.   We're not on service now, sir.   To be quite frank, I don't see that it's any of your damn business.

DIX.   If I . . . (*Notices* GRYCE, *who rises slowly.*) What the devil . . .?   Did you hear that, sir ?   I—I thought you had gone out.

GRYCE.   No, no.   No, no, no.   I don't think you actually thought about me at all.   At one time I was of some importance.   Now I am a ghost.

DIX.   Well, you've barged into this business—through no fault of your own, I admit—and I say quite plainly in your presence that I insist on seeing the books of the Branch.

COCHRAN.   And I say you can insist till you are black in the face.

GRYCE.   Gentlemen, you put me in rather a difficult position.   General, I have the privilege of knowing Mr. Cochran, and even of co-operating with him in his duties as Secretary of the Branch.

DIX.   And who the devil are you, anyway?

GRYCE.   Sir, I am a Fellow of the Royal Society of Edinburgh, an ex-member of the Senate of the University there, and in the world of metaphysics, sir, if you recognise the existence of such a world, which I gravely doubt, I have, in my day, attained some distinction.   If you had read my book on Kant, sir—spelt with a K., sir, spelt with a K.—But I don't suppose you have, sir.   I don't suppose you have.

DIX.   I don't suppose I have, either.   What has all this got to do with the books of the Branch?   You didn't write them, I suppose?

GRYCE.   No, I didn't.

DIX.   Then what are you talking about?

GRYCE.   You have asked me who I am.   I am trying, in my humble way, to tell you.

DIX.   But I thought you were the landlord.

GRYCE.   And so I am.   Do you expect me to wash my hands with invisible soap and call you my Bully Rook?

COCHRAN.   Look here, it's no good losing our tempers.

DIX.   I'm not losing my temper.

GRYCE.   Nor am I, sir.   Nor am I.

COCHRAN.   General, I apologise for losing my rag just now.   I'll be delighted to show you the books, and you have every right, as Chairman of the Rally, to ask for them.

DIX.   Very well, then.   What's all the fuss about?

GRYCE. Exactly what I was about to remark.

COCHRAN. They're a little complicated. I'll fetch them down after dinner.

DIX. Yes. But . . . wait a minute.

[*Enter* VIRGINIA *and* MISS PARKER.]

VIRGINIA. Oh, look here, what do you think? We hadn't gone down the road more than two or three hundred yards . . .

MISS PAR. When two men spoke to us. I didn't know what to do. I nearly bolted. I thought they wanted—I mean, you know what I mean.

VIRGINIA. I think they are detectives.

MISS PAR. They've been hanging about all day.

VIRGINIA. I know they were detectives. They had big boots and they smelt of whisky.

MISS PAR. Miss Dix asked them if they were, but they said No, they weren't.

VIRGINIA. Oh, but they were. They asked us if we were living in the hotel. I said, No, just for fun. You see, they asked it in a sleuth-hound way, not a " Fine night for a walk " way.

MISS PAR. You asked them if there had been a burglary or something.

VIRGINIA. They said they didn't know, but they couldn't help looking cunning. Has there been a burglary, Captain Cochran?

COCHRAN. I don't think so.

VIRGINIA. Well, there will be, unless the detectives can prevent it. I don't suppose they can. Are there any valuables in the hotel, Professor?

GRYCE. We have the Anglers' Club plate. They dine here every year. Rather a cheering function. And Mrs. Gryce has some bits of jewels and things. It appears to me, however . . .

VIRGINIA. And Mummy carries a sort of jeweller's shop about with her. Umm! Well, I suppose there's

nothing in it.   Daddy, isn't it time you dressed up and
put your medals on?

DIX.   Perhaps it is.   What were those fellows like?

VIRGINIA.   I've told you.   But I expect they've
come up for the Rally.   Hurry up, Daddy.   You know
it takes you hours.

DIX.   Nothing of the sort.   What time do we dine?

VIRGINIA.   Seven o'clock.   It's long after six now.
Do run.

DIX.   All right, all right.

[*Exit.*]

VIRGINIA.   You going to the Rally?

COCHRAN.   Yes, of course.   I am the Secretary.   I
say, may I drive you over?   I have my car here.

VIRGINIA.   No, thanks.   I'm not going.

COCHRAN.   I say, I hope you're not ill?   Got a
headache or something?

VIRGINIA.   I don't need to have headaches when I
don't want to go anywhere.   You going, Professor?

GRYCE.   Well, I haven't made up my mind.   At least,
Mrs. Gryce hasn't said.

VIRGINIA.   Oh, you *must* go.   It'll be . . . it'll be
an outing for you.   You going, Miss Parker?

MISS PAR.   Well, I hardly think I'll go.   You see, I
go to bed at half-past nine.   I can't sleep if I don't.

VIRGINIA.   Good.   Do you go to sleep then?

MISS PAR.   Oh, like a top.   In the country, at any
rate.   But it's funny.   If I'm even twenty minutes later
—of course it doesn't matter to a minute or two—but I
always find . . .

VIRGINIA.   When does the show finish, Captain
Cochran?

COCHRAN.   It goes on till to-morrow.   But the big-
wigs leave at about one.

MISS PAR.   Oh, and talking about one, it's nearly
half-past six.   I had no idea it was so late.   Well, it isn't
really late, but we're dining early, aren't we, Professor?

GRYCE.   Yes.   And now I remember, Mrs. G. told me
not to be late.

MISS PAR.   Then I'd better simply dash.   I take so
long to dress.   Thinking of one thing and another.   I
rather wool-gather.   Do you, Miss Virginia, ever?

VIRGINIA.   Not especially.

MISS PAR.   Oh, but you're so direct and brisk and so
on.   So modern, I mean.   I'm modern, too, but I
don't spring at things like a tiger or a jaguar or something
—only not striped or spotty, and really quite nice, dear,
honestly.   You mustn't mind me.

VIRGINIA.   Very well.   I won't.

GRYCE (*holding the curtain open for* MISS PARKER).   May
I draw your attention to the fact that my arm is getting
tired?

MISS PAR.   I'm so sorry.   So very courteous and old-
world of you, Professor Gryce.

[*Exeunt* MISS PARKER *and* GRYCE.]

VIRGINIA.   Does she always rattle on like Milton
Hayes?

COCHRAN.   I haven't met her before.   She seems to
have plenty of small-talk.

VIRGINIA.   Well, she does something.   Paints pictures.
At least I suppose she does.   What do you do?

COCHRAN.   I?   Oh, well, this and that.

VIRGINIA.   You mean you do nothing?

COCHRAN.   Oh, I get a bit of shooting and a little
fishing and a spot of golf now and again.

VIRGINIA.   You do nothing but kill things?

COCHRAN.   I don't kill anything at golf.   Have a
heart!

VIRGINIA.   Of course, you run this Ex-Service Men's
League, don't you?

COCHRAN.   It pretty well runs itself, don't you know.
I knock around and help to keep it moving.   I'm treasurer,
you see.

VIRGINIA.   Well, that's something.

COCHRAN.   I am much obliged to you for these few nuts. . . . I say.   You are the cheekiest little brat I have ever seen.

VIRGINIA.   I know that.   I've got no inhibitions, you see.

COCHRAN.   Inhib . . .?   Oh, I see.   Not fitted with four-wheeled brakes.

VIRGINIA.   Yes, in a way.

COCHRAN.   Pretty awkward if you ever started downhill, I should think.

VIRGINIA.   Don't you worry about that.   Life's all uphill for a girl like me.   I take things so seriously, you know.   You should, too.

COCHRAN.   Should I?   I think life's rather a joke myself.   But I've got no brains.

VIRGINIA.   Yes, you have.   You're brachycephalic, and that means you have, but they're not near the surface.

COCHRAN.   I should like you for a tutor.

VIRGINIA.   In what?

COCHRAN.   In seriousness.   I'm a bit of a rotter really.   No backbone.   Oh, I've got any amount of bull-courage and dog-loyalty and mule-obstinacy—but I haven't much character.   It's my upbringing, I expect.

VIRGINIA.   I expect it is.   You have a good face.

COCHRAN.   My people never had much truck with me.   I was born in India, you see, and then my father shot big game and my mother lived in the Riviera.   I hadn't much of a time as a kid.

VIRGINIA.   Bad luck!   I had a very good time.   But then I made most of it myself. . . . I say . . . No . . . it doesn't matter.

COCHRAN.   What doesn't matter?

VIRGINIA.   You don't have much fun here, even now you're grown up, do you?   Nothing much to be bullish and doggish and mulish about?

COCHRAN.   No.   It's rather dull.

VIRGINIA.   Do you like it dull?

COCHRAN.   I don't know.   I never troubled to ask myself.

VIRGINIA.   It looks a good place for adventures. Can't you make some?

COCHRAN.   I can't think of any.

VIRGINIA.   I'll tell you one if you like.   Only don't tell anyone.

COCHRAN.   Honest Injun!

VIRGINIA.   There are crooks in this village.

COCHRAN.   I beg your pardon?

VIRGINIA.   Crooks.   They don't send detectives out to a place like this for nothing.

COCHRAN.   I don't know.   It's a healthy sort of spot.   They may be a bit run down.

VIRGINIA.   No.   They're in the pink of condition. Listen.   Do you drink?

COCHRAN.   Do I what?

VIRGINIA.   Don't keep begging my pardon and saying " Do I what?"   I asked if you drank.   Whisky and all that sort of thing.

COCHRAN.   I am passionately fond of alcohol, if that's what you mean.   It's in the blood of my ancestors.

VIRGINIA.   Never mind about the blood.   Does it go to their heads?   Does it go to your head?

COCHRAN.   Oh, I never get soozled; no.   Indeed, I'm a bit of a three-star star, my friends tell me.   When I die, the word GLENLIVET will be found graven on my liver.

VIRGINIA.   Could you—would you make these two detectives drunk?

COCHRAN.   I'm not a philanthropist, you know.   Why should I?

VIRGINIA.   Aha!

COCHRAN.   My darling one, don't say "aha!" What is your general idea?

VIRGINIA.   Captain Cochran, they all laugh at me.

COCHRAN. No!

VIRGINIA. They do. At least, Mum and Daddy do. My own set don't, of course. But my mother thinks I'm a kid, and that a kid is a kind of silly joke. What rot it is! When you are young you bring a fresh mind to things. It stands to reason. You're not all tied up with other people's motives like older people. Don't you think so?

COCHRAN. Yes. Yes. Oh, yes.

VIRGINIA. They won't *let* me have experience. And experience is all I need. I've got a philosophy already.

COCHRAN. Quite.

VIRGINIA. Well, damn it, don't you see? Here's an experience waiting for me. I want to try myself out. I've never even seen a crook. And here's a chance to catch one practically single-handed. They won't laugh at me after that.

COCHRAN. No. I don't suppose they will.

VIRGINIA. Listen, then. Will you be matey? Will you help?

COCHRAN. If you don't mind my saying so, I think you are absolutely daft. But—yes. I'll help all right.

VIRGINIA. Sure? I mean—there may be danger. There's to be no patronising about it. I've as much pluck, probably, as you have, and I know ju-jitsu.

[MRS. DIX, *above*: "*Virginia!*"]

Oh, damn! . . . And just us two?

COCHRAN. Just us two.

VIRGINIA. Listen. I'm going to pinch the carburettor-pin of the Daimler. Then they'll all have to crowd into your two-seater and the hotel car, to go to the Rally. That'll make three main points the crooks will make for—Mummy's pearls, the show-case and the Daimler. I'll get them at the Daimler. Single-handed, mind. You're only to stand by, if you do anything at all. Besides, you're going to the Rally.

COCHRAN. Do you know, I am beginning to re-member a previous engagement. I doubt whether I'll manage to go to the Rally.

MRS. DIX (*above*). Virginia!

VIRGINIA. Coming, Mummy. Perhaps you had better bring your revolver, Edgar.

> [*Exit* VIRGINIA.
> COCHRAN *goes over to his papers, puts them carefully away, but leaves them on the table as he hears* MRS. DIX *giving tongue again.*]

MRS. DIX (*above*). Virginia!

COCHRAN (*at the door*). Hello, Herr Professor! What's the matter with you?

> [GRYCE *comes in, creeping and casting backward glances.*]

GRYCE. Well, that's a fine business! There's a pretty kettle of fish!

COCHRAN (*lights a cigarette*). Have a cigarette?

GRYCE. No. It—it would choke me. What the devil are we to do?

COCHRAN. What are *we* to do? I don't see much where you come in.

GRYCE. That's a comfort, anyway. I wish I could be sure I didn't come into it.

COCHRAN. Beyond the fact that it's all your damned fault, I don't see how you *can* come into it.

GRYCE. How can you say it's all my damned fault?

COCHRAN. You suggested my putting the money they'd collected for the new Hall into that infernal Cement Company of yours, didn't you?

GRYCE. It wasn't my Company. I was told it was a good thing.

COCHRAN. Absolutely in on the basement. Yes. And you blarneyed me into putting £2000 of other people's money down the drain. Knowing well I knew damn-all about business.

GRYCE. Well, I was told it was all right. And I

couldn't go to Mrs. Gryce. She's got—she's got no imagination.

COCHRAN. Is that right about the detectives?

GRYCE. Yes. I'm afraid it is. Oh, dear me, dear me!

COCHRAN. Who gave them the office? You?

GRYCE. My dear sir! No . . . no. I think Kelly has had his suspicions. Oh, lord! what's to be done? Do you think they'll arrest me? But they can't, of course. I wish I hadn't tried to help you with old Dix. This damned quixotry will land me in Queer Street. He's sure to think I had something to do with it. What are you going to do?

COCHRAN. I'll have to bolt, I suppose. And what then? I haven't a bean in the world. I don't see myself landing in town without a brass farthing. Look here; you'll have to come over with some money. I'm at least entitled to travelling expenses.

GRYCE. But, my dear young friend, I've no money. I've no access to any money. I've told you Mrs. Gryce has no imagination. She doesn't even give me an allowance. It's all her fault, really.

COCHRAN. Well, I'll have to dot the old General one, or something. One can't flee from justice without effects. Though I don't see why you shouldn't rob the till for me. It is the least you can do.

GRYCE. You're bringing me all out in a cold perspiration. Good God, man, you're not contemplating CRIME?

COCHRAN. Oh, I don't know. You got me into this mess. I don't see why you shouldn't do a little to help me out.

GRYCE. Look here. I object in the strongest possible way to being mixed up in this at all. I have no respect whatever for modern ethical standards. They are beneath contempt. But the consequences of running counter to them are very unpleasant. I will not languish in quod for you or any man.

COCHRAN. Then you won't be a sportsman?

GRYCE. I am asking you to be a sportsman and let me alone. You have made your own bed and you must plough it by yourself. I have plenty of worries and troubles without shouldering yours. I refuse to hear anything more about it.

COCHRAN. Very well. You're a useless old devil, anyway. Rather an attractive flapper, that.

GRYCE. You mean Miss Dix? She is an intolerable young person. An example of modern higher education at its worst. I . . .

COCHRAN. Oh, she's all right. She and I are having a romp to-night instead of going to the Rally. Much better fun, I should think.

GRYCE. Do you intend to steal that young woman too?

COCHRAN. What a nasty old fellow you are! No. No. She's asked me . . . But it's all a secret, and you don't want to hear any more secrets. By Gum! it's late. I must change.

GRYCE. I thought you weren't going to the Rally.

COCHRAN. You can think till you're black in the face. (*He goes out.*)

GRYCE (*following him*). You've promised that whatever happens my name doesn't come into it.

COCHRAN (*over his shoulder*). Yes. Yes. Yes. Pull yourself together.

                                [*Exeunt.*]
        [*The stage is empty for fifteen seconds.*
Enter VIRGINIA, *assassin-like. She holds in her hand the carburettor-pin of the Daimler.*
To her MACDONALD.
She conceals the pin in the immemorial manner of ladies on the stage and stands facing MACDONALD.]

MACDONALD. I saw you, Miss Virginia.

VIRGINIA. I didn't mean you to.

MACDONALD. What did you take from the Daimler?

VIRGINIA. Nothing. I hadn't time to.

MACDONALD. I do not know your game, Miss Virginia, but it will surprise me if the Daimler runs to-night.

VIRGINIA. It will surprise me too. What a rotten Daimler it is.

MACDONALD. Give it back to me, like a good young lady.

VIRGINIA. Give what back to you ?

MACDONALD. Whatever it was you took from the Daimler.

VIRGINIA. You go and find out what I took from the Daimler.

MACDONALD. Indeed and I will not. I will go straight to your father.

VIRGINIA. No. Don't.

MACDONALD. Then give it me back. You will only get me into trouble.

VIRGINIA. You prefer that I should get into trouble ?

MACDONALD. Now, if you don't put me in a fine dilemma with your nonsense !

VIRGINIA. Are you afraid of Daddums ?

MACDONALD. I am afraid of nobody. I respect your father because he has risen from the ranks and made the best of himself though born in a lowly station. And forbye because . . .

VIRGINIA. Because what ?

MACDONALD. There is no occasion to say. I do not fear him in any sense. He is not of my social position.

VIRGINIA. What has that got to do with it ? What is social position, anyway, these days ?

MACDONALD. A great deal. Do not misunderstand me. I did not imply that my social position was inferior to your father's.

VIRGINIA. Well, if you bother about such things, I should say it was more posh to be a general than to be a chauffeur.

MACDONALD.   It is more posh, madam, to be a Macdonald of the Isles than to be a Field-Marshal who is yet a man of the people.

VIRGINIA.   I can't make head or tail of all this, but it's quite obvious an important man like you can't go sneaking to the General about a poor girl like me.

MACDONALD.   I am afraid you are right, Miss Virginia. It is your woman's instinct.

VIRGINIA.   My what?

MACDONALD.   You think, then, that I have taken a liberty.   I should have said your young lady's instinct.

VIRGINIA.   You are a funny fool, Macdonald.

MACDONALD.   It is very friendly of you to say so, ma'am.   You will see that I take your remark in the spirit in which it was meant.

VIRGINIA.   Of course you do.   So it's all right, and we understand each other, and you'll say nothing about it to the General.

MACDONALD.   I will say nothing about it to the General.   I would do more than tell lies for you, Miss Virginia.

VIRGINIA.   Would you?

MACDONALD.   I would die for you.

[*Enter the* GENERAL.]

VIRGINIA.   That will do, thank you, Macdonald.

MACDONALD.   Very good, miss.

[*Exit.*]

DIX.   Jinny, where the devil! have you been?   Your mother's been yelling the house down, and here you are not dressed.   And did you or did you not pack my Sam Browne?   I can't find the damned thing . . . anywhere.

VIRGINIA.   Oh, yes, Daddums.   It's in my suitcase. I'll get it for you.   Daddums!

DIX.   Well?

VIRGINIA.   Macdonald just came in to tell me he's had engine trouble.   He can't get it right under two or three hours.   Isn't it damnable?

DIX. What? Where? How the devil are we to get to the Rally, then?

VIRGINIA. Mrs. Gryce can take you over in the hotel Ford. She's going, anyhow. It'll be perfectly tikh and atcha. I'm not going.

DIX. Not going? Why not?

VIRGINIA. I'm going to bed. I'm tired. I've a—a headache.

DIX. Jinny, you lie. You haven't a headache.

VIRGINIA. General Dix, did I ever tell you a lie in all my life?

DIX. No. That's what worries me. What's the matter?

VIRGINIA. I don't know why I told you a lie. Wash out and begin all over again. I don't want to go to this Rally.

DIX. Why not?

VIRGINIA. I don't know. Just womanly caprice.

DIX. But you've damn well got to go.

VIRGINIA. Well, I damn well won't.

DIX. That's like yourself, anyhow. What's wrong with the car?

VIRGINIA. You'd better ask Macdonald. I don't understand these things.

DIX. It's infernally annoying.

VIRGINIA. Yes. Isn't it? I'll get your Sam Browne. It's under a heap of camisoles and things. You needn't come up.

[Exit.]

[After a pause, enter COCHRAN, in a dinner-jacket, with medals.]

DIX. You haven't been long.

COCHRAN. No, sir.

DIX. Well, now, there's just time. Do let's go over these accounts.

COCHRAN. Very good, sir. I'll fetch them.

DIX. By the way, Cochran, I'm afraid we'll have to

ask you to drive us over to-night. We've had engine trouble.

COCHRAN. Oh? What's up? Can I help?

DIX. I haven't found out yet, but our driver is a smart fellow. It must be bad, or he wouldn't have thrown in his hand.

COCHRAN. But I'm pretty handy with cars. I wish you'd let me look at it. I'll shove on some overalls. Kelly!

DIX. Good God, no. You're dressed. You'd get dirty. Besides, the accounts——

COCHRAN. Oh, rot! Those can wait.

[*Enter* KELLY, *in the full-dress of a waiter.*]

KELLY. Sir?

COCHRAN. Got a suit of dungarees you can lend me?

KELLY. Yes, sir, I have. Dinner's just being served, sir.

COCHRAN. I shan't be a minute. Come along.

[*He goes out, pushing* KELLY *before him.*]

DIX. I say, Cochran, don't be an ass!

[*He is about to follow, but notices the manuscript-case on the table. He is in two minds.*]

It's hardly playing the game. . . . But, damn it, he's not playing the game either. (*He opens the case; finds an account-book.*)

[GRYCE *comes in.*]

GRYCE. You've got 'em at last, I see.

DIX (*starting guiltily*). Yes. At least . . . we were just going to . . . Going to the Rally, Professor?

GRYCE. No, I think not. Miss Dix has just been telling Mrs. Gryce you will require room in her car. General, I'm afraid you won't find those books very helpful. They're—they're out of date.

DIX. They're not.

GRYCE. Pardon me. I know something about it. As I have already told you, I think, I have had the privilege of being of a little assistance to Captain Cochran in the book-keeping work of the Branch. I do not pretend to be a Chartered Accountant, but what experience I had of business methods was entirely and unreservedly at his disposal. I . . .

DIX. Exactly. And now you're trying to cover his tracks with words just as he tries to put me off the scent by diving into dungarees a few minutes before dinner. I'm going to get to the bottom of this.

[*Enter* KELLY.]

KELLY. Indeed, and I hope you are, sir.

DIX. What the devil have you to do with it?

KELLY. Nothing now, thank God. I resigned my membership when I saw what was going on.

GRYCE. Will you hold your tongue, you insolent blackguard!

KELLY (*as his temper rises he relapses from his ex-Service into his Number 3 voice*). Tyach! Who are you, anyhow?

GRYCE. I have the distinguished privilege of being your employer.

KELLY. Ye ken fine you're only the Boss-Consort. I'll take no ill talk from you.

DIX. Professor Gryce, will you have the goodness to be quiet? Well, my man?

[GRYCE, *who has not hitherto heard the orderly-room rasp, collapses.*
KELLY *becomes once more an N.C.O.*]

KELLY. Sir, I have to say that me and a good many other members and ex-members of the Branch is more than suspicious of what's come of our subscriptions for the last three years. Captain Cochran's in debt to every tradesman and farmer between here and Cloy. He came here, sir, with a lot of big talk about building a new Hall. Well, there's no new Hall, and never will be, I'm thinking. I've watched him, sir, and this old man here. They've been as thick as thieves all along. And, begging your

pardon, sir, it's my opinion that that's just what they are.
Thieves.

DIX.   Have you any evidence to support this charge?

KELLY.   This last year I've seen the receipts for the
subscriptions of every man in this village. Twenty-
seven pounds, sir,—sterling. You take a look at that
book, sir. You take a look at that book. Compare it
with his entry.

GRYCE.   I tell you that's not the book. He keeps the
subscription-book at his lodge. He'll fetch it to-morrow.

DIX.   Oh, will he? He told me it was upstairs.

KELLY.   That's the book, sir, right enough. I've
kept my eyes and ears open. There's jiggery-pookery
here, sir.

[Enters COCHRAN, *with dungarees over his dinner-suit.]*

COCHRAN.   Somebody's been monkeying with your
car, General. I'm afraid there's nothing to be done
to-night.

DIX.   There's a hell of a lot to be done to-night. Will
you explain these figures to me, sir?

COCHRAN.   Certainly. Oh, yes. Certainly I will.
You see . . .

[Enter VIRGINIA, *with the Sam Browne.]*

VIRGINIA.   I've found Samuel for you, Daddums. . . .
What's the matter?

KELLY *(the waiter).*   Dinner is served, miss.

DIX.   Ah, yes. Come along, then; come along. No
time to lose. Where's your mother? She's always late.
Mister Cochran——

COCHRAN.   Sahib?

DIX.   You will dine at our table to-night, I hope?

COCHRAN.   I shall eat your salt, sir, with great pleasure.

VIRGINIA.   Oh, and our mustard too! Do come in
your dungarees. Mumsie will love it!

[She takes his arm as they go out, DIX *following.]*

THE CURTAIN FALLS

[116]

ACT II

SCENE I

The stage is empty when the CURTAIN *rises, but presently* GENERAL *and* MRS. DIX *come in.* DIX *is moody and distracted. His wife, on the other hand, is full of an all-embracing goodwill.*

MRS. DIX. Nice little dinner. But how I hate hotel port.

DIX. No need to drink four glasses if you don't like it.

MRS. DIX. But liking four glasses of port is a very different thing from liking the port. You should know that, dear one, after all those years you spent in the Sergeants' Mess. I was so proud when you became a sergeant. Dear Bombardier Dix!

DIX. Well, I'm proud of having been in the Sergeants' Mess. You learn to do a job of work as an N.C.O. You get a sense of duty. That's better than a taste in port.

MRS. DIX. Oh, do you think so?

DIX. Yes, I do. There'd be less of your aristocratic lot in nursing-homes and madhouses if they had learned to see their duty plain and do it.

MRS. DIX. You must think out some nice duties for us all one day, dear one; you're so good at that. "Duty, stern daughter of the voice of God." And while we are on the subject of stern daughters, what's the matter with Virgie to-night?

DIX. You should know better than I do. You're her mother.

MRS. DIX. I know THAT, sweetheart. But you

understand her ever so much better than I do.   You and she are rather pals, aren't you ?

DIX.   Indeed I hope so.

MRS. DIX.   Yes.   You're both so charmingly stupid.

DIX.   Jinny's not stupid.   What the devil do you mean by stupid ?   She's one of the cleverest kids I ever met. Knows more than I do myself.

MRS. DIX (*following a different train of thought*).   Y-e-s. Perhaps . . .   It's funny Virgie and I have never been friends.   We are both a little daft.   We both like adventures.   But she likes roofs and I like balconies. I suppose that's it.   Perhaps it's like the hen who hatched out a duckling.   She'll go out on the pond. . . .   Do you think she'll marry ?

DIX.   Good God! it's too early to talk about that yet.

MRS. DIX.   *We* begin to talk about it when we are five.

DIX.   Then you're a nasty lot of little sluts.

MRS. DIX.   I hope she meets some nice idiot soon.   I hope she lets me choose him.

DIX.   You!   You'd choose a policeman or a chauffeur.

MRS. DIX.   Or a bombardier, or something.

DIX.   Well, if a bombardier's got ambition . . .

MRS. DIX.   A really good chauffeur has got both ambition and nice manners.   Now *our* young fellow—I forget his name——

DIX.   For heaven's sake, Julia, don't talk nonsense. I know you're only joking, but your jokes have a habit of running away with you.   Besides, I'm in no mood for jokes to-night.

MRS. DIX.   How unfortunate for all of us. . . .   What a nice young fellow Captain Cochran is. . . .   Nice manners.   Do you know, I've a feeling that poor lad's in difficulties.   His dinner-jacket is well cut, but so old and shabby.   I noticed the lining was torn. . . .   Indeed, I don't know what we're coming to.   It is a hard life for gentlefolk.

DIX.   Julia, I wish you'd go and get your wraps on. We're dreadfully late.

MRS. DIX.   Aren't we going to have coffee?   I told the waiter to bring it in here.

DIX.   Yes.   No.   You can have it when you come down.

MRS. DIX.   I think you ought to do something for that young Cochran.   I feel so sorry for him.

DIX.   I'll do something for him.

MRS. DIX.   Couldn't you speak to someone in the Foreign Office?   I mean, he's so obviously good form. It's so nice to meet a public-schoolboy in the back of beyond.   You feel that, after all, in spite of all the queer places and the curious people, God's in His Heaven, all's right with the world.

DIX.   Hah!   I don't know.   I was a County Council schoolboy myself.

MRS. DIX.   Well, you couldn't help it, dear.   I never get morbid about it, and I don't see why you should.

DIX.   I don't see why you should stand chattering here and making me late.

MRS. DIX.   Oh, dear!   You keep pushing me about like a wheelbarrow.   I hate you.   I really do.   And the coffee will be cold, and it's probably beastly enough when it's hot.

DIX.   Go on.   Go on.

[MRS. DIX *goes out.*]

Cochran!   Come in here, will you?   No, not you, Virginia.

[COCHRAN *enters.*]

Well?

COCHRAN.   Well?

DIX.   I've never had such a dinner in my life!   I couldn't eat a bite.   I wanted to throw the plates at you. And how I'm to get through this evening!   I'll expose you, sir.   Yes, by Heaven, I will!

COCHRAN.   At the Rally, sir?

[119]

DIX.   Yes, at the Rally.   This can't go on.

COCHRAN.   And what do you suggest I should do?

DIX.   If you were a soldier or a gentleman, you would shoot yourself.

COCHRAN.   Perhaps I shall, later on. . . . You propose deliberately to spoil a pleasant evening for a lot of darned good chaps who have darned few pleasures?

DIX.   They'd have more if you hadn't stolen their savings.   Besides, I think it'll be the greatest of pleasures they could have to pitch you into the loch.

COCHRAN.   I suppose you call that playing the game— chucking an ex-officer to the mob.   You might at least stand by your class, General.

DIX.   Class?   It's the criminal classes you belong to.

COCHRAN.   Now, look here, that will do.   I've kept my temper so far, out of respect to your rank.   You've already libelled me in the presence of witnesses, and I won't have any more of it.

DIX.   It's no libel to tell the truth.

COCHRAN.   That shows all you know about Scots Law. If you say a word against me at the Rally, I'll have £5000 out of you at the Court of Session.   You'll make a stink and a scandal through the whole League. . . . And I shouldn't wonder if the boys put *you* in the loch first. They rather like me.

DIX.   The waiter fellow here didn't seem to love you.

COCHRAN.   Who?   Joe Kelly?   I'll settle with Joe Kelly before many days.   You'd take that sort of merchant's word against a gentleman?   He's a damned rotter and always has been.   Pull yourself together, sir.

[*Enter* KELLY *with the coffee-tray.*]

DIX.   Kelly.

KELLY.   Sir?

DIX.   No.   It doesn't matter.

KELLY.   If I can be of any use to you, sir . . .

DIX.   No.   Never mind.   I'll talk to you later.

KELLY.   Very good, sir.

[He goes out.]
[DIX goes over to the fireplace to think.]

DIX.   Are you going to this Rally, Mr. Cochran?

COCHRAN.   Oh, not if you'd rather not.   I wouldn't upset you for worlds.

DIX.   I don't know what to do.

COCHRAN.   I think you've rather made an ass of yourself, sir, and if I might suggest . . .

DIX.   Shut up, you.   Do you take me for a fool? You're a dirty low thief, and I'll make you sweat blood for this.   Go and get your car ready.

COCHRAN.   You remember what I told you.   I don't take talk of that sort from a Field-Marshal, let alone a second-rate little half-pay ranker.

[DIX seizes the poker.]

Scrapping won't help either of us.   Put down that poker, sir, and don't be silly.

DIX.   I'm a fool to be angry with you.   You're making me angry on purpose.   You must be a clever devil, for all your dolly looks.   Go and get your car ready.   I'll decide what to do presently.

COCHRAN.   Oh, very well.

[He goes out.]

DIX *(following).*   JULIA!   For the love of the Suffering Mike, won't you hurry!

[Enter VIRGINIA.]

VIRGINIA.   Daddums!   What a row!   You're all nervy.   What's the matter?

DIX.   Nothing, Jinny.   I'm a little off colour.   I can't move things about like I used to.   I wish you'd make your mother hurry.

VIRGINIA.   Have some coffee?   Oh, here she comes.

[Enter MRS. DIX and MISS PARKER.]

DIX.   Oh, there you are, Julia.   Come along, come

[121]

along. Is Mrs. Gryce ready? Aren't you going, Miss Parker? Get my coat, Jinny.

[*Exit* VIRGINIA.]

MISS PAR. Oh, no. I think I'll sit here and read a book, or something. I mean, there isn't much for me to Rally about, is there? I was only in a sort of canteen during the War. I was quite a kid at the time. And of course that's nothing to having been in the trenches or the Flying Corps, or even in the Special Constables like my father. Is it, Mrs. Dix?

MRS. DIX. No. I don't suppose it is. Mrs. What's-her-name—the landlady—is quite ready. I go with Captain Cowper, don't I?

DIX. Yes . . . yes, yes. Perhaps . . . No. I don't think Cochran's going. No. He's got some things of his own to carry. We'll all go with Mrs. Gryce.

MRS. DIX. What a pity. Well, well!

[VIRGINIA *comes in with great-coat and helps* DIX *into it.*]

DIX. Thanks, Jinny. Thanks.

VIRGINIA. Well, do have a good time. And you mustn't be nervous about your speech. Just think they're recruits and let yourself rip. You speak jolly well. Doesn't he, Mummy?

MRS. DIX. Beautifully. I do wish you would come, Jinny. Can't you come?

VIRGINIA. No, I won't. Mumsie, have you forgotten your coffee?

MRS. DIX. Do you know, I don't think I'll have any to-night.

VIRGINIA. It will keep you awake.

MRS. DIX. Oh, Daddums' speech will keep me awake. I always sit on the edge of my chair waiting for that H that never drops.

VIRGINIA. You—you hag! Daddums never drops his H's.

[122]

MRS. DIX.   I have just said that he doesn't, pettikins.
But it *is* so like waiting for the bomb that doesn't fall.
In those air raids, you know.   In that unpleasant War.
You were too young to notice, dearest.   You had
mumps, I remember, when they brought down that
Zeppelin.

VIRGINIA.   Had I, Mumsie?

MRS. DIX.   You had, you inconsiderate little beast.

VIRGINIA.   It showed all I cared for your silly War.

MISS PAR.   The air raid I remember best was when I
was staying with my Aunt Clementina at Hendon.   It
was most horribly dark . . .

DIX.   And we're most horribly late.   We'll talk about
the War another time, Miss Parker, if you don't mind.
Do come along, Julia!

VIRGINIA.   Yes.   Hurry.

> [*Exeunt* MRS. DIX *and* VIRGINIA.]
> [MISS PARKER *sits down at fire.   She sneezes once, twice,
> and again.*]

MISS PAR.   Oh, dear!   (*She sneezes again.*)

> [*A pause.*]
> [GRYCE *comes in, singing.*]

GRYCE.   Excuse me.   I was looking for my pipe.

MISS PAR.   What a lovely voice you have, Professor.

GRYCE.   Have they gone?

MISS PAR.   Yes.   At least they're going.

GRYCE.   You have complimented me on my voice.
Now, you may or may not mind my saying it, but your
conversation always reminded me of the leaking of a
cistern in a cheap hotel.   I suppose you know that?

MISS PAR.   I haven't really been in a cheap hotel.
Not that you would call cheap.

GRYCE.   Never mind.   That is how it presented
itself to me last night.   To-day it is different.   It is like
the sound of a little birch-shaded river running over
shingle.   Something has happened.   Not to you.   To

me. Miss Parker, has anyone ever told you, you are a most attractive woman ?

MISS PAR. Oh, yes. At Art School dances. Heaps of times. But I just got up and went away.

GRYCE. I'm an impulsive sort of a chap. But I'm true blue all through. People think I'm cold and hard. All intellect and no heart. Oh! they are mistaken. Very, very far mistaken.

MISS PAR. I don't know why it is, but you remind me of old Moriceau—he was my teacher in Paris, you know. He was ninety-eight and such an old dandy! I felt so sorry for his poor wife, but the French thought it was funny. Such a peculiar sense of humour the French have, don't you think ? (*Sneezes.*) Oh, dear! Now, I've caught a cold!

GRYCE. I ventured to suggest that as a possibility earlier in the afternoon.

MISS PAR. Yes. (*Sneezes.*) Oh, what *ought* I to do for it ? What would you do for it ?

GRYCE. Well, first of all I'd take off all your clothes.

MISS PAR. You mean you would take off all your clothes—I mean you . . . Oh, how absurd! Of course not—I——

GRYCE. Don't interrupt. It was entirely a verbal slip. My meaning was perfectly clear. Pay attention, please.

MISS PAR. Oh, I am, I am. I'm paying attention, Professor.

GRYCE. Well, then. That's all right. What was I saying when you interrupted me with your immodest remarks ?

MISS PAR. Oh, I say, look here, Professor!

GRYCE. Yes. Then you must have a hot bath. As hot as they make 'em in this public-house. With mustard in it. Then you'll get Kate to take you up a hot toddy, with nutmeg. And you'll get into bed, and then you'll take . . . Wait a bit . . . let me see. . . . Ah, yes!

You'll take two—no, three—no, six five-grain Dover's Powders.

MISS PAR.   Will that make me better?

GRYCE.   Better! My dear young lady, you will sweat your soul out.

MISS PAR.   Yes. But . . . Very well. But have you got any Dover's Powders?

GRYCE.   Yes. I'll send them up. Don't stop to argue. Off you go!

MISS PAR.   But isn't six too many? Haven't they opium in them, or something?

GRYCE.   Opium? Not a bit. No, no. No opium. At least, a very little opium. You can take my word of honour they won't do you a bit of harm. Now, off you go.

MISS PAR.   Well, thank you ever so much. I used to take aspirin, but aspirin's getting a bit—well—fast, isn't it, nowadays? I mean the associations and so on. Thank you so much.

[*Exit, sneezing.*]

GRYCE.   Let me see. Six powders. I hope it doesn't poison her. I hope not. (*Sings.*)

> I sent thee late a ro-osy wreath,
> Not so much honouring thee
> As giving it a ho-ope that the-ere
> It might not withered be.

[*He goes over to the case of plate. Tries the door gently; looks out into the hall; switches out all lights but one; opens window wide; looks out.*]

> Gaudeamus igitur
> Juvenes dum sumus;
> Gaudeamus igitur
> Juvenes dum sumus.

[*A noise of cars starting up. Of* VIRGINIA *saying goodnight. Of cars moving over gravel. Silence.* GRYCE *has withdrawn his head when the cars started, but looks out again when they have passed.*]

> Poat jucundam juventutem,
> Post molestam senectutem. . . .

> *[Comes into room, leaving window open.]*

> Nos habebit humus,
> Nos habebit humus.

Hello!

> *[Enter VIRGINIA.]*

VIRGINIA. They're off. I thought you were going too.

GRYCE. No . . . No. I didn't go.

> *[VIRGINIA is carrying an alpenstock. She lays it by the window. Sits down at fire and lights a cigarette.]*

VIRGINIA. Where's Parky?

GRYCE. Oh, Miss Parker? She has gone to bed. She has got a decided chill.

VIRGINIA. Nice she's got something decided. She *is* a hen on a motor-road, isn't she?

GRYCE. Eh? Well, you must remember, Miss Dix, that the older we get the more complicated become our experiences. It is much more difficult, as one's life silts up with millions of combinations and permutations of events, to decide between one course of action and another. Er—hum—the well-springs of action . . .

VIRGINIA. Oh, yes! Do let us talk about them.

GRYCE. No. On second thoughts, no. Don't let's have a serious conversation.

VIRGINIA. Why not? You must have picked up a lot of notions and facts and things in all these years. Besides, you are a Professor. Professors ought to be interesting.

GRYCE. I did not suggest that I was incapable of serious conversation.

VIRGINIA. I see. You think I am just a kid.

GRYCE. You are a very frank young lady. I shall be a frank old gentleman. My difficulty is not your

age but your sex. Serious conversation is one of the
noblest activities of man's mind, and it is wasted on
women.

VIRGINIA. Oh, what a lie!

GRYCE. Pardon me. I am quite prepared to justify
my observation. A great deal of harm is done by the
Western European's habit of regarding anthropomorphically the living things that surround him. Now,
if we take . . .

VIRGINIA. Anthropomorphically?

GRYCE. There now! you don't understand the simplest
sort of popular vocabulary. I'll try to make myself
clear. The European treats his dog, his ox, his ass, his
wife—even his God—as if they had the passions, the
view-points, the mysterious interactions of the mind that
he has himself. His dog is a faithful friend, sympathising
and comprehending that complication of symbolism and
abstractions he calls speech. His God is rather a common
old gentleman in a dressing-gown—unreasonable and a
little vindictive, like all old gentlemen, but still capable
of looking at some things in a common-sense, businesslike
fashion. The European's wife . . .

VIRGINIA. She's the same sort of beast as he is, surely?
Only not such an idiot.

GRYCE. Pardon me. She is not the same sort of
beast at all. That she is an ingenious animal I readily
admit. She can mimic. She is a born mimic. She
can mimic all the motions of thinking. She may even,
if she thinks it will make her attractive, exhibit to her
lovers a simulacrum of a reasoning faculty. She is a
mimetic virtuoso, as I say. But she is as incapable of
abstraction as a lizard or a toad.

VIRGINIA. Toad yourself! What absolute rot. A
woman's a reasoning being. Perhaps she's the only
reasoning being that exists. Of course, any fool knows
that there's no such thing as a woman, only a lot of women
all different, but they're alike in that. They're more

[127]

reasonable than men. They must be, or they wouldn't
be always right.

GRYCE. They're not always right.

VIRGINIA. They are. They are.

GRYCE. Dash my wig! what did I tell you? It's
impossible to argue with you. I'm wasting my time.

VIRGINIA. You seem to have plenty to waste. Now
you're sulking. I suppose you call that reasonable.

GRYCE. I am not sulking, and you are the most
impertinent besom I have ever met.

VIRGINIA. That's the *argumentum ad feminam*. You'd
better keep insulting me in the abstract, Professor. If it
comes to back chat, I'll beat you easily.

GRYCE. I'm quite sure you would.

VIRGINIA. Yes, and I can beat you at the hundred
yards, and the high jump, and ju-jitsu, and swimming
and tennis and billiards and hockey and German and
music and mathematics and modern literature.

GRYCE (*murmurous*). Little *bas bleu*, come blow up
your horn.

VIRGINIA (*without noticing him*). And I'm better-
looking than you ever were. And I've a quicker mind
and better brain than you ever had. And yet you look
down on me!

GRYCE. Yes. Yes. I suppose I do.

VIRGINIA. But why? Why?

GRYCE. Because civilisation depends on the contempt
of man for woman. When that goes, civilisation goes.

VIRGINIA. Then the sooner it goes the better.
Civilisation only exists for the benefit of a lot of perishing
duds who couldn't live for a day in a real world with no
humbug in it.

GRYCE. I could hardly expect you to appreciate
civilisation. God bless you, lassie. I don't think you've
much sense.

VIRGINIA. Yes, I have . . . Here. Listen . . .
No. It doesn't matter.

GRYCE. Oh, go on, go on. I could listen to your artless prattle all evening.

VIRGINIA. Well, look here. Do you know why I stayed behind to-night?

GRYCE. I do not. Nor have I speculated, even in the idlest fashion, or . . .

VIRGINIA. I don't suppose you know that there is going to be a burglary here to-night.

[GRYCE *laughs.*]

I'm only a poor weak woman, guided only by my woman's instinct, but I've spotted something you don't know.

GRYCE. And what is that?

VIRGINIA. There is a gang of crooks in the village. The police have followed them here. I . . . No, I won't tell you any more.

GRYCE. I like you better when you tell fairy-tales. Live on in your little world of romance. Reality is a hard thing. I'll away to my bed.

VIRGINIA. At what time do you usually turn in?

GRYCE. I am an early bird. There is nothing here to keep me up. I shut out the chills with four close walls, lay down my weary bones, and seek the end of all mankind —unconsciousness. Are you waiting up for the others?

VIRGINIA. No. I'll go presently.

GRYCE. Put out the lights, then. Good night. God bless you and send you more of the damned folly you think is happiness.

VIRGINIA. Good night. Forget what I said just now.

GRYCE. Heavens! you don't expect me to sit up all night analysing a lot of schoolgirl chatter! Me! At my time of life!

VIRGINIA. Oh, shut up! (*She sits down and takes up a magazine.*)

GRYCE. Aye, aye. Crabbed age and youth.

[*He looks out of the window, filling and lighting his pipe. He sings.*]

[129]

I will be knocking a hole in McCann
For knocking a hole in my can.

[*He potters about the room ; finds* MISS PARKER'S *box of chocolates, takes two, and puts three in his pocket.*]

McCann knew my can was new ;
And only used a day or two.

VIRGINIA.   Would you very much mind not singing ?
I have a headache.

GRYCE.   I gave McCann my can to fetch a pint of stout.
McCann came running in to say
My can was running out. . . .

[*He goes, switching out most of the lights in his passage.*
VIRGINIA *leaps out of her chair and runs to window. She leans well out into the darkness. A whistle. She draws back sharply, but looks out again.*]

VIRGINIA.   Hello !

COCHRAN.   Ssh !   I'll come in.

[*He climbs in by window. He wears a light Burberry, buttoned to the chin.*]

VIRGINIA.   I almost thought you had gone to the Rally after all.

COCHRAN.   No jolly fear !   Who's in the house ?

VIRGINIA.   Old Gryce and Parky.   I thought you . . .

COCHRAN.   No, I didn't.   The General took my two-seater—pretty thick, that—with Macdonald driving. Mrs. Dix and Mrs. Gryce went in the hotel Ford, with Kelly.

VIRGINIA.   I'm really quite glad you waited.   I'm the least bit *raised*.   Had you a row with Daddums ?

COCHRAN.   Oh, nothing much.   He's rather a testy old gentleman.

VIRGINIA.   I know.   But won't they need you at the Rally ?

COCHRAN.   No. no.   All my work's behind the scenes.

VIRGINIA. Did you manage with the detectives?

COCHRAN. I did. With Rajah's Pegs—champagne laced with brandy, you know. They'd done pretty well before I tackled them. They won't bother us to-night. And it's all right about the crooks. They're here all right.

VIRGINIA. Oh, good!

COCHRAN. I say. Let's get your mother's jewels. That'll only give us two places to watch—the show-case and the car.

VIRGINIA. Do you think that would be better?

COCHRAN. Ever so much better. Isn't this fine!

VIRGINIA. Jolly!

COCHRAN. Then show me where the jewels are. And then we'll go out into the shadows and stalk them. The moon rises in an hour. They won't be before then.

VIRGINIA. Have you got your revolver?

COCHRAN. Yes, rather. Have you?

VIRGINIA. Yes. It's a wee one, but it bites. I keep it in my stocking. I say, what fun!

COCHRAN. Come along, then.

[*They take hands and tiptoe out, putting out the lights as they go.*]

CURTAIN

ACT II

SCENE II

Scene as before. Less than an hour later. The same moon and scurrying clouds show through the window. When the audience has marvelled at the beauty of the contrivance which presents this picture, they become aware of a man and a woman entangled as for a Moving Picture fade-out. They are silhouetted against the window for an instant, and then a large cloud fades them out indeed. They are seen only dimly in what passes for darkness on the stage. This light that never was on land or sea may be produced by the pale glow of the dying fire. It is not bright enough to reveal a sofa R. *as other than a dark bulk.*

The man is COCHRAN. *The woman is* VIRGINIA—*easy game, in spite of all her emancipation, for an expert in the amatory exercises.*

VIRGINIA. I love you.

COCHRAN. It is more marvellous to hear you say so than to hear fairy music played on far-away waters.

VIRGINIA. Do you love me?

COCHRAN. Och! how do I know? My soul is away on a far journey on swift horses. It cannot tell me what it feels. I am in a maze.

VIRGINIA. Kiss me, then.

COCHRAN. Indeed I will.

VIRGINIA. How did—how did we get this way? It's never happened to me before. Am I mad, do you think?

COCHRAN. Life is all melancholy madness but this. It is madness to be generals and young ladies and poor devils of ex-service-men with no money.

[132]

VIRGINIA.   I always said so, but I didn't really believe it.   I believe it now.

COCHRAN.   You see things true, in the Fourth Dimension.

[*The moon is not seen, but a beam shoots in at the window and shines on the head of the sofa.   It reveals a red bandana handkerchief resting on a head—the head of* PROFESSOR GRYCE.   *They do not see him.*]

VIRGINIA.   One minute you were just a commonplace stranger in an inn, and the next you grew like the thingummy in the Arabian Nights, and blotted out all the world.   What were we talking about?

COCHRAN.   We were talking about the old, mad moon.

VIRGINIA.   There it is again.   All day we thought this was a dirty old hotel Lounge, instead of the silver palace the moon knows it to be. . . . Oh!

COCHRAN.   What is it, my heart's darling?

VIRGINIA.   Look there!

COCHRAN.   Hell!   Do you think he's awake?

VIRGINIA.   S-sh!   He may not be!

COCHRAN.   We'd better clear out.

[*They tiptoe once more to the door.*
GRYCE *reaches cautiously for a switch and knocks over a pile of ash-trays.   He switches on the light and sits upon the sofa, grinning like a satyr.*]

GRYCE.   Hi!   Come back.

[*They come back,* COCHRAN *dubiously,* VIRGINIA *boiling with rage.*]

VIRGINIA.   Well, of all the low, mean old skunks!

GRYCE.   I beg your pardon?

VIRGINIA.   You may well.

GRYCE.   I don't know what you mean.

VIRGINIA.   You were awake all the time.

GRYCE.   Was I?   You disappoint me.   I took it all for a delicious dream.

K   [133]

VIRGINIA. You're not a bit funny. I don't know what you are. I thought the only use of you was that you were funny. You're just a sneaking old cad, and I'm very, horribly sorry for poor Mrs. Gryce.

GRYCE. Great heavens! Is it my fault if your father's daughter chooses the public Lounge as a suitable place to cuddle a Captain? I must have dropped off to sleep, as I was perfectly entitled to do, and all of a sudden I am rudely disturbed by an—an erotic episode.

VIRGINIA. What were you doing here? I thought you had gone to bed.

GRYCE. I was under the impression that *you* had gone to bed.

VIRGINIA. Don't argue. You were here spying on purpose.

GRYCE. My dear young lady, believe me, I never had the remotest suspicion that you intended an assignation. Indeed, I should have said you were the last . . .

VIRGINIA. Never you mind about me. I didn't intend an assignation. It all happened all of a sudden. But that's not the point.

GRYCE. What *is* the point? The point seems to be, what will your father think of all this? What will Mrs. Gryce think of the uses to which her hitherto depressingly respectable hotel . . .

VIRGINIA. Oh, shut up, or I'll go mad! I suppose you'll tell?

GRYCE. Tell what?

VIRGINIA. About What-you-may-call 'um and me.

GRYCE. Tell General Dix? My dear child, what would be the good of that? What knowledge or experience has a man like that had to fit him to deal with a situation like this?

VIRGINIA. Oh, none, none. He wouldn't understand.

COCHRAN. I don't think Gryce understands the situation either.

GRYCE. I am prepared, to the best of my poor capacity, to make an effort at understanding.

VIRGINIA. Look here, I'll tell him. Professor, I thought love and all that sort of thing was all rot. But it's not. It's really plain Biology. It's not right or wrong or anything like that. It's a *fact*, if you see what I mean.

GRYCE. Go on. You interest me. How original! How novel!

VIRGINIA. I told you a lie when I said I was going to bed, but I had no notion WHATEVER of falling in love. And Captain Cochran hadn't either. I waited up to catch burglars, and he stayed behind to help. And—and it was quite a nice night, and the moon rose, and I—I suddenly realised there were more important things than burglars. *He* did too. We both sort of short-circuited and went up in a blue flame. And it was all up with both of us. I suppose it always happens that way.

GRYCE. No, it doesn't. Not a bit. Very interesting, all the same. Now, if you want my advice . . .

VIRGINIA. No, we don't, really. Please don't think I'm rude, or be offended or anything, but I'd rather you didn't give us any advice at all. We'll be quite all right.

GRYCE. In that case I'll go to bed.

VIRGINIA. All right, if you wish. We'll look after the Anglers' plate; we will really.

GRYCE. I am sure you will. My mind is at rest about the Anglers' plate. Good night. I am growing old. *O l'admirable jeunesse!*

VIRGINIA. Good night. I'm sorry I got ratty.

GRYCE. Not at all. A pleasant moon to you. Shall I put out the light?

VIRGINIA. No, don't bother, please. Good night.

GRYCE. Good night. (*He goes.*)

VIRGINIA. I thought he'd never go! That's not so bad after all. Now, darling, darling, we mustn't make love any more to-night. The burglars might have taken

[135]

the plate and killed old Gryce, and we'd never, never have noticed.

> [*She goes over to the case and tries the door.*
> COCHRAN *looks at his wrist-watch and starts.*]

Yes, it's all right.   He *is* an old chatterbox!   I believe he *was* asleep all the time.

COCHRAN.   My lord!   It's half-past ten!

VIRGINIA.   So it is.   We have wasted time.

> [*She can't resist rubbing him with her shoulder like a kitten; but he doesn't notice. His face has become sinister.*]

COCHRAN.   Yes.   I say, give me that carburettor-pin.

VIRGINIA.   Why?   What for?

COCHRAN.   I want to look at it.

VIRGINIA.   Captain dear, you're all of a dither.   What's the matter?

COCHRAN.   Never mind about that.   Be a sport; let me see the pin.

VIRGINIA.   I don't understand.   You look quite different.

COCHRAN.   Different!   I should hope so!

VIRGINIA.   Hope so?

COCHRAN.   I should have been bowling along at a level fifty, with no headlights, a hundred miles away by now.   With the loot in the boot.   And I've been fiddling away precious time toying with flappers.   I always do!   It's me all over.

VIRGINIA.   What loot?

COCHRAN.   Never you mind what loot.   Give me the pin.

VIRGINIA.   Oh—you weren't . . . you weren't just fooling me?

COCHRAN.   That?   Pretty well done, wasn't it? But too easy for anyone with my gifts.   Come along, kid; hand out.   Time's up.   I'm not going to tangle myself with petticoats any more to-night.

VIRGINIA.   I've no petticoats.   I'm a human being.
Charlie, you're only in fun, aren't you ?

COCHRAN.   Fun!   See here, I don't want to hurt you.
Hand over that pin, or I'll come looking for it myself.
(*He catches her wrist.*)

VIRGINIA.   Let go, will you ?   You dirty little village
Don Juan!

COCHRAN.   Look here; keep a civil tongue in your
head.   That is not how a lady speaks to a lover who is
about to desert her.

VIRGINIA.   You look out.   I can break your arm.
And I will.

> [*She attempts a ju-jitsu hold, but fails.* COCHRAN *breaks
> and hook-hits her under the chin.* VIRGINIA *drops like
> a log.*]

COCHRAN.   By Gum!   That's done it.

> [*He finds the carburettor-pin after a hasty search;
> wrenches open the door of the show-case and pours its
> contents into a table-cloth.*]

Pity to hit a lady. . . . But she's no lady . . . with her
infernal Japanese stunts.

> [*A car sounds on the gravel.*
> COCHRAN, *after a hurried look from the window, makes for
> the door with his burden.*
> *The stage is empty for a moment.   There is a crash, and*
> MACDONALD *and* COCHRAN *reel, struggling, into the
> Lounge.* COCHRAN *trips, and* MACDONALD *promptly
> puts a full Nelson on him.*]

MACDONALD.   You would, would you !

COCHRAN.   Look out!   You're strangling me.

MACDONALD.   I'm delighted to hear it.

COCHRAN.   Get up, and I'll go quietly.   It's a fair
cop.   I can't breathe. . . . Kamerad!   You're afraid to
let me up !

MACDONALD.   Don't be foolish now.   I could massacre
ten of your like, so I could.

[*Enter, severally, the* PROFESSOR, *négligé, with a shot-gun,* MRS. GRYCE *and* MRS. DIX.]

MRS. GRYCE.   What in all the world is all this?

MRS. DIX.   Look, he's killing him!

GRYCE.   Hi!   Look here!   Don't do that!

MACDONALD.   Have you got your gun, sir?

GRYCE.   Yes, yes.   Here it is.

MACDONALD.   Then get up on your feet, you tinker's messan that you are!   Hands above your head.   Put on all the lights, mum.   There may be more of them.

GRYCE.   Bless my soul, is that the young lady?

MRS. DIX.   Jinny!   Mrs. Pybus, help me lift her.

MACDONALD (*to* COCHRAN).   I will tear the heart out of you, you dog!

[MACDONALD, MRS. DIX *and* MRS. GRYCE *render first aid.*]

MRS. GRYCE.   Poor lamb!   Oh, poor lamb!

MRS. DIX.   Get some water.   Don't be so sloppy. She's not dead.   A very fortunate thing for you, Mr. Thingummybob.

GRYCE.   Dear me, dear me!   What a night!

MACDONALD.   Night!   The night's not begun yet. Wait you till the General comes back . . . if he ever does.

GRYCE.   What happened?

MACDONALD.   He tried to make an exposure of that man there, and the boys put him in the loch.   Kelly and I pulled him out, and then I took charge of the ladies.

COCHRAN.   He had only himself to thánk.   I warned him.

MRS. GRYCE.   It was dreadful.   A riot.   The police couldn't do a thing.

COCHRAN.   I told him they'd put him in the loch. Brass hat and red tabs and all.

MACDONALD.   Will you hold your evil tongue!   The young lady is coming round.

VIRGINIA.   Ah!   Ga!   Oh, dear!   My head!

[138]

MRS. DIX. Well, well, well, my baby! Mumsie's here. It's all right.

VIRGINIA. Hello, Mummy. I've just been knocked out.

MRS. DIX. Did you faint, mother's own darling?

VIRGINIA. Faint? I'm telling you I was knocked out. On the point of the jaw. Lumme, it's sore still!

MRS. DIX. Who did it to you, pettikins?

VIRGINIA. Oh, I don't know. My head's full of Hell's bells.

[*Alarums and excursions without.*]

GRYCE (*to* COCHRAN). Aha! Stand fast, will you! You would, would you?

COCHRAN. No. In the circumstances, I wouldn't.

[*Enter the* GENERAL, *unbraced, ungartered, wild. He has no hat. His grey hair is plastered to his forehead by the mud of the loch. He has lost one spur. A trailing green streamer of algæ is attached to the other. His British Warm is not wet, but the rest of him is.* KELLY *is holding his arm solicitously, but is quickly shaken off; the* GENERAL *stands speechless with rage, surveying the scene.*]

VIRGINIA. Hello, Daddy! Did you enjoy the party?

DIX. No, I did not. What's all this? A devil of a lot wants explaining here. And you've got the nerve to be here, Cochran!

COCHRAN. I haven't, really. It's sheer compulsion keeps me here.

MRS. DIX. Sit down, Georgie. You look tired.

DIX. Tired!

MRS. GRYCE. Do be careful with that gun, Andrew. Oh! . . . The Anglers' plate has gone!

KELLY. No, it hasn't, Mum. It's in the passage. Give me the gun, sir. (*He takes it.*)

MRS. GRYCE. And what business has it in the passage?

GRYCE. I think I can explain.

MRS. GRYCE. You think so, do you?

GRYCE.   Yes, I do think so.   And I will explain. Damn it, I must assert my manhood sometimes!

MRS. DIX.   Do go on, Professor Pryce.

GRYCE.   Gryce, madam, Gryce.

MRS. DIX.   I should have remembered that.   It's the plural of grouse.

GRYCE.   No, indeed it isn't.

DIX.   What the devil has all this to do with guns, and Virginia on the couch looking like a ghost, and Cochran with a black eye, I'm glad to see, and the passage littered with silver cups?

GRYCE.   I was on the point of explaining.   I was retiring for the night—in fact, I had retired for the night—when I became conscious of a dickens of a hullabaloo.   Throwing on a few things, I made what speed I might to the scene.   Distributed about the floor were a quantity of Anglers' Club plate, your driver and Cochran locked in mortal combat, and your daughter, sir . . . I concluded . . .

DIX.   Never mind what you concluded.   What's it all about?   It's pretty clear there's been assault and attempted robbery.   Kelly, 'phone for the police.

KELLY.   Begging your pardon, sir, the police is scattered half over the shire.   Last I saw of them, they was blowing their whistles at the road-end, while the ex-service boys was putting you in the loch, sir.

DIX.   That's true.   Damn the swine!   Oh! . . . Yes!   Jinny was speaking about two detectives earlier in the evening.   What about them, eh?   Where are they, eh?

COCHRAN.   I can help you there, General.   On Miss Virginia's most explicit instructions, I—er—dealt with them.   They are drunk.

DIX.   And you made them drunk?

COCHRAN.   I did indeed.   You'll get no sense out of them till morning—if even then.

DIX.   Why did you make them drunk?

COCHRAN.   Miss Virginia asked me to, sir.   Vicarious generosity, I suppose.

DIX.   Is this true, Jinny?

VIRGINIA.   Oh, it probably is.   Don't talk to me.   If you'd ever been knocked out, you would know a person doesn't like to be talked to.

DIX.   I see I'll have to deal with this myself.

MRS. DIX.   No, no, no.   You will do nothing of the kind.   I have had quite enough excitement to-night. And I shall probably have to nurse you through bronchitis, and I loathe that sticky antiphlogistine stuff.   Mrs. Pryce will ask the waiter to bring you a tin of mustard and a nice hot toddy with lemon and a nutmeg, and you'll put your feet in it—the mustard, I mean, not the toddy.

[*Enter* MISS PARKER, *in a nightgown and a wrap.*]

You'll drink that——— Hello! Miss Parker, this is a scream of a business, isn't it?   I'm so glad to see you still wear a nightgown, in these days of pyjamas and irritating rot like that.

MISS PAR.   Yes, I always do.   I don't know why.   I tried the other things once, but somehow I felt as if I weren't properly in bed at all.   Funny how somehow you can't just be absolutely responsible for your feelings in things of that sort.   Surely you are home very early? I heard a noise, and I came down.   I thought it was a fire or something.

DIX (*stamping*).   Oh, let's have a little silence!

MRS. DIX.   Quite right.   That's it.   Silence.   Now, off you pack upstairs to bed, and I'll see that your toddy———

DIX.   This has to be settled first, Julia.   I begin to see daylight now.   Macdonald, you caught this fellow red-handed, didn't you?   Making off with the swag, wasn't he?

MACDONALD.   I would not just say that, sir, without first giving the matter full consideration.

DIX.   Kelly, search him.

COCHRAN.   No, look here, I can explain——

KELLY.   Come away now, sir.   It's four to one.
You'll have to cry a barley.

COCHRAN.   Oh, go ahead.

> [KELLY *discovers a pistol and a pocket full of* MRS. DIX's
> *jewellery*.]

MRS. DIX.   My gracious me!   My collarette, my . . .
I say, you *have* been taking liberties, Captain Kilgour!

COCHRAN.   I've told you I can explain.

DIX.   I've no doubt you can.   But I'm too tired for
Bedtime Fairy Stories.   Kelly, I can trust you.   You
mount guard over him for a three-hour shift.   I'll relieve
you at 2.30.   Macdonald, you'll relieve me at 5.30.

MACDONALD. ⎫
KELLY.   ⎬ Very good, sir.

MRS. DIX.   And if he doesn't relieve you at 2.30, Mr.
Kelly, you won't be frightfully offended, will you?   Mrs.
Prowse, can I have that hot water and mustard and rum
and things, and a couple of extra hot-bottles, and so forth?
Do you mind?

MRS. GRYCE.   I'll get them, ma'am.

[Exit.]

KELLY.   Now then, get fell-in, accused.

MRS. DIX.   Virgie, dear, cán you walk?   That's
right.   Come with old Mummy.   George, if you stay
there chattering a minute longer I shall be very angry
indeed.

[Exeunt MRS. DIX *and* VIRGINIA.]

KELLY.   Hump yourself, now.   Quick march.

COCHRAN.   With the greatest of pleasure, Corporal.
And you'll arrange for a raw beef-steak, won't you?
My eye . . .

KELLY.   Stop the talking.   Look to your front.   Mind
that there cup.

[Exeunt COCHRAN *and* KELLY.]

[142]

MISS PAR.   How very odd it all is! Do you know, Professor, I shouldn't be a bit surprised if this were all a dream, and I woke up in a minute.

GRYCE.   Subjective reality, Miss Parker—— Oh, damn! it's time we were all in our beds. Somebody can gather up that silver to-morrow. There's a lot to be gathered up to-morrow.

DIX.   Macdonald, what the devil do you mean by talking about further consideration?

MACDONALD.   I cannot discuss my meaning now, sir.

DIX.   And why not, sir? Why not?

MACDONALD.   Perhaps, General, don't you think, if we . . .

DIX.   Will you be quiet! . . . Well? Why not? . . . Answer me, man, answer me!

MACDONALD.   I have answered you already, whatever.

DIX.   Look here, Macdonald, you're making me angry.

MACDONALD.   Not so angry as you are making me, and I am from the Highlands.

MISS PAR.   Oh, I hope they are not going to fight or anything!

DIX.   Clear out. I'll deal with you to-morrow.

MACDONALD.   I will be having no dealings with you to-morrow or any of the to-morrows to the end of time.

DIX.   You won't, won't you? (*He goes to the escritoire and writes.*)

MACDONALD.   I beg your pardon. I will fulfil the obligations entailed by a fortnight's notice. At the end of a fortnight I will give you my candid opinion of you.

DIX.   No, you won't. You're sacked. Now. Here's your wages.

MACDONALD.   I thank you. And who will drive you to-morrow?

DIX.   None of your business. I'll get a man from the village.

MACDONALD.   It is strange, but you are more tolerable when you are no longer my employer. Good night, General Dix.

[*Exit* MACDONALD.]

DIX.   And I don't know why the devil the Almighty ever made you two!

[*He grinds his teeth at* GRYCE *and* MISS PARKER. *They wilt.*]

MRS. DIX (*above*).   Georgie! Virginia wants you.

DIX.   Oh, stop howling! As if I hadn't enough to worry me! Damn Virginia!

CURTAIN

ACT III

t is just after breakfast-time. Nobody has had a very good breakfast.

    [*The Lounge is rather untidy. In it is* MISS PARKER, *alone, and palely loitering.*]

    To her GRYCE.]

MISS PAR. Oh, hello!

GRYCE (*moodily*). Hello.

MISS PAR. (*inanely bright*). You are up very early this morning, Professor. I mean, the rest of the crowd is just having breakfast, and they're much later than usual, of course. But still, it's not ten o'clock yet, and I thought you liked resting in the morning.

GRYCE. A miraculous lot of rest I had last night. They routed me out at six to mount guard on the prisoner. You'd have thought it was a sort of favour, too.

MISS PAR. Well, so it was, in a way, wasn't it? I mean, to trust you, and so forth, after everything.

GRYCE. Trust! The general impression seemed to be that I was hand-in-glove with the gang, but could easily be bullied and blackmailed into ratting. I was never so insulted in my life.

MISS PAR. They couldn't have quite *meant* that, really, could they?

GRYCE. I know quite well what they meant. But I'll show them.

MISS PAR. I'm sure you will. Look here, why did you try to poison me last night?

GRYCE. Poison you?

[145]

MISS PAR.   Yes.   I asked Mrs. Gryce this morning
how many Dover's Powders one ought to take, and she
said, "Two at the outside."

GRYCE.   What are you blethering about, woman?

MISS PAR.   Well, you told me five or six or something,
and oh, please don't mind my saying so, but you said it
deliberately, just like a Borgia or something.   And then
when they all said you had something to do with the
burglary, I got most frightfully suspicious, though I
haven't a suspicious nature, really.

GRYCE.   Yes, you have.   You have an abominable
nature.   Why should I try to poison you?

MISS PAR.   That's what I've been asking myself all
night.   I—I thought you might know.

GRYCE.   Oh, hell and a thousand furies!   Oh, cats
and monkeys!   I'll have a nervous breakdown.   I know
I shall.   See here, you may as well know.   I didn't try
to poison you.

MISS PAR.   Thank you for that, anyhow.

GRYCE.   I wanted you to sleep and not to interrupt
with your infernal half-witted jargon.

MISS PAR.   Not interrupt what?

GRYCE.   Never mind.   It's of no importance.

MISS PAR.   Then you only tried to drug me, not poison
me?

GRYCE.   Yes, I did.

MISS PAR.   But it's pretty bad to drug people, too,
isn't it?   Of course, I didn't take the Dover's Powders.
My cold felt so much better after the hot bath.

GRYCE.   Well, I advised that too.

MISS PAR.   Yes.   It's quite true.   You did.

GRYCE.   I suppose you'll say I tried to drown you.

MISS PAR.   Oh, no, no.   Of course not.   That
would be silly.   Besides, I locked the door.   But, look
here, you may think I look a fool, and I may be, of course,
but I'm not an absolute imbecile.   I earn my own living
and all that sort of thing.   And I don't feel the least bit

disposed to let the matter rest.   I'll have a chat with Mrs.
Gryce.   She's so sensible.

GRYCE.   I forbid you to discuss my private affairs with
Mrs. Gryce.

MISS PAR.   But, Professor, I don't even know what
your private affair was.   It's only all this drugging and
poisoning I want to know what to do about.   Oh, here
are the Dix's.   That sounds so like a music-hall trapeze
act, doesn't it ?

[*Enter* MRS. DIX *and* VIRGINIA.   *Following them politely,*
the GENERAL.]

MRS. DIX.   Good morning, Miss Cartle.

MISS PAR.   Miss Parker.   It doesn't matter really,
but it's my name.   Good morning, Mrs. Dix.   Good
morning, Virginia

VIRGINIA.   Good morning.   How is your cold ?

MISS PAR.   Ever so much better, thank you.   I had a
blazing-hot bath and two bottles.   Hot-water bottles, of
course.   I must have caught it in good time.   A cold
may be such a nuisance if it goes on and on and on and
on . . .

VIRGINIA.   Yes.   What are you going to do now,
Daddums ?

DIX.   Well, I shall want this room in the first place.
You and your mother had better go for a walk.   Perhaps
Miss Parker will go with you.

VIRGINIA.   Indeed we won't.   We must see this
court-martial.   I've never seen a court-martial.   Have
you, Mumsie ?

MRS. DIX.   Good Lord, no !

DIX.   It isn't a court-martial.   Don't speak irre-
verently of sacred subjects.   It's more a—a sort of Court
of Inquiry.   I don't feel like dragging the police into
it.   Especially since I've seen those two detectives this
morning.   Somehow . . . sort of delicacy . . . ex-
officer and so forth. . . .

MRS. DIX. Besides, it's quite enough to be dragged through a loch without being dragged through the Sunday papers.

DIX (*she has surprised him as much by her incisive tone as by what she says*). Julia!

MRS. DIX. Yes, dear?

DIX (*after a pause*). Yes. Well, I shall have to look into the whole business. You won't want to be here, will you?

MRS. DIX. Oh, I don't know. It's raining cats and dogs outside.

DIX. Virginia?

VIRGINIA. No walks. I'm evidence, besides.

DIX. Oh, well. (*To* GRYCE.) Here, you.

GRYCE. Were you addressing your remarks to me, sir?

DIX. Yes. Go and get Kelly, and bring the prisoner here.

GRYCE. General Dix, the sooner you and I come to some sort of understanding . . .

DIX. Do as I tell you. Jump to it.

[GRYCE *goes out.*]

(*To the ladies.*) Now, sit down out of the way, and keep quiet.

[MRS. DIX *smiles indulgently and sits down in the best chair in her best manner.* MISS PARKER *effaces herself.* VIRGINIA *stands on the fender, looking more subdued than usual.* DIX *takes his state behind a little table. To him, processionally—*

COCHRAN, KELLY, MACDONALD, GRYCE *with* MRS. GRYCE *behind.*

MRS. GRYCE *goes round and stands behind* MRS. DIX. *The rest stand by the door.*]

KELLY (*officiously*). Accused 'n h'escort, sir.

DIX. All right. All right. This isn't Orderly Room, Kelly.

KELLY. Very good, sir.

DIX. Cochran.

COCHRAN.   Good morning, sir.

DIX.   It seems you're a crook, Cochran.

[COCHRAN *is silent*.]

Well?

COCHRAN.   What do you want me to say, General?

DIX.   I want you to answer my question.

COCHRAN.   You haven't asked me a question.

MRS. DIX.   He's quite right, George.   You haven't.

DIX.   Julia.   Please.

MRS. DIX.   You must be fair, you know.

DIX.   I am fair.   God bless my soul!   I've tried thousands of cases.   Thousands.

MRS. DIX.   I know, dearest one, I know.   But even if it had been a question you couldn't have asked it.

DIX.   And why not?

MRS. DIX.   You hadn't warned him, you know.   You ought to warn the prisoner the very first thing.

DIX.   Will you kindly let me do things in my own way?

MRS. DIX.   But you can't administer the Law in your own way.   Otherwise it wouldn't be the Law, would it? Except in India, of course.

DIX.   My dear, I'm not going to argue with you.

MRS. DIX.   Of course you're not, sweetheart.   Don't let me interrupt you any more.

DIX.   I certainly won't.   Look here, Cochran.   I want your account of what happened last night.   You needn't give it if you don't want to; but if you do, please note particularly that I don't want any lies.   I've a nose for lies.

COCHRAN.   I suppose you know what you've let yourself in for?   I'll tell you in front of all this mob if you like.

DIX.   If you mean assault and illegal detention and all that, I know all about it.   It's not the first time I've taken responsibility.   And if you object any more to the presence of witnesses, I'll have the whole damned village in.   There's been plenty of underhand work here already.   Are you going to tell your story?

L   [149]

COCHRAN. Oh, if you like. . . . My parents were poor but honest gentlefolk who traced their ancestry back to the days when this old land of ours was young indeed. The fortunes of our house, since the hot, mad days of the '45—that wild and passionate adventure—have undergone many vicissitudes. In 1784 . . .

DIX. This isn't a joke, as you'll pretty soon find. Tell your story properly.

COCHRAN. I'll tell my story in my own way.

DIX. You can tell it in your own way in the news-papers, when you get out of jail. But that's years ahead. Virginia dear, are you feeling fit enough to tell us what happened last night? Or would you rather these people cleared out?

VIRGINIA. Oh, no, not a bit. Where do you want me to begin?

DIX. At the beginning. Go on.

VIRGINIA. Well, first of all I pinched the carburettor-pin.

DIX. You pinched the carburettor-pin?

VIRGINIA. From the Daimler.

DIX. What the . . . Whatever for?

VIRGINIA. So that the car wouldn't go.

DIX. Didn't you want the car to go?

VIRGINIA. What a silly question. And how you bark at me when I ask silly questions.

DIX. But I don't understand. Macdonald told me . . .

VIRGINIA. Macdonald couldn't tell you anything. He was on his honour.

DIX. *His* honour!

MACDONALD. You will pardon me, sir, but I object to the tone in which you mention that word. I am, as you know, a Highlander.

DIX. Oh, shut up. Jinny, I don't understand.

VIRGINIA. Of course you don't, Daddy. You don't know all the facts yet.

[150]

DIX.   Go ahead, go ahead.   By Gad, I'll get them somehow.   Why didn't you want the car to go?

VIRGINIA.   Because—well, because it was the biggest car, and I didn't want Captain Cochran to go.

DIX.   You—you weren't—you're not in love with the fellow, are you?

MRS. DIX.   Darling!

VIRGINIA.   No.   At least, I wasn't.   And I'm not. I wanted him to help me with the burglars.   To catch them.   So it all came out as I'd arranged, and . . .

DIX.   What burglars?

VIRGINIA.   The burglars who were after the Anglers' plate.

DIX.   But he was after the Anglers' plate himself.

MRS. DIX.   Now, now, now, George.   That's what you're trying to find out.   You don't *know* it yet.   You're just a mass of prejudice.

DIX.   I am nothing of the sort.

MRS. DIX.   You are.   Do get on with the court-martial, or whatever it is.   You aren't getting anywhere.

DIX.   If only you wouldn't butt in . . .

MRS. DIX.   Darling, you *know* I *never* butt in.   Go on, Virgie dear.

VIRGINIA.   So we waited at the window, as quiet as mice.   Captain Cochran had encouraged the detectives to get drunk.   So they wouldn't spoil the fun, you see. I asked him to.

DIX.   You did, did you?

MRS. DIX.   Saying "You did, did you?" is bullying the witness.

DIX.   Julia, what the devil do you know about it?

MRS. DIX.   I know *all* about it.   Don't you remember? I saw Mother and Lucy and Jessie Sturgeon all through their divorces?   Don't be so silly.   Do get on.

VIRGINIA.   So we waited and waited and waited.   All of a sudden I heard a low whistle from somewhere near the big elm across the road.   Captain Cochran said he heard it too, and went out by the front door to reconnoitre. I stayed all crouched down by the window. After what seemed ages, the suspense became too great. I popped up my head to look out. I got a glimpse of an evil face. The mouth and nose were muffled in a yellow silk handkerchief, but I'll never forget the eyes. They had heavy red eyebrows and no eyelashes. The left eye had a—had a decided cast. There was a long scar running down the right cheek. The face was—the face was livid in the moonlight. I stood petrified.

DIX.   How did you see the scar when this fellow's face was muffled in a handkerchief?

VIRGINIA.   It wasn't muffled so badly as that. Every detail was horribly, horribly clear. Then he hit me. With a bit of lead piping, I think. I saw thousands of sparks and flashes, and a wave of unconsciousness swept upon me, but I managed to struggle to the hearthrug. I had time to see two dark figures come in by the window and make for the show-cupboard. Then Captain Cochran came in, and there was a fight. I can't tell you any more. I must have fainted.

DIX.   Why in the name of the Suffering Saints didn't you tell us all this before?

VIRGINIA.   I felt so absolutely rotten. And you never asked me.

DIX.   It sounds darned thin to me.

VIRGINIA.   Do you suggest that I am a liar?

DIX.   No. Of course not. But people often dream things when they get a clout on the head.

VIRGINIA.   Daddy, I swear to you, honest Injun, I didn't dream this. I *know* I didn't.

DIX.   And how did his pockets happen to be bulging with jewellery, and what was he doing with the Anglers' plate?

KELLY.   Yes, what was he doing? . . . I beg pardon, sir.

VIRGINIA.   He was getting the jewellery when the

burglars arrived. I expect he barged into the passage
with the plate when he got it from them. I don't know
anything about *that*.

DIX. Here, you. (*To* GRYCE.) You were in the
hotel all evening. Did you hear or see anything of this?

GRYCE. Well, I saw Macdonald and the Captain
implicated on the floor. I assisted Macdonald to over-
power him. I thought, naturally enough, that the
Captain was mixed up in the affair. I see now I was
wrong. And now you mention it, I did see two dark
figures hurrying down the road. I thought nothing of it
at the time.

DIX. Cochran, why have I had to wait all this time
to get this story? Why didn't you speak?

COCHRAN. Because I question your right to inquire
into my actions at all. You've been most infernally
high-handed all through. You told me off like a pick-
pocket over those books, without taking the least trouble
to verify the facts. You stole my car. You neglected
my friendly warning, and suffered for it. You came
back like a raving lunatic and vented your spite on me.
It was no part of my duty or inclination to put you right
on matters of fact. There's your carburettor-pin. Are
you satisfied?

DIX. No. I'm not satisfied. Macdonald . . .

MACDONALD. Sir?

MRS. DIX. George, that's quite enough. You've
made a horrible mess of your court-martial, and any more
of it will give me a heart-attack. Don't pay any attention
to him, Captain Parkinson. He's a darling old thing,
but he's had a trying night, and he's never at his best in
the morning, anyhow.

DIX. Julia, that young man has stolen trust money,
and I'm going to make him sweat for it.

MRS. DIX. But, George, it wasn't his fault that those
men threw you in the pond.

DIX. It wasn't a pond, it was a loch; and, besides,

that has nothing whatever to do with the case.   He
stole trust money.   That's the point.

MRS. DIX.   Well, he can pay it back, can't he ?

DIX.   How do I know ?

MRS. DIX.   Haven't you asked him ?

DIX.   Of course not.

MRS. DIX.   Of course not ?   I should have thought
your first thought would have been how those nice old
comrades who threw you in the pond were going to get
their money back.   They were your old comrades too,
you know.   You said so in your speech.   But you don't
seem to worry about their hard-earned savings.   Oh,
dear me, no!   You just go ramping and stamping about,
calling poor Captain Kilpatrick a thief because he isn't
much good at book-keeping and mathematics and things.
We've not all got clever business heads like you,
darling.

MRS. GRYCE.   Now, that's quite right.   I'm sure it's
all been a mistake, and only wants a little explanation
and good-will on both sides, and it'll be all right.   It's
not everyone that can get their books to balance, especially
with that husband of mine helping him.

MRS. DIX.   How good of you to speak up so nobly,
Mrs. Gryce; but the General and I will manage this
all right for ourselves.   Now, George, the rain is off.
You go for a nice sharp walk round the village before
you finish packing, and I'll have a little cosy chat with
Captain Macadam, and there'll be nothing at all to worry
about.   It only wants a little sympathy and understanding,
a thing like this.   I remember when Father got drunk
in Mess one night and Major What-was-his-name hit
him with the port-decanter for saying Annie Kilbride was
a scarlet slut, it *all* came right.   All what's needed is
somebody with a little common-sense.

DIX.   Julia, I must ask you not to interfere.   You
must not interfere.   You don't understand these things.

MRS. DIX.   George, you are making me angry.   And

if I get angry, I shall have my *migraine* to-morrow.   And it will be all your fault.   Virginia, take your father away.

VIRGINIA.   Daddy, Mumsie's getting excited and all worked up.   Do come out for a little.   The rain has stopped.   The hills are lovely.

MRS. DIX.   Captain Macpherson, will you please go up to our sitting-room ?   I shall be up presently.

COCHRAN.   Very well, Mrs. Dix.

[*He goes.*]

MRS. DIX.   Mrs. Prichard, I think that will be all.

[MRS. GRYCE *bridles, but goes.   Her husband is irresolute, but she hurries him out.*]

KELLY (*to* DIX).   I'll keep an eye on him, sir.

DIX.   Go to hell !

[KELLY *goes there.   Nobody notices* MISS PARKER, *who has opened a book—down-stage.*]

MRS. DIX (*sitting down wearily*).   Oh, dear !   So that's that.

DIX.   I respectfully beg your pardon, but that isn't that.   Not by a jugful.

MRS. DIX.   May I ask what you mean ?

DIX.   I mean that damned rogue isn't going to save his brass neck because you've taken a fancy to him.

MRS. DIX.   What a vulgar old person you can be, George, when you really try.

[VIRGINIA *sees* MISS PARKER.]

VIRGINIA.   Hello !   Miss Parker.   You still here !

MISS PAR.   Oh, yes.   I am.   I was just finishing a chapter.   Albert Huxley, you know.   I mean, I didn't realise . . .

VIRGINIA.   Oh, it's a public Lounge.   You needn't keep on explaining yourself.   Only Dad and Mumsie are going to have a row.

MRS. DIX.   Isn't she a frightful brat, Miss Ponsonby ?   Do wait and have a chat.

MISS PAR.   Oh, no.   I was just going.   I've some

letters and things to write. To my aunt and all sorts of people.

MRS. DIX. But won't you finish your chapter?

MISS PAR. No, really . . . at least, it's nearly finished, and I've such a lot to do, what with one thing and another. I'd better perhaps . . . I do hope . . . By the way, General, while I'm here I think perhaps I ought to tell you that that old Gryce is a proper old rascal. I think it's quite possible he was at the bottom of all the trouble. I could tell you a thing or two about him, only—you want to talk.

DIX. Go on, go on. What about Gryce?

MISS PAR. He tried to poison me. At least, not exactly that. Only indirectly, in a sort of way. . . . Or not really poison. . . . It was more a case of drugging. . . .

MRS. DIX. We are keeping Miss Polson from her correspondence. Good morning, my dear.

[MISS PARKER *is blown out by the radio-active emanations of* MRS. DIX'S *noblesse.*]

There, you see! You're a gossip, that's what you are.

DIX. Look here. This has gone on long enough. . . .

MRS. DIX. I agree with you. Go away. Your parade-ground voice rakes through my head like grape-shot, or whatever it is.

DIX. Julia . . .

MRS. DIX. Go away.

DIX. Julia, for God's sake, be reasonable.

MRS. DIX. Reasonable! Reasonable! Do you want me to stamp about and yell and get red in the face? Do you call that reasonable?

DIX. No, but . . .

MRS. DIX. Then go away.

DIX. Oh, what's the use? What IS the use? I'll go upstairs to my packing. The sooner we are out of this madhouse the better.

[*Exit.*]

VIRGINIA. Mother, why are you shielding Cochran?

[156]

MRS. DIX.   I haven't the remotest idea.

VIRGINIA.   But there seems to be no doubt he stole all those poor chaps' money.

MRS. DIX.   " Converted it to his own use," I think.

VIRGINIA.   The man's a damned sweep!

MRS. DIX.   My precious! Haven't you eyes? Good gracious me! he's got breeding in every inch of him, that boy!

VIRGINIA.   Got what in every inch?

MRS. DIX.   Breeding. Don't you know a gentleman when you see one?

VIRGINIA.   Gentlemen don't convert trust money to their own uses.

MRS. DIX.   Don't they, though! Don't they! Really, I must arrange for you to meet some nice people. You don't appear to know a thing.

VIRGINIA.   Well, I think it makes it worse if he's a gentleman.

MRS. DIX.   Of *course* it does, pettikins. *Ever* so much worse. Now, if I haven't left him up in the sitting-room, waiting for me, and George is certain to bump into him. Touch the bell, sweetheart.

VIRGINIA (*rings bell*).   Mumsie, he should go to prison.

MRS. DIX.   Oh, no, no. He'd hate it. Oh, porter (*as* KELLY *appears*), will you give Captain Macadam my compliments and tell him I should like to see him here?

KELLY (*the waiter*).   Yes, madam.

[*Exit* KELLY.]

MRS. DIX.   Thank you *so* much.

VIRGINIA.   Do you want me to go, Mumsie?

MRS. DIX.   You? No. Why? Do you think he is my lover, or what?

VIRGINIA.   Oh, no. I didn't think that, *of course.*

MRS. DIX.   Now, that ' of course ' would have offended me, seventy years ago. How callous we old women become! And *à propos des bottes*, why did you tell a pack of lies to save that slack-mouthed, watery-eyed budmash from all that he nobly deserved?

VIRGINIA. They weren't . . . How did you know they were lies?

MRS. DIX. Everybody knew they were lies except your father. Isn't he the dear thing?

VIRGINIA. Mumsie, I hate to keep anything from you . . .

MRS. DIX. You can't keep anything from me. I've got low tastes too. Your daddy was a bombardier when I ran away with him. Only he had a clean crime-sheet and he wasn't the sort who would beat his wife unless he was badly mishandled.

VIRGINIA. Mumsie, do you think my heart's broken? It feels all dull in here.

MRS. DIX. That's excitement and a little indigestion. No. Hearts are more difficult to break. It takes years sometimes.

VIRGINIA. I expect you're right. Oh, my God, I'm ashamed! I think I'll die of shame. I never knew what it meant before.

MRS. DIX. Of course you didn't, dear love. But everybody gets to know some time. I only hope it won't make you too frightfully good.

VIRGINIA. You see, it's all the vegetative nervous system and the endocrine glands, I know. I keep telling myself that. But I don't believe myself. Something's sickened me right to the soul.

MRS. DIX. You're a very proud soul, Virgie. It's very *comme il faut*, and it doesn't approve in the least of its dear, delicious, beautiful, vulgar little body. Souls haven't much sense of humour, you see. You've only got to go to one of those too-wonderful spiritualist circles to find *that* out. I remember your grandfather's soul spoke to me through a little trumpet, and he had grown so dull and correct. Not a bit like what he used to be. Are you fond of this thief person?

VIRGINIA. Oh, not now.   NOT now!

MRS. DIX. And you don't want to marry him?

VIRGINIA. Heavens! no.   Mumsie, how can you!

MRS. DIX. Oh, I " can " ever so many things, you'd never imagine.   If you don't want to, it's all right.   But I thought at one time he might be quite suitable.

VIRGINIA. But he's a thief!

MRS. DIX. That's only because he has no money. Daddums will get him a job, and then he won't have to bother about doing any more stealing.   It's no use talking about it if you don't want to, but I should like to see you married.   It's such a settling thing.

VIRGINIA. You're being horribly, horribly cruel.

MRS. DIX. It isn't very nice of you to say that, Virgie. You needn't marry Captain Thingummy if you don't want to.   Marry that Highland young man—you know —who drives the Daimler.

VIRGINIA. Mumsie, you're an old ass!

MRS. DIX. I know. I know. . . . And now run away and forget all about it. Or remember it in the right way. Yesterday and yesterday. The past is only material for amusing stories, and even they needn't be true.

VIRGINIA. It gives us experience, too, I suppose.

MRS. DIX. Experiences, you mean, lovikins. I don't want my lamb ever to be experienced.

[*Enter* CAPTAIN COCHRAN. VIRGINIA *retires to window.*]
Oh, come in, Captain. . . . Dear me, I've forgotten your name.

COCHRAN. My name's Cochran, Mrs. Dix.

MRS. DIX. Of course. How stupid of me. One of the Tir-a-drum Cochrans?

COCHRAN. They are cousins of mine.

MRS. DIX. Your mother wasn't Fanny Riches, was she?

COCHRAN. Yes, Mrs. Dix, she was. Mrs. Dix, I want to say . . .

MRS. DIX. Sh! That accounts for a great deal. How much do you owe this Band of Hope, or whatever it is?

COCHRAN. I haven't the least idea.

MRS. DIX. Then don't you think you'd better get some clever accountant to give you an idea? And then you could get the Tir-a-drum people to pay it back.

COCHRAN. I suppose I'll have to do something like that. (*Emotionally*) Oh, Mrs. Dix, if you only knew—if there was anything I could say . . .

MRS. DIX. I've done nothing. I only wanted to know whom it was you kept on reminding me of. Fanny Riches! Well, well, well. How is old Fanny, by the way?

COCHRAN. She's dead, Mrs. Dix. Died in East Africa, two years ago.

MRS. DIX. I remember. That's where he took her. How absurd of him. Well, I'm so sorry. I don't suppose we can offer you a lift to Edinburgh?

[COCHRAN *falls on his knees and kisses her hand.*]

Now, now. Don't be silly. Look here, I don't suppose two tenners are much good to you, but you'd better have them. Go away and be a good boy, and try to be a credit to your—to your father.

COCHRAN. Good-bye, Mrs. Dix. By Jove, you are a topper!

MRS. DIX. Cheer-oh!

[*He goes.*]
[VIRGINIA *is waving frantically at the window.*]

VIRGINIA. Professor! Professor! Do come here. I want to talk to you.

MRS. DIX. Virginia! Don't bring that nasty, mouldy, smelly old man in here.

VIRGINIA. There's something I want to ask him.

MRS. DIX. Then I'll go upstairs. I'd better, anyway. The General-Sahib will put his wet flannels on top of his sword if I don't stop him. You'd better hurry too. We must be off.

VIRGINIA. Right-oh, Mumsie.

[MRS. DIX *goes.*]
[*The* PROFESSOR *encounters her awkwardly, apologises with his bourgeois elaborateness, and comes in.*]

Professor, I've only got a moment. But there are one or two things. First of all, I want to thank you for being so sporting and backing me up.

GRYCE. Not at all. Not at all.

VIRGINIA. Then I want to know—dead secret and all that—why you poisoned Miss Parker, and what you were doing in the Lounge at that time of night.

GRYCE. Miss Dix. I have your secret. You shall have mine. And yet . . .

VIRGINIA. Oh, do tell me. Please do. It can't make any difference.

GRYCE. It can, curiously enough; though I don't know why it should.

VIRGINIA. It can't, it can't. I'll never see you again. I'll never even think of you again if you don't wish it. Tell me, Professor.

GRYCE. Well. As a matter of fact, I was carrying on a guilty *liaison* with the hotel cook. And she disappointed me.

VIRGINIA. Oh! Is that true?

GRYCE. She went to the Rally with the butcher's son.

VIRGINIA. I never heard anything so disgusting. You ought to be ashamed of yourself. Good-bye. I *won't* even *think* of you.

[*She goes.*]
[GRYCE *fills and lights his pipe. He sings :*]

GRYCE. Pour un peu d'amour,
Un peu d'amour;
Je donnerais bien mes nuits, mes jours,

[161]

> Pour t'entendre, dans cet instant suprême,
> Murmurer tout bas, tout bas, " Je t'aime ! "

(Changing his tune.)

> " I triumph, I triumph ; the last word is
> spo-oken ! "

[*Enter* MISS PARKER *and her book.*]

MISS PAR. Oh, hello, and all that sort of thing.

GRYCE. Hello. Isn't it a funny world ?

MISS PAR. Well, funny—peculiar, not funny, ha-ha, I should say. Is that extraordinary English family away yet ?

GRYCE. " Extraordinary," you say ? I should say fantastic, but not extraordinary. They are typically English. They are quite sure they know what's right without turning it up in the dictionary.

[MACDONALD *enters.*]

MACDONALD. I beg your pardon, sir, I was looking for Mrs. Dix.

GRYCE. She hasn't finished packing yet. Singular affair that, last night, Macdonald.

MACDONALD. Very peculiar.

GRYCE. Come in for a minute.

MACDONALD. Mrs. Gryce has some objections to my presence in the Lounge.

GRYCE. Damn Mrs. Gryce.

MACDONALD. Very good, sir. In any case, I am a chauffeur no longer. I can come in. (*He comes into the room.*)

GRYCE. Captain Cochran came out of it rather well, I thought.

MACDONALD. For the present, yes.

GRYCE. Now, now, you mustn't say " for the present." It's all over and done with. The detectives, even, have gone back to Glasgow. It's all over.

MACDONALD. Indeed and it is not.

GRYCE.   Don't be so foolish.   You know it was all a mistake.   There was no question of Captain Cochran making a get-away with the plate and things.   The idea is absurd.   It was quite natural, of course, for you to make the mistake you did, but . . .

MACDONALD.   I care nothing for your plate and things. He could steal the whole hotel from over your heads, and what would I care?   But his conduct to the young lady I will not excuse, and for that he will suffer if I have to follow him over the whole of Africa.

MISS PAR.   Why Africa?

MACDONALD.   Either there or anywhere else, if I get my two hands upon him . . .

[VIRGINIA *enters, dressed for the journey.*]

VIRGINIA.   What *are* you talking about, Macdonald?

GRYCE.   Last night appears to have gone to his head. I've told him the whole thing is settled.   The detectives went back to Glasgow on the early bus.   Their reports should be interesting reading.   There will be no prosecution.   It's all clear.   And this chap talks about chasing poor Cochran all over Africa and man-handling him when he catches up.

VIRGINIA.   Why, Macdonald?

MACDONALD.   You will never know why till the world falls into the sea.   I will be helping with the luggage . . . *your* luggage.   The General's can fend for itself.

[*He goes.*]
[*They stare after him.*]

MRS. DIX (*above*).   Virginia!   I want you.

[*Enter* MRS. GRYCE.]

MRS. GRYCE.   Your mamma wants you, dearie.

[VIRGINIA *goes out, amazed.*]

GRYCE.   Yes,   I . . . Well . . . Yes . . . Well, have they paid the bill yet, my love?

[163]

MRS. GRYCE. Oh, yes. (*Sits down.*) I nearly paid them to go away. Kelly's loading the baggage. What a carry-on! There's one comfort—I don't suppose they'll ever come back.

GRYCE. They'll recommend the Anglers' Arms to all their friends. They'll say they've been very comfortable here. That's what their sort call comfortable.

MRS. GRYCE. Well, it's not what I call comfortable— stirring up wasps' nests. Thank the Lord they'll be away in a few minutes. The Captain's paid his bill too.

MISS PAR. I *knew* he was really all right at heart.

MRS. GRYCE. It's not for us to judge. What I say is, whatever happens, what's the use of making unpleasantness?

[*Enter* GENERAL *and* MRS. DIX.]

MRS. DIX. Oh, Mrs. Watson, there you are. I wanted to thank you for being so good to us. We have been most comfortable. We shall certainly mention your most delightful little inn to all our friends.

MRS. GRYCE. It's very kind of you, ma'am, I'm sure.

DIX. I'm afraid we've been rather a nuisance to you, Mrs. Gryce.

MRS. GRYCE. Oh, dear me, no; it's a great pleasure.

DIX. I'd have liked to clear things up more fully, but I'll look into it later. In the meantime, I'm glad to have been of any service.

GRYCE. The trained hand of the man of affairs is always a pleasure to watch. I'm afraid we had been letting matters drift a little.

DIX. Indeed you had. Is the new man—What's-his-name—ready with the car?

VIRGINIA. But, Daddy, Macdonald . . .

DIX. Never mind Macdonald. We'll—we'll talk of that later.

MRS. DIX. Good-bye, Miss Thomson. I do hope you will look us up whenever you are in Town, and—and sing us something. Or is it Eurythmics you do?

MISS PAR.   No. I paint. Flowers and landscapes and so on.

MRS. DIX.   I am the stupidest woman out of captivity. Don't you think so, Professor ? Haven't I got a silly face ?

GRYCE.   Madam, it is impossible to tell whether your face is silly or not.

MRS. DIX.   That sounds as if it might be quite nice. And you must be a judge yourself. You are so picturesque yourself. Like a ruined Abbey. Isn't he, Virgie ?

VIRGINIA.   I suppose so. Mumsie, what's this about Macdonald ?

MRS. DIX.   He was impertinent to your father, dear. An offence that obviously ranks with blasphemy. Well, well, well. Are we all ready ?

OMNES.   Good-bye. . . . Good-bye. . . . Safe journey. . . . We'll all see you to the door. . . . So good of you. . . .

MRS. DIX.   I feel as if we were all quite old friends.

[*Exeunt* OMNES.]

[*After a pause, enter* COCHRAN. *From the shelter of the window-curtain he sees the motor-car go off. Then he shrugs his shoulders and comes down-stage, lighting a cigarette.*]

[*Enter* KELLY.]

COCHRAN.   Oh, hello, Kelly. So that's all ended happily.

KELLY.   Sez you.

COCHRAN.   I beg your pardon ?

KELLY.   Granted.

[*He goes to the fireplace and fiddles with the poker—not menacingly but to disguise his emotion.*]

COCHRAN.   Well, I'm off. I don't suppose I shall see you again. Catch.

[*He rolls a Bradbury into a ball and tosses it to* KELLY. KELLY *catches it.*]

M   [165]

KELLY.   What's this?

COCHRAN.   Small token of my esteem.

[KELLY *throws the note in fire.*]

I say, my dear old chap!   What a thing to do!

[MACDONALD *appears behind him.*]

KELLY.   Hullo, Mac.   Here he is.

COCHRAN.   What's the idea?

MACDONALD.   The idea?   I have the curiosity to see what else you can do with your fists forbye hitting young ladies.   Put up your hands, you dirty brock!

COCHRAN.   Look here.   Keep the fun clean.   No. Honestly.   Two to one, I mean.

KELLY.   Come on, Mac.   Owre the bags, and good luck tae us!

[*They advance on* COCHRAN.   *He quails.*]

QUICK   CURTAIN

THE DANCING BEAR

A COMEDY IN THREE ACTS

*None of the characters or incidents in this Play is
intended to suggest actual individuals or happenings.
Nor is the Play intended as a satire upon any actual
society or group of people. It is to be read and played
purely as a work of imagination.*

*This play was first presented by the Scottish National Players at
the Lyric Theatre, Glasgow, in February* 1931, *with the
following Cast:*

CHARACTERS

MRS. MURDOCH	Meg Buchanan.
MRS. GOBIE	Esther Wilson.
MRS. DICKSON-WATSON-DICKSON	Hester Paton Brown.
PROFESSOR NISH . . .	Moultrie Kelsall.
MISS SOULIS	Elliot Mason.
MR. MURDOCH . . .	James Anderson.
MR. GOBIE	H. C. Stark.
MR. PRINGLE . . .	Sheridan Aitchison.
MRS. NISH	Mae Watt.
MISS BAIGRIE . . .	Nan Scott.
MR. BETTS . . .	Hal Stewart.
MISS MURDOCH . . .	Jean Stuart.
BELLMAN KILGOUR . .	Charles Brooks.
COLIN KILGOUR . . .	James Gibson.
JEAN	Elsie Brotchie.
A VOICE at Mrs. Gobie's.	
MISS HENDERSON . . .	Marie Daeblitz.

GUESTS at Mrs. Gobie's.

VOICES from a Charabanc, and A BLACKBIRD.

The play was produced by W. G. Fay.

TIME.—The Present.

ACT I.—September at the Seaside.

ACT II.—February in Glasgow.

ACT III.—April at the seaside.

[168]

Note.—If it is desired to play " St. Eloy and the Bear " separately, the passages referring to production hitches (see pp. 216 *et seq.*) may be cut out and the following lines substituted :—

A two-legged thing that makes me dance and tumble. . . .

GASTON.   My dear old creature, don't stand there and mumble.
           Dance down the road and think.   And I expect
           You will be somewhat heartened to reflect
           That you have left all other bears behind
           In brain power ; and the strongest of mankind
           Are babies to you.   Off you go then.
MIRABEL.   Shoo !
BEAR.   You put an interesting point of view.

[He goes out.]

The play goes on as before till the line " And I shall not require a cook. . . . wild " (p. 219).

*[*GASTON *flees in terror.   The* BEAR *eats* MIRABEL.*]*

BEAR.   Holy St. Eloy, unto thee I lift
           My not ungrateful paws.   If on the whole
           I cannot thank thee for the equivocal gift
           Of a tormenting, wayward, sorrowful soul,
           At least I thank thee for the eye to see
           The wit to grasp, the stomach to enjoy
           Whatever on this earth seems good to me.
           I magnify and thank thee, Saint Eloy.

CURTAIN

SYNOPSIS OF THE CHARACTERS

which may be read as a guide by modest actors creating the parts.

PROFESSOR NISH is the incumbent of the McCracken Chair of Fundamental Principles in the University of Glasgow. He is also a graduate of that University but conceals the damning fact as far as possible. He is between forty and fifty, and combines a remarkably youthful appearance with an aged and even stricken manner. He is far from being such a fool as he appears to be. But, on the other hand, though he is a secret hard worker, he is a man of no great ability. Realities of all sorts terrify him and he has grown a thick hedge of mannerisms to protect himself against his fellow-creatures.

MRS. NISH is also a graduate of Glasgow University. But her attitude is that of one who has " passed her examinations " in literature and science and doesn't need to bother any more. She is pretty, too, but she passed her examination in that when she collared Professor Nish, and she pays little or no attention to her appearance.

MISS BAIGRIE is a handsome, talented trollop who would like it to be thought that she has no inhibitions.

MARY HENDERSON is a little grey-haired woman with a limp and a black ebony stick to support it. She has been in three lunatic asylums and still bears about her their ruined day.

MISS SOULIS, the lady-novelist, is a difficulty to the critics. They hardly know whether to align her with the frosty magnificence of Rebecca West or

[171]

with the guilty splendour of Elinor Glyn. She hates them for that, and none the less that she doesn't know where to align herself. She is greedy, ignorant, proud, noisy, tall, flabby, and not ill-looking.

KITTY MURDOCH is not a bad sort of girl at heart. Her schooling and her environment have made her the idiot that she is.

JEAN is simply an ordinary, competent woman who gives to her profession of domestic service the utter honesty of purpose and efficiency she would give to any other profession into which it pleased God to call her. Lady Rhondda is apt to assume that all women are like her, but unfortunately they aren't.

BETTS is an intelligent flibbertigibbet. It is he and such as he that terrify a city like Glasgow into believing that it really is as provincial as it looks. He is the only member of the cast with a really expensive accent.

COLIN is the hero of the play. It is not intended that he should be a good poet, but he has enough fire in his belly to make him acutely uncomfortable. Apart from his poetry he is a decent enough young fellow. He can be played in any recognised manner so long as the actor realises that he is not a Russian but a Scot.

MURDOCH is a money-grubbing brute who tolerates the Arts because of some queer strain in his ancestry.

MRS. MURDOCH is a roustabout nobody.

MRS. GOBIE is Mrs. Leo Hunter on a smaller physical and mental scale.

MR. GOBIE is a successful warehouseman like his father before him; but he has been educated at Glenalmond and he admires his ass of a wife. These two facts make him rather a figure of fun in a Scottish community.

MRS. DICKSON-WATSON-DICKSON is a sweet, humble,

plebeian soul whose husband has left her an enormous
quantity of money made by gambling, luck and frank
stealing.

PRINGLE is a beast of a successful parson, with a noble
presence and a dirty little mind.   He is driven into
this profession, as girls are said to be driven on to the
streets, by economic pressure.

KILGOUR is a talkative, sardonic hypocrite of a Scot.

THE OTHERS are stage caricatures at the discretion of
the Producer and his Players.

THE DANCING BEAR

ACT I

[JEAN *at door, with a basket, speaking to someone off.*]

JEAN. Aye, I know. It canna be helped.

[*Noise off.*]

Uhuh. . . . Mercy, here they're coming. I'm away to the kitchen garden.

[MRS. MURDOCH, MRS. GOBIE, MRS. DICKSON-WATSON-DICKSON.]

MRS. MUR. Hey, you men! The rain's off. Do you hear me?—the rain's off.

MURDOCH (*without*). All right, mother.

MRS. MUR. Well, come on out. It's a lovely evening, going to be. Us ladies are going along to look at the chrysanths. Aren't they the lazy gang, Mrs. Gobie?

MRS. GOBIE. Oh, Henry will make them come all right. He's passionately fond of chrysanthemums. Quite Japanese he is in that way, anyway.

MRS. DICKSON. Gracious! it's offle damp.

MRS. MUR. Yes. isn't it, Mrs. Dickson-Watson-Dickson? We'll stick to the path. (*They pass out.*)

[*Enter* NISH *and* MISS SOULIS.]

NISH. You know, I think we hardly realise the extrod'ny wa-wa-wa—— Push—those Renaissance fellahs derived from Ronsard and Ariosto.

MISS SOULIS. No. I don't think we do, do we?

NISH. No. And that's why we get quite hysterical, don't you think? When the whole bunch seem, as it were, to go in off the deep end, don't you think?

[175]

MISS SOULIS.   Oh, I do, I do.   I do think so.   I often, often have.   (*They pass.*)

[*Enter* GOBIE *and* MURDOCH.]

MURDOCH.   So, thinks I, my lad, if that's the airt the wind blows, we'll see.   So I says, " Look you here, Mr. Wyllie, if I was to foreclose to-morrow——" and, mind you, for all he knew there was nothing to hinder me doing it. . . .

GOBIE.   Quite, quite, quite, quite, quite.   After you, sir, after you.

MURDOCH.   Ye see?   Hey?

GOBIE.   Quite, quite, quite.   (*They pass.*)

[*Enter* MISS BAIGRIE, MRS. NISH *and* PRINGLE.]

PRINGLE.   And just as things were getting what one might call really—well, remarkably interesting, down came the blind.

MRS. NISH.   Mr. Pringle!   What an awful like story for a minister!   Miss Baigrie here, too.   She's astonished at you, I'm sure.

MISS BAIGRIE.   Nothing astonishes Miss Baigrie, sweetheart.

PRINGLE.   I'll astonish you one of these days, you stiff-necked, perverse brat!   (*They pass.   Pause.*)

[*Enter* BETTS *and* KITTY.]

BETTS.   Do you particularly want to see the chrysanthemums?

KITTY.   I do most decidedly not.

BETTS.   Then let's go back, and you'll play me a spot of Chaminade, and I'll eat chocolates.

KITTY.   No, no.   We mustn't waste the first bright blink of the day.   There's a watery flicker of sunshine that will do you good.   All handsome men are sunburned.

BETTS.   Ah!   And do I stand here and get all damp and sloppy to improve my sex appeal?

KITTY. You don't need to stand unless you like.
Park your hips on the doings, here.

BETTS. But the seat is wet.

KITTY. What's that you've got there? *Vogue?*
We'll sit on it. It's thick and soft and doughy. Do
you smell the burning leaves?

BETTS. I think it's a loathsome odour, if you don't
mind my saying so. They used to burn them in the
garden of a perfectly emetic school my dismal parents sent
me to. Luckily my glands all swole up in the first term
and they had to take me home.

KITTY. Filthy luck for them!

BETTS. For whom? My parents? Not at all. I
was the sunshine of the home. "Little Sunshine" they
called me.

KITTY. You're not so sunny to-day.

BETTS. No. I'm off my oats a little.

KITTY. I noticed that. Why is it that wet earth is
the only wet thing that smells nice?

BETTS. I beg your pardon?

KITTY. I know wet trees and grass and flowers are
all right, but they never get properly soaked. Wet
blankets and boots and dogs are horrid. I can't think of
another wet thing that smells nice.

BETTS. Napoleon brandy does, and stamps after you've
licked them. So there is nothing in what you say.

KITTY. No?

BETTS. No. As you were remarking, I am not at
the top of my form.

KITTY. Aren't you enjoying your week-end?

BETTS. Not a bit.

KITTY. Why not? The duodenal ulcer bothering
you?

BETTS. Mind your own business. No. I'm in love.

KITTY. Oh! Who with?

BETTS. You. Will you marry me?

KITTY. My dear sir——!

[177]

BETTS.   You rather like me, you know.

KITTY.   I suppose I do.   Lord knows why.

BETTS.   Well, what about it ?   You don't want me to ruin the knees of my good bags on this dirty ground, do you ?   You don't expect me to say that you cannot have failed to have noticed the nature of my sentiments towards you ?

KITTY.   It would be a pity to spoil such beautiful bags.

BETTS.   A thousand pities.   Come along.   It's quite a normal and customary sort of contract, and I don't see why we should get the wind up about it.   Are you on ? I pause for a reply.

KITTY.   Well, you're all right in a way, and sometimes you amuse me quite horribly.   But could you keep me amused for years and years and years ?

BETTS.   I'd have a shot at it.   You see, I admire you most frightfully, and when you appreciate me I go all lofty.   A lifetime of being appreciated by you would make a man of me.   And you're an intelligent sort of little skirt.   We'd be rather a wow as married people.

KITTY.   Maybe we would be rather a scream.   We could muck in with quite an amusing crowd.   Would we live in Glasgow ?

BETTS.   Are you being funny ?

KITTY.   I say, it might be rather a mouldy trick not to stay for a bit and liven the place up a little, don't you think ?

BETTS.

A loaf of bread, a pint of fizz, and thou
Singing beside me in Auchenshuggle,
This Auchenshuggle would be Paris *Plage* enow.

We're engaged now, aren't we ?

KITTY.   Oh, are we ?   Yes, I suppose so.

BETTS.   Shall I kiss you ?   I only kissed you once before, and I was a little tight at the time, if you remember.

KITTY.   No.   Not here.

BETTS.   Where, then ?

KITTY. Oh, some old where. Listen, Ronnie; I thought we had got it over without any of that sort of rot.

BETTS. O.K. with me, chief.

[*A bell is heard on the roadside of wall. It is accompanied by a voice, but the words are at first indistinct through distance.*]

What's that heart-sickening and gloomy sound? Do they buy and sell old clothes in this frightful part of the country?

KITTY. No. It's old Tam Kilgour, the village bellman.

BETTS. But how nice! I thought the charabancs had exterminated the poor old wretches.

KITTY. It would take a fleet of tanks to exterminate old Tam. All the licensed premises along the coast have been trying to kill him for the last fifty years. And they've only made him sadder and sadder and sadder.

BETTS. He's a sad bellman, then? He doesn't play fantasias from sheer joyousness of heart?

KITTY. No. He only really enjoys announcing funerals. Listen.

KILGOUR (*behind the wall*). Lost on or near the vicinity of the Esplanade, a fawn-coloured Pekinese bitch answering to the name of Toto. Finder will be rewarded on returning same to Mr. McNicol of the " Black Bull."

BETTS. Why " returning same," do you think? I say, let's have him in and ask him.

KITTY. If you like. You won't find him very amusing.

BETTS. But I might amuse him, you know.

[*He goes to the wicket and shouts.*]

Hey, Bellman!

KILGOUR (*at the wicket*). What's your wull?

BETTS. Oh, good afternoon. It has brightened up into a fine day.

KILGOUR.   Aye, if it keeps.

BETTS.   Do you see any reason why it shouldn't keep ? It's been allowed to get a bit damp, of course, but . . .

KITTY.   Good afternoon, Mr. Kilgour.   Which of McNicol's Pekes is that you are crying ?

KILGOUR.   It is one of last year's litter, Miss Murdoch. It was aye a wandersome wee de'il.

KITTY.   I hope nothing has happened to it.

KILGOUR.   It is in the hands of Providence, like the rest of us.

KITTY.   By the way, talking of dogs . . .

BETTS.   We were talking about a Pekinese.

KITTY.   Well, it's a sort of a dog.   Talking of dogs, do you think your son is likely to bring back my wee Cairn to-day.   I was down at the smithy yesterday, and he said the wee boy was practically well.

KILGOUR.   I think it is very possible that Colin will be up to-day.   Very possible.   (*He gives vent to a strangled and melancholy guffaw.*)

KITTY.   That's nice.   Poor little Rob was so miserable with his distemper.

KILGOUR.   The wee beast's no richt better yet, miss. But as you and me are aware, Colin has his ain reasons for wanting to come up to the House.

KITTY.   Has he ?   I hadn't heard of any other reason.

KILGOUR.   Hey ?   Ye didna ken he had taken a notion to the lassie McLeish ?   It's all owre the village.

KITTY.   McLeish ?   Oh, you mean Kate, our table-maid.   Well, she's a real nice lassie, Mr. Kilgour, and I think you should feel very glad your son has such good taste.

KILGOUR.   Aweel, I'm thankful enough.   But it's no Kate—that's the McLeod.   It's Jean, Jean McLeish. Auld McLeish, the weaver's Willie that went to Glasgow's dochter.

BETTS.   A complicated relationship.

KITTY.   Oh, yes—Jean.   When's the wedding to be ?

KILGOUR. Oh, they're no promised yet. It's just a notion he's ta'en. I'm real glad in a way. He's a queer lad, and I was feared he might he catched by one of they summer visitors—a wheen of cow-hocked Jezebels.

KITTY. You are very hard on the summer visitors.

KILGOUR. Hard, do you say? I wish I was their father.

BETTS. Oh, Mr. Kilgour! What gross philoprogenitive ambitions!

KILGOUR. It was parental authority only I wished for, sir. The *locum parentis*, merely, if you ken the Latin by-word. I wouldna sire the best o' the shauchly besoms. They have nae thought, nae ambeetion but to expose their persons to the day and to the scorn of the judeecious. Each year the frontiers of modesty do further and further recede. There they go, stoitering along the promenade wi' their high-heeled shoon and in a' their nakedness, and yet canna arouse a single lasceevious thought in the mind o' the beholder. But it'll no' pay me to stand havering here. I'll be stepping. Good day to you, Miss Murdoch. Good day to you, sir.

BETTS. Look here. What is your fee for crying a bit of news?

KILGOUR. That depends on the news and how long it would tak' to wale it.

BETTS. Miss Murdoch and I are engaged

KILGOUR. I'm sure I congratulate you.

BETTS. Will you cry that round the town?

KITTY. Ronnie, don't be an ape!

KILGOUR. In what terms would you wish it to be cried?

BETTS. I'll leave that entirely to you.

KILGOUR. I will get my son Colin to compose something. He is a great hand at the literature. And what's the name, sir?

BETTS. Ronald Mackenzie Crathie Mavrogordato Betts.

KILGOUR. Thank you, sir. I'll remember that. I
will send you my account in due course. I think you
said money was no object?

BETTS. I didn't, but you can spread yourself as much
as you like.

KITTY. Ronnie . . .

BETTS. Only don't call Miss Kitty a cow-hocked
what-do-you-call-um.

KILGOUR. I would never think of taking the liberty.
Good day to you, Miss Catherine. Good day to you,
sir.

[*He goes.*]

BETTS. We Scots are a strong, silent race.

KITTY. You're not professing to be a Scotsman, are
you?

BETTS. Yes. Mother's side. Father was born within sound of the boom of Big Ben. I never told you about
my father?

KITTY. I've forgotten if you did.

BETTS. He was one of the first Englishmen to colonise
Scotland. He early decided that London was no good to
him.

KITTY. All the Heids o' depairtments were Scotch.

BETTS. They were. Nobody but a Scotsman was
prepared to take the necessary dog's abuse or to crawl
so continually on the belly of his manhood . . .

KITTY. Ronnie Betts——

BETTS. Shut up. I'm speaking. So he emigrated
to Glasgow, where his London gutter wit and sterling
English insincerity soon brought him an easy fortune and a
bride who was almost County. Result—me. I inherit
my father's facile smartness and vulgarity and my mother's
mental and physical slovenliness. My love of the beautiful
I have supplied for myself.

KITTY. And where did you get your taste for neckties?

BETTS. From Mother. That is part of my sense of
humour.

[182]

KITTY. I suppose making Kilgour yell our private affairs all over the town is part of your sense of humour too?

BETTS. No. Father's vulgarity. Do you mind?

KITTY. No. I'm pretty *bourgeoisie* myself, if it comes to that.

BETTS. I hope he says: "Oyez, oyez, oyez" and "God Save the King." Do you think our nuptials will be any sort of menace to the King his peace?

KITTY. If our kids take after us they will.

BETTS. Who is this literary merchant? This son, who is going to write the merry stuff?

KITTY. Colin? Oh, rather a pet. He writes verses for the newspapers. Oh, and a book too. He works in the smiddy, and he's a bit of an amateur vet., too. He's Rob the terrier's particular medical man. I expect he . . . Oh, here he is.

[*Enter* COLIN.]

Hello, Colin. You've brought the wee man?

COLIN. He's not just right yet, Miss Catherine, but I've brought one or two of the pills, and you can just give them to him yourself.

KITTY. Diddums, the little angel beast! And was they good to him in the hospital? And did he fall in love with his nursey-pursey, and forget all about his poor old mamsy-pamsy?

BETTS. Kitty, *please!* You are making me feel quite sick.

KITTY. Give a paw to Uncle Ronnie, darling. That's a clever wee man.

BETTS. How do you do?

KITTY. Would you mind taking him round to the kitchen door? Just call for Kate . . . No, no, I mean Jean—and she'll take him from you.

COLIN. Very well, miss.

KITTY. Thank you so much. Oh, no, stop a bit. There's Jean in the kitchen garden. I'll call her.

COLIN.   Och, I wouldna bother her, miss.

KITTY.   It's all right.   Jean!   Jean!

JEAN (*off*).   Yes, Miss Kitty?

[*Enter* JEAN, *with basket.*]

Yes, miss?

KITTY.   Will you show Mr. Kilgour where to put Rob to beddy-byes?

JEAN.   Certainly, miss.   Will you please step this way?

COLIN.   I'll take your basket.

JEAN.   Not at all.   I'll manage fine.

COLIN.   No.   No.   Gie us a hold of it.

JEAN.   Watch! you'll spill the peas, and cook 'll be in an awful state.

COLIN.   Please yersel'.

[*Exeunt* COLIN *and* JEAN.]

BETTS.   How I should love to have two pairs of eyes looking at me like that!

KITTY.   Looking at you like what?

BETTS.   Oh, I don't know.   As if the heavens had opened—or something unusual like that.

KITTY.   What eyes are you talking about?

BETTS.   The dog's and the man's.   How is it done, Kitty?

KITTY.   Is it too much to ask you not to be a fool? If you had ever been in love you would know the heavens could—could flype themselves, and he'd think of nothing but Jean or Kate or whatever her name is.

BETTS.   But I am in love, damn it.   That's what makes me so simpatico.   If you haven't knocked a couple of hot sonnets out of that there poet, I am wrong.   And I never am.

KITTY.   Never are what?

BETTS.   Wrong.   Are you tired of shivering out here?   In any event, all the comment must be squeezed out of the chrysanthemums by this time, and we are liable to be attacked by a band of massed yammerers at any moment.

KITTY.   But really, Ronnie, that's all rot about Colin. He doesn't admire me a bit.   He thinks I'm a parasi'ic capi'alist and a bum stiff.

BETTS.   Oh, he does, does he?   Well, he probably as good as means what he says.   And in any event he is hardly worth catching pneumonia over.   What about a spot of Chaminade?

KITTY.   All rightie, you bullying brute.

[*They go.*]
[*After a short pause, enter* COLIN *and* JEAN.]

JEAN.   It's all right.   They're away.   You can go this way.   It'll save you the walk round by the front gate.

COLIN.   Yes.   It will that.

JEAN.   It looks like being a fine evening after all.

COLIN.   Aye.   I wouldn't wonder.

JEAN.   You'll be busy up by at the smiddy the night?

COLIN.   No . . . No.   I'm done for the day.

JEAN.   I was just saying to Kate I was wondering what I would do with my night off.

COLIN.   Aye.   There's not much doing in this part of the world.

JEAN.   No.   It's awful dull, whiles.   But it's real peaceful if you were living here, like.

COLIN.   Aye, it's peaceful.

JEAN.   There'll be some nice walks round by the shore that us folks coming down for the summer ken— know nothing about.

COLIN.   Aye.   There's some bonny spots.   Well, I'll need to be stepping.

JEAN.   They're telling me there's a right of way round by the Sandman's Corrie.   Where'll that be, now?

COLIN.   It's no' very easy to find it you don't ken the neighbourhood.   You'll ken Patie Fleemings' croft?

[185]

JEAN.   No.   I don't think I do.

COLIN.   It's the wee theekit hoose Wast the Kilsant Road end.

JEAN.   I think I know the house you mean. . . . If I was to go there . . . ?

COLIN.   There's a footpad round the back of the croft. You canna miss it.   But you'll need to mind yoursel' on the rocks. . . . You should get one of the lassies frae the village to go wi' you.   There's rough characters about. . . . Good evening to you, Miss McLeod, and thank you.

JEAN.   Mr. Kilgour, you're not vexed I didna let you carry the basket?

COLIN.   What basket?   Oh, yon!   No.   See here . . . Miss Murdoch—I mean, the family 'll be for Glesca next week, maybe?

JEAN.   Aye, they're saying so.

COLIN.   Well, I'll be stepping.

JEAN.   Ugh! mercy me, there's the whole jing-bang of them back again.   I'll have to run.   Good night.

> [*Exit* JEAN.]

MRS. MURDOCH (*without*).   Oh, is that you, Kilgour? Wait a minute.   There's a something . . .

> [*The Party enters, talking loudly and all together.*]

MISS SOULIS.   I think your little place is just too simply perfect, Mrs. Murdoch.   Lucky, lucky you to have a place like this to fly to!

MURDOCH.   So I just rang up my broker, and I said to him plump and plain: " Look ye here, McPherson, if you had the smeddum of a louse you would know that with the market in the state it's in . . ."

GOBIE.   Quite, quite, quite. . . .

MRS. GOBIE.   Doesn't it remind you of " fringed grot, rose pool " and so on?   I do think God must walk in your garden, May dear.

MRS. MUR.   Well, I'm sure I hope——

MRS. DICKSON (*displaying her dress*). I am sure I'm glad if it's all right, Miss Baigrie. My niece Annie wasn't awful well pleased with it.

MISS BAIGRIE. Tell her to go and boil herself. The garment's all right. It grows out of your unconscious like ectoplasm, sweetheart.

MRS. DICK. I don't know. I feel a wee bit like a shop-girl in it.

MISS BAIGRIE. A shop-girl! What a hope. My good woman, have you ever *seen* a shop-girl? (*She walks away from* MRS. DICKSON.)

MRS. DICK. She's a funny young lady that, Mr. Pringle. Here to-day and gone to-morrow, like a grasshopper.

PRINGLE. Did you ever hear the little poem about the young lady of Blighty?

MRS. NISH. No. And we don't want to hear it.

PRINGLE. Mrs. Nish knows it, evidently.

MRS. MUR. Kilgour, I wish you'd ask the smith to come up and look at the mangle. The laundry-maid says it's breaking her heart.

COLIN. Very well, mum.

MURDOCH. Hello, Kilgour. How's the po'try getting on?

MRS. NISH. Oh, have you got a poultry-farm? My sister is thinking of keeping hens. . . .

MURDOCH. No, no. Po'try. The stuff you write. Rabbie Burns stunt. Kilgour's a great poet.

MISS SOULIS. Oh, are you?

PRINGLE. Let me see. Kilgour, hadn't you a book reviewed in the " Scots Observer " last week?

COLIN. Yes, sir. I had.

PRINGLE. Jolly well spoken of, too. The Swan of Duthie Bay, what?

MISS SOULIS. But how interesting!

MURDOCH. I never knew you had a book published, Kilgour.

[187]

COLIN. It was only a wee thing. Printit in Edinburgh.

MISS SOULIS. But how splendid! I'm a writer too, you know.

COLIN. Is that so, mum?

PRINGLE. This is the famous Miss Rosemary Soulis, Mr. Kilgour. You'll have read some of her books?

COLIN. I can't say that I have, but I'll can get them out of the library.

MISS SOULIS. You must send me a copy of your book, Mr. Kilgour. I know a good many people, you know— influential sort of people in that sort of line, you know— and I'd simply love to do anything I possibly could.

COLIN. I'm sure I'm very much obliged to you, mum.

MISS SOULIS. Not at all, not at ALL! I'll love it. Do you know, I was just saying to myself, how *likely* to find a poet in this simply idyllic little place. And here you are, aren't you? Isn't it psychic of me?

MRS. GOBIE. Oh, don't say you are a medium, Miss Soulis! Are you?

MISS SOULIS. I sometimes think I am. Ouch! It frightens me. Do you remember the fourteenth chapter of my book, "*Cadenzas*"? Do you know, I think I wrote that in a trance?

NISH (*aside to* MURDOCH). Do you know, I think so too.

MISS SOULIS. I haven't the least recollection of writing a word of it. Only I can hear my typewriter click, click, click like a musical instrument playing through a dream. My thoughts were far away.

MRS. GOBIE. Ah, where were they? Where were they?

MRS. NISH. It's a great mystery.

GOBIE. There are more things in Heaven and Earth.

MISS BAIGRIE. I've had that experience too. One morning I brushed my teeth three times because I couldn't remember whether I had done them or not.

MISS SOULIS.   Indeed? . . . And were you born here, Mr. Kilgour?

COLIN.   Not just here.   Down the village a bit.

MISS SOULIS.   Ah! Within sound of the sea. How I wish I had been born within sound of the sea. I suppose the waves beat their rhythms into your brain?

COLIN.   Maybe they did. I never right thought of it.

NISH.   I hardly think, wa-wa-wa, it could be on the waves, you know, Miss Soulis. Otherwise all the inhabitants of this sea-board would be poets. And they are not.

MISS SOULIS.   But I'm sure they are, aren't they, Mr. Kilgour?

COLIN.   No. I'm the only one.

MISS SOULIS.   Oh!

MISS BAIGRIE.   Professor Nish, I bet you sixpence I can beat you at skiffies.

NISH.   Wa-wa-wa, what are skiffies, Miss Baigrie?

MISS BAIGRIE.   You know. Making flat stones bounce on the water. Come down to the beach, dear ones, and I'll show you.

MISS SOULIS.   What fun! Let's all go down to the beach.

MRS. GOBIE.   Oh, yes, let's. That's Ducks and Drakes! Won't you come, Mr. Murdoch? I should like to back Henry against you. He is really terribly good at Ducks and Drakes.

GOBIE.   Now, now, dearest! You exaggerate.

MRS. GOBIE.   Yes, you are. I used to swoon with admiration on our honeymoon at Zurich. It is the only thing I remember about our honeymoon.

MURDOCH.   Come along, then.

   [*The Party goes out, in some confusion, leaving* MRS. MUR-
     DOCH *and* COLIN.]

MRS. MUR.   You'll remember about that mangle, won't you, Colin?

COLIN.   Yes, Mistress Murdoch. I'll take your message.

[MRS. GOBIE *comes back.*]

MRS. GOBIE.   Oh, I forgot to ask you. Are you ever in Glasgow, Mr. Kilgour?

COLIN.   Whiles I am, mum.

MRS. GOBIE.   I wonder if it would amuse you to come to one of my little evenings? Quite informal Bohemian little things, you know. Just a few nice people. We have a little music and talk. Do say you'll come.

COLIN.   I would feel highly honoured, mum, but . . .

MRS. GOBIE.   You don't need to dress unless you like. Literary and artistic people, you know. Kitty Murdoch comes and helps me with them, so that will be somebody you know.

COLIN.   Well, mum, I will be very pleased.

MRS. GOBIE.   Splendid. Miss Soulis is very charming, isn't she?

COLIN.   A very nice-spoken lady, mum.

MRS. GOBIE.   I thought you'd think so. She'll probably be at one or two of them also. Though she doesn't live in Glasgow, of course.

COLIN.   No, mum.

MRS. GOBIE.   I can't imagine anyone living in Glasgow unless they have to. But Henry has his business there, and we simply can't afford to retire.

COLIN.   No, mum.

MRS. GOBIE.   Yes. And, by the way, so stupid of me! What is the name of your book?

COLIN.   It's called "*Driftwood*," mum. The Mackerel Press printed it.

[KITTY *and* BETTS *appear at the French window.*]

MRS. GOBIE.   "Drifting!" What a good title! So nice! "Drifting." I'll get Rosemary Soulis to lend me her copy when you send it to her.

COLIN.   It's very kind of you, mum.

[190]

MRS. GOBIE.   Oh, but I'm so INTERESTED.   I write a little myself.   Oh, just little things.   Plays and little jingles for children.   But those dear people will be wondering what has become of me.   *Au revoir*, Mr. Fordyce.   I'll write you a little note.

COLIN.   Good afternoon, mum.

[MRS. GOBIE *goes.*]

KITTY.   Hello, Colin.   Don't tell me those people have been persecuting you.   I knew old Rosemary would nose you out sooner or later.   What did they say to you ?

COLIN.   Nothing much.   About poetry and such-like.

KITTY.   Did Rosemary patronise you ?

COLIN.   Not that I noticed, Miss Catherine.   I'm not very accustomed to be patronised.

KITTY.   And what was old Gobie wanting ?

COLIN.   Nothing special, Miss Catherine.

KITTY.   Colin, I've never read your book.   I wish you would lend me a copy.   Will you ?

COLIN.   I'll be pleased if you will accept one in a present.

KITTY.   Oh, you mustn't think of doing that.   I'll let you have it back.   Bring it up to-night, will you, if you've nothing better to do ?

COLIN.   I'll be very pleased to.

KITTY.   I won't be in.   We are all going along to a dance at Kirnbeg.   But you might just leave it with Jean.

COLIN.   It's Miss McLeish's evening out.

KITTY.   Oh, is it ?   Well, you might happen to meet her in the village and give it to her.

COLIN.   No.   It just happens I have a copy in my pocket.   I'll give you that, miss, if you don't object.

KITTY.   Oh, that's kind of you.   Are you sure you don't need it ?

COLIN.   No.   You're welcome.   It's a wee thing tashed.

KITTY.   No. It's lovely. Thank you very, very much.

COLIN.   You're welcome.

BETTS.   Oh, look here. I don't suppose your governor has told you yet about our little commission for you ?

COLIN.   No.

BETTS.   He'll be asking you to write a little epithalamion for bell accompaniment.

COLIN.   An epithalamion ?

BETTS.   Yes.

KITTY.   Ronnie, do shut up.

BETTS.   Why should I shut up ? I won't shut up. It's a sort of a joke, you see. You see, Miss Murdoch and I have just become engaged, and we'd like to have it announced, or have our banns cried, or whatever it's called, in proper style, you see. And we talked it over with your governor, and we thought it would be rather touching if it were done in verse. Ballad metre.

COLIN.   And you are suggesting that I should write this verse for you ?

BETTS.   Yes, that's the idea. Quite short, you see, with a pretty ring of sentiment in it.

COLIN.   Well, I'll see you damned first.

BETTS.   Oh, I say, don't take it that way !

COLIN.   There's no other way to take it. If you werena such a wabbit-looking crult I'd hit you a clout on the jaw.

BETTS.   Look here . . .

KITTY.   Kilgour, what *do* you mean !

COLIN.   I'm sorry, Miss Catherine. I forgot myself. I'm sorry.

[*He goes out quickly through the wicket.*]

BETTS.   Well, my—hat ! I seem to have annoyed the gentleman.

KITTY.   Well, of course you did. You're hurt his feelings.

BETTS. Well, he has hurt mine. What did he call me? A " wabbit-looking crult "? What the devil's a crult, Kitty? Or is it one of those things a young girl ought not to know?

KITTY. I think it's the weakling puppy in a litter. The one they drown. He had no business to speak like that to you.

BETTS. They were certainly harsh words. Let's have our revenge. Let's read his blooming book aloud.

KITTY. No, no!

BETTS. Yes, yes. He didn't call *you* a wabbit-looking crult. Give me the book.

KITTY. Oh, don't be an ass. I don't feel comic just now.

BETTS. Let's have a course of divine poesy, then. For nerves it has aspirin looking silly. Kitty! I am beholding the most entrancing object at this moment that I ever saw in my life. Do you know what it is?

KITTY. No, and I don't care.

BETTS. It is your right ear. Look at it.

KITTY. I can't, damn you.

BETTS. Ah, passion-weaving involucrum! (*He kisses her ear.*)

KITTY. Don't, you beast. You tickle.

BETTS. Then give me the book.

KITTY. I won't.

BETTS. Give me the book. I should be sorry to come the rough stuff on a delicately-nurtured female, but . . .

[*After a short struggle, he gets the book.*]

KITTY. Oh, you crult! You've broken my finger!

BETTS. It serves you right.

KITTY. You *are* a cad!

BETTS. I know. I know.

KITTY. A cad—a cad—a cad!

BETTS. Sit down, and keep quiet. I'll find you something too absolutely too in a minute.

KITTY. I think you're a pig.

[193]

BETTS. I am much obliged. Shut up. . . . Ah, here we are.   Listen to this.

KITTY.   I won't.

BETTS.   Do be quiet. (*A pause.*) Here's a bit of guid braid Scots.

AUTUMN LEAVES.

> The pliskies o' the wastlin' win'
> Brumble amang the boughs abune;
> Aboot the bole the wee leaves spin
> And ca' their brithers,
> " Let go your haud an' drap doon shune
> Tae dance wi' th' ithers."

I've often thought that sort of stuff must be very easy to do.   I could do it myself in my sleep.   What do you think of this?

> The smeerin' smook abune the byke
> Mak's glink the cadger ow're the dyke;
> And gey auld-farrant in the syke
> Forbye, ye ken.
> The cottar whustles on his tyke
> Frae but the ben.

> The lyart clarts gang tapsal teerie,
> Wi' chafline flegs I'm unco weary.
> A handsel for ma bonnie dearie. . . .

KITTY. That's absolute gibberish, and not a bit clever.

BETTS. Not?   Then let's try some more of the poet Kilgour, as you seem to appreciate him better.   Here is a rollicking piecie about a kintra funeral.

> Over their heads a lark is singing,
> Their heads are bowed, their steps are slow;
> She cannot mark the plovers winging,
> Nor count the peatstacks in a row,

> Nor ponder on the road we go.
> The kirkyard stands upon a hill. . . .

Dear old Professor Housman! Hey! What's the matter with you?

KITTY. I don't know. I'm going into the house.

[*She runs into the house, feeling desperately for her hand-kerchief.*]

BETTS. Good lord! . . . Kitty! I say, Kitty!

[*He walks irresolutely to the window and back; then downstage, where he stands thinking. He says pleasantly enough and quietly.*]

> " Tread lightly on the cloths of Heaven,
> For you tread on my dreams."

(*Or words to that effect.*)
Oh, hell! What a life!

[*He throws the book of Poems at the garden-seat, and goes out by the wicket. He cannons into MRS. MURDOCH.*]

Oh, I say, I *am* sorry!

MRS. MUR. What a fright you gave me! I thought my last hour had come.

BETTS. Did you? I'm so sorry.

MRS. MUR. I've come in to see about feeding all you people. You'll be wanting dinner early to-night. Where's Kitty?

BETTS. She went into the house a moment ago. I think she has a headache, or something.

MRS. MUR. Well, she has no business to have a head-ache, and the whole house upside down. Her and her headaches!

[*She bustles into the house.*]

BETTS. Oh, Mrs. Murdoch!

[*There is no answer. Instead, a rumour of sound is heard from the wicket. MURDOCH comes in first, and holds the door open; then PRINGLE, registering deep concern;*]

then GOBIE, *dripping wet and supported on either side by* MRS. GOBIE *and* MISS SOULIS, *dabbing him with inadequate hankies ; then the* NISHES, *and* MRS. DICKSON-WATSON-DICKSON, *embarrassed. Finally, after an interval, a depressed* MISS BAIGRIE.]

I say! This is a sorry sight!

MISS SOULIS. Yes, isn't it terrible ? Poor Mr. Gobie! Miss Baigrie pushed him into the sea.

GOBIE. Oh, come, come! No, no. It was a pure accident.

MRS. GOBIE. Accident!

MISS BAIGRIE. Yes, it was. I never meant him to fall in.

MRS. GOBIE. Then why did you push him ?

MISS BAIGRIE. I only touched him. The jetty was slippery.

MURDOCH. Now, now! There's no need to go over it again. We'll have to get Mr. Gobie a hot bath and a change. Come along, Mr. Gobie. You'll be feeling first-rate in a wee minute.

[*The procession enters the house, all except* MISS BAIGRIE.]

BETTS. Did you push him in, Connie ?

MISS BAIGRIE. Of course I did. It was his own fault.

BETTS. Why ? What had he been doing ?

MISS BAIGRIE. Nothing. Just being him. I couldn't stand it any longer.

BETTS. I suppose some day you'll set about your twelve children with a hatchet. You seem to be that sort of woman.

MISS BAIGRIE. Oh! Twelve! Have a feeling heart, sweetheart! Have you got a gasper for the poor ickle sing ?

BETTS. I don't know that I should give you one. You are quite evidently in disgrace.

MISS BAIGRIE. I know. I'm a bad, bad woman. But Heaven help me, I can't help it, so help me. (*Giggles.*)

Silly little rabbit! Honestly, you would have done it yourself. Standing on the edge of the jetty, quacking like a duck!

BETTS.   Who pulled him out?

MISS BAIGRIE.   Old Murdoch, of course. Professor Nish moaned, and the holy man groaned, and the women made noises like pigs being killed. Tragedy in real life is very unsatisfactory, don't you think?

BETTS.   There is no tragedy in real life. Only a *reductio ad absurdum.*

MISS BAIGRIE.   . . . as they used to say in the 'eighties. . . . I'll take you on at Snooker pool.

BETTS.   You are an impenitent devil, and I have a good mind to skelp you.

MISS BAIGRIE.   I'm sure you have, but we'll have Snooker pool instead. Come on. . . . Oh, wait. What's that?

[*The bell is heard approaching.*]
[*The lighting now suggests early twilight.*]

KILGOUR.
Tae a' whom it may Concern
(An' it concerns the hale o' ye in this case):
A wedding has been arrangit and will
Shortly take place
Atween R. Betts Esquire o' Glesgie,
Wha has been shot by Cupid's darts,
And Miss Katherine Murdoch o' the Hollies, Duthie,
Weel kent in these parts,
Who in the affairs o' this village has always ta'en
The keenest interest.
So we all jine wi' one accord
In wishing them the best.

MISS BAIGRIE.   What a perfectly orgiastic idea! Is that you and Kitty?

BETTS.   Yes, I suppose so.

MISS BAIGRIE.   Oh, well! I hadn't really any hope. Was it your idea—the bellman?

KILGOUR.   To all whom it may concern.   A marriage has been arranged——

BETTS.   I say, Kilgour——

KILGOUR (*appearing*).   Sir?

BETTS.   Look here, please consider it off, after all.

KILGOUR.   The engagement, sir?   I'm real sorry, and I think you're making a mistake . . .

BETTS.   No, no.   The noising it abroad.   I've changed my mind about that.

MISS BAIGRIE.   Oh, what a shame!

KILGOUR.   Very well, sir.   As you wish.   I'll no say I wasna a wee bit surprised at the order.   And my boy Colin, he simply wouldna take in hand to make up the bit verse.   I had to do it a' mysel'.

BETTS.   You did it very nicely.

KILGOUR.   There's the maitter o' a fee.   I had cried it a guid furlong or mair before you stoppit me.

BETTS.   There you are.   Good evening to you.

KILGOUR.   And good evening to you, sir.   You are a gentleman.   It's cleared up into a braw-like night.

[*He goes.*]

BETTS.   Now come along, and we'll smash the balls and tear the blasted billiard-cloth to shreds.

MISS BAIGRIE.   Doesn't the poor darling like being engaged?

BETTS.   You shut up.   Come along.

[*Empty stage.   Sunset glow.*]
[JEAN *enters, cat-like.   She goes to the wicket and looks down the road ; comes back to the garden-seat ; finds the book ; throws at the upper windows of the house a look of cold fury ; sits on seat and opens the book.*]

JEAN.   Wee book!   They flung ye awa' and forgot ye, wee book, the same way as they'll fling awa' the maker o' ye! . . .   They're no guid eneuch for ye, wee book.   They canna unnerstan' ye.

MRS. MUR. (*from the house*).   Jean!

[198]

[JEAN *buries her face in the book and begins to cry.*
   A charabanc passes. The PASSENGERS *are singing the*
      following dirge :

   Who am I ?   Nobody at all.   ^
   How and why did you happen to fall ?
   Now I see that dreams come true,
   Lucky me to have lovable you. . . .

MRS. MUR.   Jean !   Jean !   Where are you ?

JEAN (*under her breath*).   Ach !   How am I to ken
where I am ?

CURTAIN

ACT II

Some months later. A large drawing-room at MRS. GOBIE'S *Glasgow house. Part of it is curtained off to form a sort of stage, and at the edge of the proscenium of this stage a little rostrum stands. It is draped with a Spanish shawl, and a small megaphone lies on it. A few chairs and a great many cushions are scattered about.*

> [MRS. GOBIE *and* KITTY *come in, followed by* JEAN. KITTY *is in evening dress.* MRS. GOBIE *has been surprised in the middle of dressing, but displays no false modesty about it. She is* vrai enfant de Boheme.]

MRS. GOBIE. I'm so glad you've come, Kitty. I'm not nearly ready. You are such a comforting dear thing. I'll never, never learn to be punctual. They'll be here in a minute, and look at me! Now, listen; I just want you to chuck the cushions about anyhow. A little more *dérangé* than last time, if you see what I mean. They sat like a Gospel Meeting last time, and it's so important to muddle them up a bit. Jean 'll help you. I suppose the performers are all ready. I heard somebody coming in. We are a very small party to-night, Kitty. This damned 'flu has done its best to spoil everything. I do think it might have been more considerate. Half my *pièces de résistance* aren't coming. Sachs can't come, and Clithero's got pneumonia, and Bessie Sproat, who plays the bass viol, has got Badminton elbow, and Halliday Spinks's wife is having a baby— though I don't see what that's got to do with him. But I must absolutely fly. I've got to get Henry into his dress-shirt, too. I do hope Rosemary Soulis will turn up. She's so unreliable. I've had to wire for your

[200]

local poet at Duthie Bay. He has just published a new book, so he should be quite amusing. Now I must run. You'll be a dear and see that everything's all right, won't you ?

[*Exit.*]

KITTY. I've seen you before somewhere.

JEAN. Yes, miss. I was at The Hollies for a wee while with your Ma.

KITTY. Of course. You're Jean. You threw up your place the night—— Oh, yes. In October, when all those people were down for the week-end. I don't blame you at all. When did you come to Mrs. Gobie's ?

JEAN. Last week, miss. I'm still a bit strange.

KITTY. I don't wonder. Push the sofa a little. And take away those cushions on the chest. Someone is sure to strike matches on it if they sit there. What time is it ?

JEAN. About twenty minutes from nine.

KITTY. Let me see. They were invited for half-past eight. We have still a little time. Push that rostrum over there further back. . . . I went down to Duthie Bay last week, to bring up some things.

JEAN. Did you, miss ?

KITTY. It's spoilt by the new people. All coast places are spoilt by the new people. I often wonder why they don't go on going to wherever they went before. Oh, there's a bit of news, too. You remember the old Bellman—Mr.—Mr. Kilgour ?

JEAN. Yes'm. I mind him fine.

KITTY. He's been left a fortune.

JEAN. A fortune, miss ?

KITTY. Yes. A brother of his stole some money from his employer, forty years ago, and ran away to America. He did very well there *too*. . . . Old Tam comes in for about fifteen hundred a year. Isn't that nice ?

JEAN. Yes'm. Very nice. Would you like this wee table out of the way ?

KITTY.   No.   They're having coffee or cocktails or something, aren't they?   Better leave it.

JEAN.   Kilgour 'll be quite a gentleman now.

KITTY.   Oh, yes.   He doesn't need to be civil to anyone, now.   He's going to devote his life to his hobbies. . . . Collecting china dogs and learning the speeches of Abraham Lincoln by heart.

JEAN.   That'll be nice for him.

KITTY.   It'll be very jolly for Colin too.

JEAN.   It'll make no difference at all to Colin.

[*They look at one another.*]

KITTY.   I'll go and see if Mrs. Gobie wants any help. I don't think there's anything more to do here.

[*Goes out* R.]

VOICE.   Just step this way, sir.   The mistress 'll be down presently.

[COLIN *comes in* L. *He is dressed in a good tweed suit and carries a bunch of papers.*]

COLIN.   Oh, hullo, Jean.   I didn't expect to see you here.

JEAN.   No.   I've just come to this place.

COLIN.   Well, well.   It's a great surprise. . . . I thought I was late.

JEAN.   So you are, a wee bit.   But all the rest are later.   It's a funny-like party, so far as I can see.

COLIN.   What's the curtain for?

JEAN.   They're goany do charades, or something. Some of them are dressing up for it already.

COLIN.   Oh! . . . It's funny you being here.

JEAN.   It's funny *you* being here, if it comes to that.

COLIN.   Aye.   Maybe it is, in a way.

JEAN.   You're the great man now, I'm hearing.

COLIN.   What way?

JEAN.   With all that money, and writing books.

COLIN.   I don't care for it much.   It's awful like being in a zoo—in a cage.

[202]

JEAN.   How do you get on with all they swells?

COLIN.   You mean my manners? If they don't like my manners they can leave them. I've mair to do wi' my time than learn their monkey tricks. ‸ I'm the best o' the bunch o' them.

JEAN.   You are that . . . Colin, you're gentry now, and I'm only in service, and we'll maybe no' see each other again, so I'll tell you this. I fun' your book in the—— I fun' your book, and I took it to my bed and read it all through, and I was greeting a' nicht. . . . Now here they're coming. Away you and sit down.

[JEAN *exit*, L.]

[*Enter* MR. GOBIE, R. *He is in full evening dress.*]

GOBIE.   Ah, how do you do, Mr. Kilgour. It was very good of you . . .

COLIN.   I'm pretty well, thank you. I have the asthma now and again——ever since I was a wean. But I haven't had any wheezling for twa-three weeks now. How is yourself?

GOBIE.   Very well, thanks. It was good of you to come.

COLIN.   And I hope your good lady is keeping brawly.

GOBIE.   Yes. She's appearing in our little play to-night. That's why she's not here to receive you. Have you met the authoress?

COLIN.   I met Miss Soulis down at Duthie in October.

GOBIE.   No, no. Not that authoress. The authoress of the play. Miss Mary Henderson. A nice little body.

COLIN.   No. I never even heard tell of her. I didna know it was a full-dress affair.

GOBIE.   Oh, some of us dress and some of us don't. It's Liberty Hall, you know. Quite informal and go-as-you-please. Quite, quite. Will you have a cocktail?

COLIN.   Yes, thank you.

[JEAN *brings forward a tray of dry Martinis.*]

[*Enter* KITTY, *in a hurry.*]

[203]

KITTY.   Mr. Gobie, Mr. Gobie! When are you going to get dressed ?

GOBIE.   Eh ?   Yes, Kitty, I'm going just now.

KITTY.   Mrs. Gobie is in a frightful state. She's fretting like gummed velvet.

GOBIE.   Like what ?

KITTY.   Oh, never mind like what ! Like gummed velvet.   Do hurry up.

GOBIE.   Yes, yes, yes.   Perhaps I had better. *(Goes up stage and examines footlights.)*

KITTY.   Oh, hello, Mr. Kilgour.

COLIN.   Good evening, Miss Kitty.   I am very glad to see you.

KITTY.   Thanks.   This is a comic place for you to find yourself, isn't it ?   You see what happens to you for writing books.

COLIN.   Och !   I feel like a fish out of water.

[GOBIE *crosses to table with cocktails.*]

KITTY.   You just hold my hand and I'll see you through. *(Takes him over* R.)

VOICE.   Mr. and Mrs. Murdoch.

[MR. *and* MRS. MURDOCH *come in. As they are the wealthiest people among the party, there is a stir.*]

GOBIE.   How nice of you to come, Mrs. Murdoch. And how splendid that you were able to bring your husband.

MRS. MUR.   We nearly couldn't get.   So Kitty's here ?

GOBIE.   She is lending a hand with our little play.

MURDOCH.   Is Mrs. Gobie doing something in it ?

GOBIE.   Yes, she is dressing now, otherwise she would have been here to receive you.   I have a small part in it myself, so I'll be leaving you presently.   Everybody makes himself at home here.   This is Mr. Kilgour.   I think you have met before.

MURDOCH.   How are you, Kilgour ?

MRS. MUR.   Good evening, Colin.

COLIN.   I have the asthma now and again.

MRS. MUR.   Is Miss Soulis coming to-night?

GOBIE.   Oh, I hope so, I hope so.   I do hope so.
She said she would.   Such a lot of people have disappointed us, but I don't think *she* will.   She is so
anxious to see the little play.

MURDOCH.   What is the play?

GOBIE.   It's a little thing we are entering for the
Drama Festival.   A symbolic little thing.   Rather an
expressionistic little thing.   Ha-ha!   It should be quite
amusing.   Quite!   Quite!   Tchekovian little thing
with a rather pretty touch of old-fashioned sentiment.

MRS. MUR.   I hope we'll be able to understand it.

GOBIE.   Oh, it's not a bit modern.   I wouldn't have
anything modern.   I put my foot down there.   No tin
scenery and fog-horns for me.   Now do you mind if I
run away?   You won't think me frightfully rude?   I
have to change, you know.

MURDOCH.   What are you in the play, Gobie?

GOBIE.   Who?—me?   Oh, it's a sort of—you'll
laugh—it's a sort of animal part.   Quite.   Ha-ha!

MURDOCH.   Are you the hin' legs of the elephant,
hey?

GOBIE.   No, no.   There isn't an elephant.   Very
eccentric.   Very original.

MURDOCH.   They tell me there's a lot to be made off
play-writing.

GOBIE.   Quite.   But I must go.   Ruth will be
fretting like gummed velvet.

MURDOCH.   All right.   Don't let us keep you.

[GOBIE *trots out*, R.]

VOICE.   Mrs. and Professor Nish.

KITTY.   How do you do, Mrs. Nish.   How do you
do, Professor.   Mrs. Gobie has just gone to dress.

MRS. NISH.   I hear we are to have a real treat to-night.

I hope I'll understand it. The last one was too deep for me.

KITTY.   You know Mr. Kilgour, Professor?

NISH.   No, I don't know that I do. Howdydo.

COLIN.   I'm very well, thank you, now. I had a touch of the asthma twa-three weeks by. How are you yourself?

NISH.   Very well, thanks. I hope they are not going to give us any of that damned modern music to-night.

KITTY.   Well, you know, I'm afraid not. Herr Sachs and Miss Sproat rather disappointed us to-night.

MURDOCH.   'Evening, Professor.

NISH.   Oh, good evening, Mr. Murdoch. Wa-wa-wa—filthy weather, isn't it?

MURDOCH.   Yes. Mother made me come; but I'd been just as happy at home, with a good cigar and a book. I suppose there'll be music.

NISH.   No. I believe not.

MURDOCH.   Thank God for that.

VOICE.   Mr. Pringle. Mrs. Dickson-Watson-Dickson.

[ENTER *the above-mentioned*.]

NISH.   I say, Pringle, have you been wa-wa-wà praying, or anything?

PRINGLE.   Continually, my dear boy. And watching, too. Why?

NISH.   The Almighty has smitten old Sachs with—ah —boils or something equally—ah—providential—and we're to have no modern music.

MRS. DICK.   Now isn't that an offle pity?

NISH.   No, madam, it isn't. My cat Alabaster has an—ah—an unconscionable habit of wa-wa-wa-walking up and down the keys of my piano; but he lacks the— the—higher cerebral faculties that enable old Sachs to make such a discordant beast of himself.

MRS. DICK.   You're an offle man, Professor. I think Mr. Sachs plays lovely.

NISH.   He plays with a damnable disregard for other people's feelings that puts the mere dumb brute to shame. We may be wa-wa-wa—emancipated, but let us at least be gentlemen.

MRS. DICK.   Oh, hello, Mrs. Nish.

MRS. NISH.   Oh, hello, Mrs. Dickson-Watson-Dickson.

MRS. DICK.   Dear me, isn't it offle? I never know yet whether to call you Mrs. Nish or Mrs. Professor Nish.

MRS. NISH.   Ugh! just call me Jessie. . . . Oh, hallelujah! Cocktails.

MRS. DICK.   Where? Are those them?

MRS. NISH.   Yes. Have one. They look awful wicked, don't they?

MRS. DICK.   Not relly.

MRS. NISH.   No, no. Go on.

MRS. DICK.   Quite nice. Relly. What do you do with the wee stick?

MRS. NISH.   Do you know, that's funny. I never know what you do with the wee stick. I nearly poke my eye out with it always.

MRS. DICK.   Ugh! Surely you should know. You're an M.A.

MRS. NISH.   Oh, an M.A.! Our cook's an M.A.

MRS. DICK.   Our cook's a pure fiend. Honest, I really think she is. The things that woman 'll singe. You wouldn't think it possible, so you wouldn't.

MRS. NISH.   You come some night and eat one of the M.A.'s dinners. You'll find out what's possible. Nothing's impossible to Cathie, except to cook a decent meal.

MRS. DICK.   I don't know what we're coming to.

MRS. NISH.   No more do I. I say, we'll just have another cocktail.

MRS. DICK.   It's all this Labour Government, as the saying is.

MRS. NISH. Oh, I don't know. . . . Here, it's an awful shame of Ruth Gobie hauling up this poor Kilgour to recite his poetry. Making a fool of himself before us all.

MRS. DICK. But the Professor's to recite too.

MRS. NISH. Ugh! He's a Professor. It's his trade to make a fool of himself in public. But I always say there's a place for everything and for everybody.

MRS. DICK. That's what I always say too, Mrs. Nish.

MRS. NISH. Colin's a decent-like lad, but there's no sense in giving him notions above his station. Now I saw him and Kitty Murdoch in Fuller's—— Ahem! As you were saying, you can't get a cook-general for love or money. . . .

KITTY. Oh, Miss Henderson. Very nice of you to come. Have you met Mr. Kilgour, the poet? Miss Henderson has been dying to meet you for some time, Mr. Kilgour. We are doing one of her shorter plays to-night.

COLIN. Pleased to meet you.

MARY. Oh, are you? Why?

COLIN. Oh, well . . . you see . . . I am . . .

MARY. Do you write plays too?

COLIN. I'm starting one.

MARY. What's it about?

COLIN. Well, it's about a kind of a poet, who—well, he falls in love with this girl, and—well, her father is a sort of an earl, and he's only a kind of a working lad. . . .

MARY. I see. I see. And then the plot thickens. Are you happy, Mr. Kilgour?

COLIN. No, I am not. And that's the truth.

MARY. You should be happy, shouldn't you? Knowing how to write verses. It is splendid to know how to write verse, isn't it? Everybody thinks so.

COLIN. I suppose it's fine, in a way.

MARY. The flying's all right, but it's the tumbles

[208]

that are so nasty, aren't they ? Well, good-bye, and try to be good. It's very difficult for poets to be good.

[*She fades into the crowd.*]

NISH. It's wa-wa-wa—described, I believe, as a Poetry and Drama Evening. Tchehe!

MURDOCH. Oh, is it ?

NISH. I expect it will be quite loathsome enough without the music. There is one comfort—that appalling creature Rosemary Soulis hasn't put in an appearance. . . . You know her, Miss Henderson ?

MARY. No. Well, I hardly do. I've met her.

NISH. She's—wa-wa-wa—she's a sort of mixture between Catherine of Aragon, Mrs. Jellaby and the Ten Plagues of Egypt. She pervades, if you see what I mean. AND her BOOKS! I read one once, when I was ill. When I closed that book, my dear, I felt—wa-wa-wa— I felt as if I had been eating apricot-jam in the back seat of a talkie-house. . . .

MARY. That must have been a interesting sensation. You don't like her, then ?

NISH. Some day I'll kill that woman.

VOICE. Miss Soulis.

NISH. Talk of the devil!

[*Enter* MISS SOULIS.]
[*Exit* KITTY.]

MISS SOULIS. Professor! You darling to be here! You are the very man to tell me all about Glopz.

NISH. What are they ?

MISS SOULIS (*with a silvery laugh*). Sebastian Glopz, you absurd person. Do tell me about him. I have only had time to glance at his new book but everybody's going mad about it.

NISH. As a matter of fact, I have met Glopz on his native heath. He is—wa-wa-wa—the man who put the pest in Buda. I disliked him as intensely as an attack of neuralgia would allow me.

[209]

MISS SOULIS. The Professor is at his naughtiest to-night. Isn't he, Mrs. Dickson-Watson-Dickson? And there is dear Mr. Kilgour! What a marvellous evening it looks like going to be!

[KITTY *appears through the curtain.*]

KITTY. Will everybody sit down somewhere, please? The play is just going to begin.

PRINGLE. I suppose we may sit anywhere?

KITTY. Oh, yes. Anywhere. (*She disappears.*)

PRINGLE. I suppose you have heard, Mrs. Murdoch, of the poor old gentleman who had something to sit on but couldn't find a place to put it?

MRS. MUR. No. Tell me about him.

PRINGLE. That's all, ralley.

MISS SOULIS. Do sit by me, Mr. Kilgour. I suppose you have heard what the play is all about?

COLIN. No, Miss Soulis. I haven't heard tell.

NISH. It's a . . . By the way, the authoress is here. She ought to have inside information.

MRS. MUR. Yes. Come away, Miss Henderson.

MARY. It's a sort of little play of St. Eloy and the Bear. Deary me, I do hope nobody's been reading out of little books on how to write plays. But everybody does, nowadays. Even newspaper men, who are such busy, busy bees. And then they know how it *ought* to be done, and they can't enjoy a *thing*. You know—the man who gave King Dagobert good advice about his trousers. It's mediæval.

MRS. NISH. I hope it's quite proper?

PRINGLE. You mean you hope it's not!

MRS. NISH. Mr. Pringle, I'll throw something at you!

MRS. DICK. What's that? Haven't they got the scenery fixed yet?

MISS SOULIS. Hush! That means they are going to start.

MRS. DICK. It's funny without an orchestra.

[210]

ST. ELOY AND THE BEAR

A Play within a Play,

by

MARY HENDERSON

PERSONS :
  ST. ELOY, *a Saint.*
  GASTON, *a Page.*
  MIRABEL, *a Circus Girl.*
  TOUTOU, *a Bear.*

SCENE.—*Beside a haystack on the Doullens Road.*

> [ST. ELOY *is sleeping on top of the haystack, his halo tilted over his nose.*
>
> GASTON *is sitting on the ground against the stack, playing* Pont d'Avignon *on a tin whistle.*]

GASTON.   Be still, my pipe, and let the twilight make
             Its own cacophonies.   Frogs in the darken-
                ing lake
             Chant their asthmatic vespers.   Starlings
                tell
             Their restless bedfellows to go to hell.
             The byre-ward kine tone their contralto
                moo
             Sorrowfully.   And I am mournful too.
             Sad intimations of the death of the day !
             But who is this who picks her mannered
                way
             Among the poplar-shadowed primroses ?

> [*Enter* MIRABEL, *leading a* BEAR *by a pink ribbon.*]

             Monster-attended ?   Ha !   Good   even-
                ing, miss.
             Nice evening for a walk.

[211]

MIRABEL.   Yes, is not it ?
GASTON.   But nicer, don't you think, perhaps, to sit
            Beside a comely stranger, and to mark
            The coloured evening deepening into dark ?
MIRABEL.   Well, yes, perhaps I will. But not to
            mark
            The coloured thingummies deepening into
            dark,
            But just because my darling Toutou, there,
            Whom I am taking to the Doullens Fair,
            Has dreadful corns upon his poor old paws,
            And I am tired and hungry.   And because
            I like this haystack.   Is it yours ?
GASTON.   Ah, no,
            I have no haystacks.   Have you far to go ?
MIRABEL.   I told you I was going to the Fair
            With Toutou, my unrivalled Dancing
            Bear.
GASTON.   Ah ! Can it dance.
MIRABEL.   You bet your socks he can !
            Come, do a turn for this young gentleman.

                            [*The* BEAR *dances.*]

            Presto ! Houp-la ! Kiss Auntie. Did
            you ever
            Think that a dear fat bear could be so
            clever ?
GASTON.   Clever ?   I'm pretty dull, but I could do
            All these uninteresting antics too—
            Especially " Kiss Auntie."   Do sit down.
            And I am pink-and-white, and he is brown.
            A horrid walking door-mat.   I can write
            Sonnets—while he can only growl and
            fight
            And cadge for buns and climb his bear-pit
            pole. . . .
            Besides, he hasn't an immortal soul.

                            [212]

MIRABEL.   Oh! what a lie! He has a feeling heart.
He has a soul as well . . .

GASTON.   Jesting apart.
A little earlier I heard you say
That you were hungry. Will you have
    some hay?

MIRABEL.   I've never eaten hay.

GASTON.   Neither have I.
'Twill be a new sensation. Shall we try?

                        [*They eat hay.*]

MIRABEL.   It is quite palatable. What is your name?

GASTON.   Gaston.

MIRABEL.   Is that all?

GASTON.   That's all.

MIRABEL.   What a shame!

GASTON.   Oh, I don't know. It suits me pretty
    well.
What do they call you, darling?

MIRABEL.   Mirabel.

GASTON.   Ah! Golden belfries chiming honey
    sweet!
Oh, Mirabel, your feet! Your little feet!

MIRABEL.   Please leave my feet alone. You go too
    far.
Alas, I know you now for what you are!
You are a courtier. The sort who cling
Round stage-doors, blossom-laden like the
    Spring,
And twice as treacherous and insincere.

GASTON.   *Sanct Ciel!* What boots sincerity, my
    dear,
When one is drowning in the rapids of
    passion?

MIRABEL.   What made you speak of Toutou in that
    fashion?

GASTON.   Of Toutou?

P   [213]

MIRABEL.   Yes, my loveliest of bears.
      You hurt his feelings.

GASTON.   Ha! A lot he cares!
      His feelings exist in your imagination.

MIRABEL. Is that your view? Good-bye, then.

GASTON.   Oh, damnation!
      You stupid woman, don't you see I love
       you?

MIRABEL. I value Toutou infinite leagues above you.
      He has an immortal soul—as splendid as
      A clergyman's.

GASTON.   He hasn't.

MIRABEL.   Yes, he has.
      He loves me dearly.

GASTON. I congratulate you.

MIRABEL. You spiteful pig, I hate you, hate you, hate
      you!

  [ST. ELOY *wakes up, straightens his halo, and peers at
  them through his spectacles.*]

ST. ELOY. Ahem, aha!

MIRABEL.   Good gracious, who is he?

ST. ELOY. It's only me, my children.

GASTON.   Who is me?

ST. ELOY. In point of fact I—well, I am St. Eloy.

             [Sensation.]

      It is my evening custom to enjoy
      Upon this haystack saintly meditation,
      But voices raised in shrill recrimination
      Broke in upon my dreams—I mean my
       med-
      Itations, and it came into my head
      I might be of some service. What's ado?

MIRABEL. Oh, well, you see, it's this way.
      (*To* GASTON) Listen, you.
      I'll ask the Saint himself, and then you'll
      see

       [214]

	Whether he's got a soul.
GASTON.	Okay with me.
MIRABEL.	(*To* ST. ELOY) Has Toutou got a soul? Tell us, please do.
	Please tell us.
ST. ELOY.	Is this gentleman Toutou?
MIRABEL.	No, this is Toutou.
ST. ELOY.	Hum!
GASTON.	I told you so!
MIRABEL.	Darling, I'll kill myself if you say no.
ST. ELOY.	Dear, dear! you will? Well, well, but . . . There, there, there!

I think we can arrange. Come here, nice bear.

[*He takes something from his scrip and gives it to the* BEAR. MIRABEL *is in tears.*]

There, there, good fellow.

GASTON.	Mirabel, stop that row.
MIRABEL.	Look here, sir, has he a soul?
ST. ELOY.	He has one—*now.*

[*He vanishes.*]
[GASTON *and* MIRABEL *stare at each other and at the* BEAR.]

GASTON.	Quaint sacerdotal gerrymandering.
MIRABEL.	What an unsatisfactory old thing! He wriggled like a lizard on a grid, But he gave in.
BEAR.	Yes, I suppose he did.
MIRABEL.	Gaston! What's that? I've all come over weak.
	Didn't you hear?
GASTON.	I did. Bear, did you speak?
BEAR.	I think I did. I think so. Let me see.

There's something . . . Why have you done this thing to me?
Why this, of all intolerable wrongs?
Eating—and dancing to your little songs—

And sleeping. That was all. And now
    what is ?
Why could I not be spared these mysteries ?
This haystack's bitter beauty, and the
    West
Shot with the sun's hot anger—weariest
Of all these things, the pitiful tragedy
Of Mirabel's fading fragility.
Why do they not remain a pleasant heap
Of stuff to eat; to warm me when I
    sleep ? . . .
A two-legged thing that makes me dance
    and tumble . . .
That makes me dance. Makes me
    dance . . .
(Dash it all ! I can't hear you !)

PROMPTER. I've lost the place.

BEAR. Then find it again, for goodness' sake !

PROMPTER. The page has gone missing. Go on to
" But I love you . . ."

BEAR. But I love you.

GASTON. No, you don't. I say that.

BEAR. I beg your pardon !

GASTON. Well, how do you expect me to carry on
when you dry up in the middle of your lines like that ?
I knew you didn't know it. But it's all the same with
you poofling amateurs. All right on the night ! You see !

MIRABEL. Connie, Connie ! Now, now, now.
You're spoiling it. It'll be quite all right. No, no,
leave the tabs alone. Go on from " But I love you."

GASTON. Oh, all right. But I'm sure to fluff now.
Beshrew my waistcoat, sweetheart, but I
    love you;

MIRABEL. Essential of my being !

GASTON.   Angel face !
Go on now, Gobie. Don't stand staring
    there. We can't hold this all night.

PROMPTER. How this new universe is a lonely place!
BEAR.   How this new universe is a lonely place!
GASTON.   Go on, go on!
PROMPTER. 'Tis lonelier than the roaring Pyrenees
           Where my dam bore me . . .
BEAR.   'Tis lonelier than the boring Pyrenees
           Where tumtitumto-tum . . .
GASTON.   Keep silence, please.
BEAR.   I'm only saying what is in my part—I
           mean my heart.
GASTON.   My dear old creature, don't stand there and
           mumble,
           Dance down the road and think.   And I
           expect
           You will be somewhat heartened to reflect
           That you have left all other bears behind
           In brain-power.   And the strongest of
           mankind
           Are babies to you.   Off you go, then.
MIRABEL.   Shoo!
BEAR.   You put an interesting point of view.

                                    [*He goes out.*]

GASTON.   And so the pretty moments pass,
           Till now arrives the loveliest,
           And tiny harpers in the grass
           Play gentle lovers to their rest;

           And Hesperus, above the West,
           Smiles through the pansy-coloured light
           Gaily, but trembling a little, lest
           He miss the lovers' first good-night.

           The thousand marriage gifts of sight
           Go.   But a million fragrances . . .
MIRABEL.   Gaston, excuse me.   Tell me this.
           Do you think Toutou is all right?
           That silly miracle worries me.

                      [217]

GASTON.   My darling dearest, don't you see?—
                 The only actually talking-bear—
                 What a success at Doullens Fair!

MIRABEL.   Perhaps you're right.   He should go over
                 big.
                 Father once had a calculating pig.
                 No other pig was fit to stand beside him.

GASTON.   What happened to the pig?

MIRABEL.   Alas, we fried him!
                 We had sad breakfasts for a time.   Ah,
                 well!
                 Let us forget the sad things.

GASTON.   Mirabel!

                                [Re-enter the BEAR.]

                 Look here!   What do you want?

BEAR.   I have been thinking,
                 Yonder where, bathed in gore, the sun is
                 sinking.

GASTON.   Well, kindly go on thinking long, long
                 thinks,
                 Like intervals to Carolinan drinks.

MIRABEL.   Darling, I say.   Isn't it rather queer,
                 We shouldn't have minded Toutou being
                 here
                 Before he had a soul?

GASTON.   Please run away.

BEAR.   No.   There is something I should like to
                 say.
                 Mirabel, I have now made up my mind,
                 And as I am the strongest of mankind
                 And wisest of all bears, I really feel
                 It to be time I had a righteous deal.
                 This lady hasn't fed me a square meal
                 For upwards of two days.   I quite intend
                 That she shall do so now.   This is the
                 end.

MIRABEL. Gaston!   His eye has got a nasty look!

GASTON. Stand back!

BEAR.   And I shall not require a cook.
Clear out, young man.   Now, come along,
   my child.
That little knife will only make me wild.

[The BEAR *closes with* GASTON.]

MIRABEL. Ah!   Ah!   Ah!   (I say, do black out,
   there!)

PROMPTER. The electrician has gone for a drink of
water.

MIRABEL. Oh, that's too bad!   I'll scream again.

[Does so.]

PROMPTER. Here he comes.   Just wrestle for a bit.

BEAR. Oh, I say!   Do be careful with that
dagger!

GASTON. Well, don't be so blinking naturalistic!

BEAR. Well, I'm supposed to be hugging you.
Ow!   Now you've gone it!

[Lights go out.]

You've injured me very seriously.

MIRABEL. What's the matter, dear?

BEAR. My arm!   She's stabbed me!

PROMPTER. Curtain!   Curtain!   Quickly!

*[Lights go up.   The curtain has fallen on the little play.
There is rather embarrassed applause.]*

PRINGLE. I say, is Mr. Gobie all right?

BEAR *(taking off his head).*   Quite, quite, quite, thanks.
It was nothing.   It doesn't hurt.   It's all right.

PRINGLE. Good.

*[Applause breaks out again.   Cries of " Author! "
MISS HENDERSON appears.]*

MARY. Ladies and gentlemen.   Thank you so much.
And what a good thing Gaston didn't kill the Bear, isn't

[219]

it ?   It would have destroyed the whole *meaning* of the play, if you understand me.   However, it's nice he didn't. Thank you so much.   It didn't end quite as I intended. The bear really ate them, you know.   But thank you all the same.

> [CURTAIN.   *End of the Play within a Play.*]
> [*The* GUESTS *arise in some confusion.* MRS. GOBIE, MISS BAIGRIE *and* BETTS *come in from the stage, still in their costumes, and make for the cocktail-table. Everyone sets up a loud appreciative jabber.*]

MRS. DICKSON.   I think it was simply luvly !

MRS. GOBIE.   Wasn't it streptococcal about those lights ?   A young man Henry brought in from the warehouse was supposed to be looking after them.

MISS SOULIS.   I do hope Mr. Gobie wasn't hurt.

MRS. GOBIE.   Oh, he got a little scratch from Connie's dagger.   She is a careless brat.   Kitty's putting some iodine on it now.

MISS SOULIS.   I do think you were all perfectly splendid.

> [MISS BAIGRIE *comes down-stage sulkily, carrying a cock-tail, and sits on a cushion near* COLIN.]

MISS BAIGRIE.   Pretty poisonous mess, don't you think ? We had quite a good bear, and he had to go and get 'flu, and that little fool went and mucked it up.   Potty play, too.   Do you like Levinski's stuff ?   We did a thing of his last year.   I was a dope fiend in a quayside pub, and Ronnie Betts was a masochist, and old Ruthie Gobie was a bawd.   There's some pleasure in playing in a thing like that.   However, we had to give that Henderson bird a leg up.   How did you like me ?

COLIN.   I thought you had some very good points.

MISS BAIGRIE.   Isn't that frabjous !   I must tell Ronnie.

> [MRS. GOBIE *beats a little gong.*]

Oh, hell! What's this now? You get no peace in this joint.

MRS. GOBIE. Professor Nish is going to read us one of Cyril Wilkin's poems. Is Mr. Kilgour there? Oh, there you are, Colin. How do? Mr. Kilgour will then give us some of his " Beach Wrack," and then we'll all go downstairs and have some sandwiches and coffee.

[*The* PROFESSOR *mounts the rostrum.*]

NISH (*taking up the megaphone*). I take it one is not expected—ah—to employ this—wa-wa-wa—this Sitwell stunt?

MRS. GOBIE. Not unless you like, Professor. Isn't he sweet?

NISH. I met Cyril Wilkin at Oxford in 1925. Poor fellow, he looked all shot to pieces. He was taking hashish, I imagine, at the time, in—wa-wa-wa—poison-ous doses. I tried it once, but it made me horribly sick. I was rather a disappointment to—wa-wa-wa—to poor Cyril. He liked everyone to share his—ah—his intensity of existence. He told me that what he admired most of all in his verse was the short experiment in the free stanza one is going to—wa-wa-wa—read to you now. . . . One's own impression is that it rather—wa-wa-wa —derives from . . . But this isn't a wa-wa-wa leckchah. . . . I don't mind telling you in confidence one is sick and tired of giving leckchahs, and . . . Ah—well— wa-wa-wa—I shall now read you the poem.

What are we looking for in this mud?

So glutinous, so opaque,
So thundering muddish as it is.

Surely, surely, in its sticky liquescences
Something . . . oh, something,

[221]

Lurks shyly in the black track
Of the soft sigmoidous worm
Undulating to heaven.

Pultaceous, moonless mud;
Brackish to the sucking lips
Suffocating. . . .

Prehensile, resisting forward shove
Or shuddering flight.

Palpitating, fetid, pest-bearing,
Cloying. . . .

What are we looking for in this mud?
Can it be we shall find a Star?

[*Applause.*]

MISS BAIGRIE.   I do think it's enormously clever to be
so perfectly beastly. Do you like writing loathsome
poems too, Mr. Kilgour?

COLIN.   I don't think the Professor read that one
awful well. And I didn't think much of it, anyway.

MISS BAIGRIE.   Miss Soulis, Miss Soulis! Mr. Kilgour doesn't think much of Wilkin.

MISS SOULIS.   Oh, don't you, Mr. Kilgour? I
wonder why, now? I think I see what you mean, but
I do think a poet should have a grasp of Reality in addition
to his more sublimatory functions, don't you think? Or
don't you? *I* think Wilkin is so *mathematical.*

MRS. GOBIE.   Perhaps Mr. Kilgour thinks that perhaps Wilkin did better work. A poet is so seldom a
judge of his own work, don't you think, Colin?

COLIN.   I think he's the only one who's a judge of his
own work.

NISH.   Oh, I say! What about Shelley? What
about poor dear Byron? To say nothing of Blake!
Oh, Mr. Kilgour! Now, now, now!

COLIN.   Well, it's no' very easy to say offhand why a

person says a thing like that. It comes to you, and you just say it. You can't quite explain why you come to the conclusion that what you say is, in a way, true. Though you know fine somehow that it is. It just kind of comes to you, if you see what I mean.

[GOBIE *comes in as he is speaking.*]

MISS SOULIS. I see. I see. It's frightfully difficult, isn't it, to get at the, so to speak, sources of all that sort of thing? There are deep waters, Mr. Kilgour, deep waters. We may never know the true explanation till we die.

COLIN. Well, anyway, the real swank reviews all pick out the ones of my poems that I thinks the best and say they're the best in their opinion too.

MISS SOULIS. I don't think that proves anything. I have no high opinion of critics. They are the greatest argument against free education . . .

MRS. GOBIE. Rosemary dear, I hate to interrupt you, but we are all dying to hear Mr. Kilgour, and the sandwiches are ready.

MISS SOULIS. Ah! We mustn't keep the sandwiches waiting.

MRS. GOBIE. And now, Colin, please.

[COLIN *mounts the rostrum.*]

COLIN.   TO A LADY

" Peeweet! Come awa, come awa," says the plover,
    wheeling and flying.
" It isna there that the thing that I ken o' is lying.
" Come awa, come ahint the dyke," says the lying
    plover.
" I ken your game fine," says the lover.
" I'm your marrow mysel'," says the lover.
" For I hae a secret too, hid bye," says the glaikit
    herd,

[223]

" And there's naebody keens it ava; for they kenna
        the word
O' the wee tell-tale in the bush and the lark in the
        skies,
That tell where my secret lies.
The wee burn yammering down through the birks wi'
        his myriad bells,
The chickling grouse that whirrs from the heather, he
        tells, he tells . . ."

Mrs. Gobie, I'm sorry to say you'll hae to excuse me.
There's something . . . You'll hae to excuse me.

MRS. GOBIE.   Oh, what a pity!   And you were reading so beautifully.   And we were all dying to know
what the secret was.   However . . . Perhaps after you
have had some sandwiches, you will read us some more.
Have a cocktail, if there's one left.

COLIN.   I'm vexed I've disgraced you, ma'am, and
spoiled your party.

MRS. GOBIE.   Not a bit, not a bit!   My dear, poets
often take stage fright when I get them to read their own
stuff.   Now do go downstairs, everybody.   You take
them down, Henry.   Is your wrist quite better, dear ?

GOBIE.   Oh, quite, quite, quite.   The furry gloves
protected it.   Kitty put some iodine on it.   It nipped
like anything.   Come along, come along, come along.

[*The Party goes out, all but* KITTY, MRS. GOBIE *and* COLIN.]

MRS. GOBIE.   Oh, you've got a cocktail.   That will
do you good.   I often take the most frightful panics even
now when I'm doing my own stuff.   Oh.   You're
there, Kitty.   Do try to cheer Colin up.   And bring him
down when he's feeling better.   He must be hungry.

[*She goes.*]

COLIN.   Oh, God!   What'll you be thinking of me ?
KITTY.   Tuts!   Don't be silly.   We all get stage-
fright now and again.

COLIN.   Yon wasna stage-fright.

KITTY.   Oh ?

COLIN.   I ken I'm naething to you but a common village lad; and I ken I'm naething to them but a kind o' a freak in a show.   You'll be thinking my heid's turned wi' a' thae notices in the papers and getting ta'en up by the swells.   Well, it's no'.   I ken I canna write verse.   Yon auld Gobie could do it better nor me.   I havena had the education.

KITTY.   What absolute rot, Colin!   Your poems are simply lovely.

COLIN.   I maybe ken more about my poems nor you do.   It maks me grue, whiles, to read them.   But I'll tell you this.   Almighty God has put something in me that naebody else has got; and it gars me struggle and struggle in an agony to say what's to be said on God's behalf.   And some day I'll say it. . . . So it cam' ower me when I was peacocking in front o' thae fleeching, yammering mauks . . . like a dream I had o' promen-ading down the main street wi'oot even my sark. . . . What's it their business what I think and what I feel ?

KITTY.   I think I understand.

COLIN.   I maun fecht it out till the Word comes— alone.   And there's nae loneliness like that.

KITTY.   It's terrible to be alone like that.

COLIN.   Listen to me.   I canna lie to you.   There was mair to it nor I've said.   You mind that blasted jingle I read the noo ?   It was about a secret.   And there I was blashing it out to the whole roomful of them . . . when you came in.

KITTY.   Colin . . . Tell me . . . Was I part of the secret ?

COLIN.   You were part of the secret.   You came by me as the Queen of Elfland came by True Thomas on Huntly Bank.   You showed me a way to come by the Word that I daurna follow.

KITTY.   You daurna ?

COLIN.   Och!   I daurna.   I'm just a rough country tyke.   You're a lady.

KITTY.   Colin . . . Oh, Colin!

COLIN.   What's the matter? . . . Oh, Catherine, you're a' lit up with love for me!   Oh, my dear, you wouldna choose the Hell of a poet's wife for the likes of me?

KITTY.   I would.   I would.

COLIN.   My dear!   My dear!

KITTY.   Oh, Colin!   This is me for the first time.

COLIN.   Aye.   It takes you like that.

KITTY.   How do you know?

COLIN.   Och, it's my trade to know.   That's what poets are for.

KITTY.   What a funny trade!

COLIN.   It's no' just what you would term funny. Ach! we're wasting time.   Come on up to the skies again!

KITTY.   Colin!

[*They embrace.*]
[JEAN *enters.*]

JEAN.   I beg your pardon, miss.   Mrs. Gobie says . . .

KITTY.   How dare you come into a room without knocking!

CURTAIN

ACT III

*The scene is the same as in Act I. It is early Spring. A black-
bird is singing.*

> [NISH *is discovered, considering the daffodils.*
>
> *To him,* MISS SOULIS.]

MISS SOULIS. Professor!

NISH. Eh? Oh! Ah! I was considering the
daffodils.

MISS SOULIS. Were you? Ah, Spring, Spring!

NISH. A devilish season, in my—wa-wa-wa—humble
opinion.

MISS SOULIS. Oh, do you think so? Well, perhaps
it is. Perhaps it is. We are so, so horribly far from
Nature, now, that it is strangely disturbing when she
takes her revenge upon us.

NISH. Perhaps that's it. I suppose my lumbago is
only a—wa-wa-wa—an expression of some atavistic,
biological immortal urge.

MISS SOULIS. Perhaps you are right. How true and
how sad that the most beautiful things in the world—
those—those inspired longings are so often so torturing.

NISH. I don't call my lumbago the most beautiful
thing in the world—or even one of them.

MISS SOULIS. I was not speaking of your lumbago,
though of course I do really and truly sympathise with
you. They have all gone to the Church.

NISH. Whatever for?

MISS SOULIS. Oh, for some sort of rehearsal for to-
morrow's ceremony. It is such a weeny little church,
and the bridesmaids are to be in voluminous Early Italian
dresses. They wanted me to go, but I couldn't bear
to. The Spring, I think. It affects me very strangely.

NISH. It affects others—ah—very strangely, too. Rather an odd marriage, don't you think?

MISS SOULIS. Odd? I don't think so. The only odd thing is that anyone should have the courage in these horrible days.

NISH. Oh, I don't think marriage requires courage. It isn't courage that makes a bolting horse go slap into a shop-window. It's sheer damned panic.

MISS SOULIS. Panic? And yet . . . in a sense it is. They are possessed by Pan. That's what makes it so beautiful. You must admit it is charming, Professor. If I had had your classical education I should work it into such a sweet little tale. You know. Kitty could be a patrician maiden betrothed to a young philosopher in Athens; and they could be walking by the side of a dark forest, when out comes a wild young faun, and away they go, Kitty and the faun, into the green depths.

NISH. Yes, yes, yes. But the faun probably eats peas with his knife, and says, "Pleased to meet you." And he has, no doubt, any number of—wa-wa-wa—relatives with hairy legs. It's all right in a story, but it won't wash in real life. In any case, why didn't they slip off to a registry-office, instead of coming down here with all the pomp of their heathen ceremony? It's a bit of rather disagreeable posturing, if you ask my opinion.

MISS SOULIS. In a sense you are right. Marriage is such a personal sort of thing, don't you think? But still, it is rather a noble gesture to say, "Go on, you people, make as much fuss as you like. We don't care."

NISH. Nasalheim says . . .

MISS SOULIS. Nasalheim's books are extremely cynical and nasty, and I don't believe you believe a word he says. You are a strange man, Professor.

NISH. Oh, ah!—not particularly.

MISS SOULIS. You are. You are. Why do you always avoid *me*?

NISH. I don't avoid you, my dear lady.

MISS SOULIS. I think I know why you avoid me, but I won't tell you . . . just now. . . . I love that tender south-west wind; don't you ? Or don't you ? You are such a curious personality.

NISH. I'm a very ordinary sort of chap, really . . .

MISS SOULIS. I find your personality so intriguing. What do you think of mine, I wonder ?

NISH. Well, it is rather an awkward question—wa-wa-wa—to answer offhand . . .

MISS SOULIS. Do I look old and faded ?

NISH. No. You certainly do not. In point of fact, you are quite extraordinarily—wa-wa-wa—quite a fine figure of a woman.

MISS SOULIS. Have I allure ?

NISH. I believe you have.

MISS SOULIS. I thought I had. . . . Professor, do you know what is wrong with my work ?

NISH. Well, to begin with, if one may say so, you are rather confusing at times in your manner of handling your punctuation. I counted no fewer than twelve semi-colons . . .

MISS SOULIS. No, no. It's not that. . . . But you must have noticed what I mean. You are sensitive in these things. I'll tell you. Tell me if I am right. I am lacking in emotional experience.

NISH. Well, I shouldn't have thought . . .

MISS SOULIS. I know. I know. I have suffered, in a way. But I don't mean that. You've read Georges Sand, Professor ?

NISH. Yes. Yes. Oh, yes.

MISS SOULIS. How she enriched her work by her—by her—well, experiences. Where would she have been without her—her *friendship* with Chopin, with de Musset, with . . . Oh, you know what I mean. I am writing as if I were swathed and suffocated in the bondage of convention. I want to tear all that off.

Q   [229]

NISH. I say, Miss Soulis—wa-wa-wa—I mean to say. . . .!

MISS SOULIS. You are an Oxford man, aren't you?

NISH. No. Not exactly. Glasgow, to be absolutely candid. But a lot of my people went to Oxford.

MISS SOULIS. I thought you were in some way connected with Oxford. You are so cosmopolitan—I mean broadminded in the broadest sense. Professor Nish, I want you to take me to Paris.

NISH. Oh, I say! Why?

MISS SOULIS. Why do people take people to Paris?

NISH. Well, I mean to say—what would Mrs. Nish say?

MISS SOULIS. She need never know.

NISH. My dear girl, she keeps all the books. She knows to a penny what I spend.

MISS SOULIS. I would stand all the expenses.

NISH. Oh, damn it! It isn't done, you know.

MISS SOULIS. Oh, don't be so provincial.

NISH. I'm not a bit provincial. And if it comes to that, what could be more provincial than going to Paris for a—wa-wa-wa—*liaison*?

MISS SOULIS. Everywhere else is so—so blameless.

NISH. Well, blameless or not, it is extremely nice of you to suggest it, but, really, it's out of the question.

MISS SOULIS. It isn't. It isn't. It isn't. I know you don't love me, but you could learn to.

NISH. Miss Soulis, I hardly think you have any idea—wa-wa-wa—of the regard I have for you. I should never dream of compromising you in the—wa-wa-wa—most negligible respect. What you have said to me to-day I shall blot absolutely out of my mind.

MISS SOULIS. You are afraid to run away with me.

NISH. That too I shall forget. It is unworthy of you.

MISS SOULIS. Very well. We shall cut the past ten minutes out of our lives. They shall be as if they had never been.

NISH. They shall be as if they had never been.

MISS SOULIS. I should die of shame if I thought——

NISH. Rosemary, apart from all other considerations, one is a gentleman.

MISS SOULIS. I think I'll go and write some letters.

NISH. And I shall go on considering the daffodils from where I left off.

MISS SOULIS. Yes. They're lovely, aren't they?

[*She goes into the house.*]

NISH. Au revoir. . . . Dear me! Well, well, well!

[*Enter* PRINGLE, *by the wicket.*]

PRINGLE. Hello, Nish. You here?

NISH. Ah, yes. I made a long week-end of it. I am putting up at the village pub. And you?

PRINGLE. I'm staying there too. I've just arrived. I looked round to see if I could have a word with the organist. I don't know who he or she is.

NISH. " Have you Sir Pandarus of Troy become? " Are you—ah—officiating to-morrow?

PRINGLE. Oh, yes, rather. They *would* have me to bump them off.

NISH. Ah . . . Women are curious creatures, Pringle.

PRINGLE. Yes. Aren't they? That reminds me . . .

NISH. I often think you must miss a lot in your profession, old boy, going about in that kit.

PRINGLE. Oh, my job has its compensations too. " All the nice girls love a padre."

NISH. I wasn't referring to that—wa-wa-wa—aspect, and perhaps you will allow one to say that one is rather surprised that *you* should.

PRINGLE. I suppose I'm to consider myself told off, as usual, for my frightful vulgarity. Well, it may surprise you to learn that a parson's a man like anybody else.

NISH. Wa-wa-wa—of course he is, old boy. But he hasn't quite the same romantic occasions as one of the unsanctified. Now—wa-wa-wa—you wouldn't call me a particularly attractive sort of a chap?

PRINGLE.   I certainly would not.   Rather the reverse.

NISH.   Yes.   Well, to give you an instance of the sort of thing that happens—wa-wa-wa—only this—ah—only the other day, a most charming woman, intellectual, refined, of good social position——

PRINGLE.   Sounds like a cook-housekeeper.

NISH.   She was not a cook-housekeeper.   You wouldn't believe me if I told you her name. . . . This lady made a most sensational proposal to me.

PRINGLE.   Did she want you to join a Galsworthy Club?

NISH.   No.   She wanted me to go to Paris with her.

PRINGLE.   And are you going?

NISH.   Well, as a matter of fact, I'm not.

[*Enter* MRS. NISH, *with* MR. *and* MRS. MURDOCH.]

MRS. NISH.   Berti-ie!   Oh, there you are, Bertie. We must hurry along if we are to be in time for lunch.

NISH.   Oh, by Jove, yes.   They must be nearly at the prunes by this time.

MRS. NISH.   Come away, Bertie.   Oh, how do you do, Mr. Pringle.

PRINGLE.   How do you do.

MRS. MUR.   Oh, good afternoon, Mr. Pringle.   It was real nice of you to come down.

MURDOCH.   How're ye, Pringle?   Are you for some lunch?

PRINGLE.   Well, no.   I had a spot of lunch before leaving.   But I'll watch you eat, if you don't mind.

MRS. MUR.   Not at all.   Not at all.

[PROFESSOR *and* MRS. NISH *take leave, and go.*]

PRINGLE.   May I just wash my hands?   I've got very grubby on the journey.

MRS. MUR.   Certainly.   You know the way?

PRINGLE.   Oh, I think so.   Yes.   (*He goes into the house.*)

MRS. MUR.   Ah-hee!

MURDOCH.   Aye, you may well!

MRS. MUR.   Och, well!

MURDOCH.   But it's no' "Och, well," and fine you know it.

MRS. MUR.   Well, it canna be helped now, anyway.

MURDOCH.   It could have been helped if you'd only taken a telling.

MRS. MUR.   Now, Gavin, you know perfectly well there was no telling about it till the mischief was all done.

MURDOCH.   Could you not have kept an eye on her?

MRS. MUR.   Ugh!   I've got a squint already trying to keep an eye on yon one.   We must grin and bear it.

MURDOCH.   Well, once and for all, you'll no' see me grinning at the wedding of my only daughter to a village bellman's brat.   Is this what I've wrought for for all these years?

MRS. MUR.   No.   You've wrought for fun and because you were gey greedy on the siller.   Now, I've enough to do without you girn-girn-girning, so you'll just try to be as nice as you can.

MURDOCH.   Him and his poetry!

MRS. MUR.   Ugh, you like his poetry fine.   You were greeting over that bit about the funeral only last week.

MURDOCH.   I wasna greeting.   I had a bit of cigar-ash in my eye.

MRS. MUR.   Well, stop greeting now, anyway.   I never saw the like of you. . . . Who's that?

[*Old* KILGOUR *appears at the wicket.*]

Good afternoon, Mr. Kilgour.

MURDOCH.   Afternoon, Kilgour.

KILGOUR.   Good afternoon to you, sir and madam. I hope you're brawly this fine spring weather.   The wind's in a good airt for bringing things oot.

MURDOCH. Aye, I see it's brocht you oot, for once in a way. We've not heard so much of you, Bellman, since you jined the gentry. How d'ye like being kind of weel off?

KILGOUR. Ach, it's no' so bad. There's an old saying that it's easier for a camel to get through the eye of a needle than for a rich man to enter the kingdom of heaven. But there's aye compensations. Mebbe, you and me is no' jist sae ta'en up wi' the kingdom of heaven as we were, sinsyne, Mr. Murdoch. Heaven lies about us in our infancy, the man says, and I'm beginning to see that it's a kind of infantile notion.

MURDOCH. You're a blasphemious auld runt. Have a cigar?

KILGOUR. Thank you kindly. I'll put it in my pocket; it's near time for my denner. I thocht I'd look in in passing. Aye, just that.

MURDOCH. You did, did you?

MRS. MUR. I'll away and leave you to your blethers. I've another new housemaid, Mr. Kilgour. And you know what they are.

KILGOUR. Aye. Thowless besoms. Thowless besoms. Good day to you, mistress.

[MRS. MURDOCH *goes in.*]

Aye. Just that . . . Mr. Murdoch, there's a wee thing I thocht you and me micht hae a word aboot in the by-gaun. It's about Colin.

MURDOCH. Well?

KILGOUR. Well, the laddie's got his head in the clouds, as ye can understand, and I canna get his buits lower nor the kirk steeple, never mind aboot terra cotta, as the sailors say.

MURDOCH. Aye. I can understand that.

KILGOUR. There's nae sense tae be got oot o' him at a'. Haud your tongue. Business? He'll no' touch it wi' the tongs.

MURDOCH. I had the opinion mysel' that that's just the puir, wandering Willie I have had wished on me for a son-in-law.

KILGOUR. Ach! We was in love once oursels. But there is a great necessity for us two business men tae dae his considering for him. Now, for instance, there's the question of a marriage settlement.

MURDOCH. Look you here, Kilgour. There'll be nae marriage settlement in a marriage I don't approve of. I tell you straight, they're piping a tune I don't care for, and the piper can just whistle for his pay.

KILGOUR. But I thocht when you was puttin' up sic a grand wedding, and the reception in the Burgh Hall, and . . .

MURDOCH. Well, you can think again. Besides, yon's the wife's doing, no' mine. And now, you've had my last word.

KILGOUR. That's final?

MURDOCH. That's final.

KILGOUR. Murdoch, I was just thinking there's another compensation for not getting into the kingdom of heaven.

MURDOCH. Eh?

KILGOUR. I can call you a ticht-fistit auld scrunt. And that's a great preevilege.

MURDOCH. I'm a scrunt, am I, you drunken Bellman?

KILGOUR. You are that, sir. And furthermore, your countenance is disfigured with vanity, your belly with gluttony and your soul with avarice. And you're a puir, wee, chitterin' muck-raker wi' it a'. You're no' fit company for man or beast. Ye can buy dirt for a farden an' sell it for a maik, and that's aboot a' under God's heaven ye can dae. Ye puir sowl, I'm sorry for ye.

MURDOCH. Ye're drunk!

KILGOUR. Drunk? How would I be drunk? There's naebody but cadgers 'll drink wi' me now I'm gentry.

[235]

Here. Tak' back your cigar. I'll awa tae my cheeny dugs.

MURDOCH.   See here; stop a bit. I've a word or two to say to you.

KILGOUR.   Well. Come awa wi' them.

MURDOCH.   You're a most impertinent fellow.

KILGOUR.   Ach! awa and chase yoursel'. Ye havena the guts for a guid blackguarding match. Puir soul, I'm sorry for ye.

MURDOCH.   I'm sorry for myself, that a daughter of mine is marrying into a nest of tinkers the like of you yins.

KILGOUR.   *You're* sorry, ye creeshy gomeril! An' here's my son, a fine upstandin' young fellow, thirled tae a deuk-heided daw like your dochter. Sakes! The life she'll lead him! I wasna for 't, and I'm no' for 't. Goad! I seen him carrying her bag frae the station. There's a bonny bit wife for you! There's a helpmeet! It's a valley de chamber the hizzies are wanting; no' a man. It'll be a sorry day for me the morn, mind, I'm tellin' you. And I wish you a very guid day, Murdoch, and, man, you've an e'e in you like a biled haddie.

[*He goes out by the wicket.*]

[MURDOCH *is about to follow him but thinks better of it, and stamps back to the house, terrifying the audience with the threat of apoplexy.*]

MURDOCH (*as he goes*). Of all the blasted impidence! There's a fine thing! What in Heaven's name are we coming to?

[*He disappears.*]

[*After a short pause,* KITTY, BETTS, MISS BAIGRIE *and* COLIN *come in, in that order.* COLIN *is sulky and self-conscious in wedding garments.*]

KITTY.   Well, thank Jessie Matthews that's over. What a giggling lot of idiots, my dear, charming brides-maids are; and what a dud you look, Colin, in your morning clothes.

MISS BAIGRIE.   I think it was a hearty great shame and absolutely irredeemably silly to make him put them on for the rehearsal.

KITTY.   Well, he's never worn a morning coat and a topper in his life before, and I'm not going to have him disgracing me to-morrow.   I meant the whole thing for a slap in the eye for the village, and I'm not going to leave any sort of chance for them to sneer at me afterwards.

BETTS.   Ahem!

KITTY.   What's the matter with you, Ronnie?   Have you caught a cold, or what?

BETTS.   No, curiously enough, I haven't; though thank you for speiring.   No.   Are you open to receive a bit of mild criticism from a discarded lover and prospective groomsman?

KITTY.   No, I don't think I am.   You weren't very helpful, either.   You were either sulking or tickling Connie all morning.

BETTS.   As for sulking, I may surely be allowed a little appropriate melancholy on such an occasion?   As for tickling Connie, she liked it, and it was my Boy Scout's good act.

MISS BAIGRIE.   Oh, are you old enough for the Scouts?

KITTY.   Oh, shut up.   What is your criticism, Ronnie?

BETTS.   Did you notice in the church a stained-glass window behind the pulpit?   It represented an old gentleman stealing their supper from a covey of crows.

KITTY.   It is Elijah being fed by the ravens.

BETTS.   How neat!   How appropriate!   But that's not the point.   Did you notice the colour of his bathgown?

MISS BAIGRIE.   Yes, it was a yelling sort of vermilion. It would make rather jolly lipstick.

BETTS.   It might.   But I'll tell you what it *will* do. You are dressing your bridesmaids in burgundy-coloured

Early Italian costumes? Now, doesn't it occur to you that Elijah's bath-gown and your bridesmaids' wedding garments will simply scream at each other all through the ceremony? It will make me sick. I know it will.

KITTY. Heavens! It will make the dresses look frightful.

BETTS. If you had married me, as you said you would, I should never have allowed you to make such a bloomer. What do you think, Colin?

COLIN. I think it's not very genteel to talk like that.

BETTS. Talk like what?

COLIN. Well, to be always talking about. . . . well, your having been engaged, and that.

BETTS. I say. I'm not ashamed of having been engaged to Kitty. What about my broken heart, eh? Do you call it genteel to grouse at me because I try to pass off my tragedy with a light laugh?

[COLIN *wanders out of wicket.*]

KITTY. This is serious.

BETTS. I know it's serious. Look at the sky. It is as if Nature could bear it no longer, and was about to break down.

KITTY. Oh, yes! It's going to rain! It's been one thing after another. . . .

[*A gong sounds.*]

BETTS. Ah! Lunch, lunch, lunch! Come along. We can at least eat.

KITTY. Eat? How can I eat? Connie darling, you've got to get into your bridesmaid's kit and nip along with me to the church.

MISS BAIGRIE. Now, sweetheart?

KITTY. Ronnie's quite right. It will spoil the whole show if those two shades of red scream at each other.

MISS BAIGRIE. Well, let it spoil the whole show. It's a punk show. I'm hungry.

KITTY. Don't be a beast.

[238]

MISS BAIGRIE. If you will go and dress your poor un-
sophisticated bridesmaids up like a lot of Borgias, at least
you needn't starve them, sweetheart.

KITTY. Will you go or will you not?

MISS BAIGRIE. I'm not going to trail through the
village looking like an utterly esoteric Botticelli virgin
on two successive days. And you can put *that* in your
cigarette-holder.

BETTS. You'd better give her lunch first, Kitty.
You'd really better. It's going to rain like Billy-oh.

KITTY. Oh, rot!

MISS BAIGRIE. Darling, sweetheart, you're getting
quite psych-asthenic. Come and have some soup,
darling.

KITTY. Oh, damn Elijah and his crows! Do you
think they could hang a curtain over it?

BETTS. Oh, listen, Kitty. I'll put a brick through
it after lunch. I promise you. I'm too weak now—
from want of food. Take her other arm, Connie.
We'll support her into the house.

[MRS. MURDOCH *appears at the French window.*]

MRS. MUR. What in all the world are you people
doing? Gavin's in a bad enough temper as it is, and
he's about bitten the head off poor Mr. Pringle, and Miss
Soulis has gone to bed, and the tureen's on the sideboard,
and what like a state we'll be in for the wedding to-
morrow, don't ask me!

BETTS. Mrs. Murdoch, your daughter has had a
serious blow.

MRS. MUR. But everything's all right, isn't it? I
saw to most of it myself.

BETTS. It's about Elijah and the bridesmaids' dresses.

MRS. MUR. Elijah who? They're from Daly's.

BETTS. Now, that's funny. I don't believe I know
his surname. Do you, Connie?

MISS BAIGRIE. Search me.

KITTY. It's the prophet Elijah, Mumsie.   He doesn't go with the wine-coloured frocks.

MRS. MUR.   I don't know what you're all blethering about.   He went up to heaven in a fiery chariot.

KITTY.   It's the two shades of red.   It'll be—it'll be pandemonium.

MRS. MUR.   Mercy me!   I never thought of that.

KITTY.   Yes.   Isn't it dreadful?

MRS. MUR.   Oh, deary me, deary me!   Now you mention it, they'll look awful.

BETTS.   They'll look like two kinds of Hades.   It'll be symbolic, in a way.

KITTY.   What the devil do you mean?

BETTS.   It was a thought that crossed my mind.

KITTY.   I don't want to know about your mind.   It's a beastly mind.   What did you mean by that remark just now?

MRS. MUR.   Kitty, Kitty!   Behave yourself.

KITTY.   Well, I want to know what Ronnie's hinting at.   And I will know.

MRS. MUR.   There now, my lamb.   He never said anything.   You're just overwrought with all the excitement.

[MURDOCH *appears at the window.*]

MURDOCH.   What the—— Here am I standing here, and I've been waiting for my lunch for the last half-hour. Are you coming in, or are you not?

MRS. MUR.   Wheesht, wheesht, Gavin.   We're coming. Away you go in, Miss Baigrie, and you too, Ronald. He's in an awful tiravee the day.

BETTS.   Oh, righto!   Come on, Connie.

[MISS BAIGRIE *and* BETTS *go in.*]
[COLIN *comes back.*]

MRS. MUR.   I wonder at you!   What'll they think of you?   That's an awful like way to go on.

KITTY.   Ugh!   I've half a mind to chuck the whole business.

MRS. MUR.   Kitty, you'll do no such thing. . . . Oh, there you are, Colin. This is an awful like carry-on. But never you heed it, Colin. When I was a girl they wouldn't let the young man see the young lady for a week before the wedding. And a very good rule too.

KITTY.   I'm sorry, Colin.

COLIN.   Don't mention it. It's all right.

KITTY.   But you understand, don't you?

COLIN.   Yes, yes. I understand fine.

KITTY.   Come in and have lunch, won't you?

COLIN.   No, thank you. I'll have to be stepping. Is that all you need me for to-day?

KITTY.   I think that's all. You're a dear darling! Mumsie, I'm all right now. I'll be good.

MRS. MUR.   Come on, then. See and no' be late to-morrow, Colin.

KITTY.   Cheery-oh, old thing.

COLIN.   Good-bye.

> [MRS. MURDOCH *and* KITTY *go into the house.*
> (*The rain-storm becomes very immediate.*)
> COLIN *stands looking at the house in a dazed way. Everything is very still.*
> *The wicket opens slightly, and* JEAN, *in a neat walking-dress, insinuates herself in.*]

JEAN.   Oh! I didna notice. . . . It's you, Mr. Kilgour.

COLIN.   Yes.

JEAN.   It's my day off. I just took a run down to see Cook. She was good to me, here. I thought they would all be at their lunch and I could get in by the wee gate. You're an awful swell the day!

COLIN.   God! yes. Look at me!

JEAN.   You look awful nice.

COLIN.   Do I?

JEAN.   Not that I didn't like you better in your leather apron down at the smiddy. But you make a fine gentleman.

COLIN.   Oh, a fine gentleman!

JEAN.   Now I'll have to away round and see Cook. I had no business to come in this way at all.

COLIN.   No, Jean.   Wait.   Wait a bit.

JEAN.   But we canna stand clavering here.   They'll come out and find me, and I would get my heid in my hands.

COLIN.   Wait, I tell you.   Wait!

JEAN.   Colin!   Colin!   Let go my wrist.   That's no' the thing at all!

COLIN.   Jean, I must talk to someone.   I'm just fair bursting.   For God's sake, Jean, wait a wee minute.

JEAN.   What's like the matter with you, laddie? You're looking all disjaskit.

COLIN.   Ugh!   I dinna ken what's the matter wi' me, Jean.   I'm just a plain ass.

JEAN.   No, you're not.   Colin—is she—is she no' guid to you, Colin?

COLIN.   Aye, she's guid to me.   I'm no guid enough for her.   And yet, kind of, in a way I am.   I don't know what's come over me.

JEAN.   A'body feels funny the night before a wedding.

COLIN.   It's no just feeling funny.   I'm feeling fair hellish.

JEAN.   Do ye no' want to get married to Miss Murdoch?

COLIN.   I do not, and that's a fact.

JEAN.   Oh!

COLIN.   This is the first time I've admitted it, even to myself.   I've maybe no' seen the next ten years clearly till this minute.   Maybe I've held my e'en awa from these ten years in case I couldna abide them.   Oh, Jean, I'm in for it.   I'm in for a living hell. . . . Jean. . . . Ye've heard tell of Shelley . . . and Byron . . . and Burns?   Well . . . I'm made like them in a way.   I canna write like them, if ye understand me, but some way I've gotten the twist they a' had.

JEAN. Aye. I've read about yon yins. You've got a kind of look of them in a way. They were funny ones, those chaps. They didna treat women awful well.

COLIN. In a way they did. There's no' a woman worth her salt that wouldna raither an hoor ahint a dyke wi' Rabbie than be an Emperor's lawful wife. They're not like ither folk, poets. Treat women decent! There's mair nor one kind o' woman that marries a poet. There's ae kind thinks she's gotten a pedigree dog! Aye, she's guid tae him! She'll spend the day kaiming his coat. She'll sit up wi' him a' nicht when he's for the distemper. And she'll teach him tae give a paw, and tae die for his country, and tae—tae BEG! He'll win prizes at the Show for her. He'll look bonny in the weekly papers. Ach! hell blast it! Geordie Byron, Geordie Byron, wi' the daughter o' the horse-leech sook-sooking at your heart's blood! What were you to dae? What am I to dae?

JEAN. But there's anither kind o' woman, Colin, is there not? You said there was anither kind o' woman.

COLIN. Aye. They say there is.

JEAN. She'll be a kind o' woman you wouldna look at twice, for she hasna the wit for play-acting and make-believe. She couldna see onything in you but a queer mix o' a man and a wean and an angel and a devil.

COLIN. Aye. There'll be a woman like that.

JEAN. It's no likely she'll be gentry. They're awful keen on dugs and horses and tame beasties, the gentry. But they're awful feared of folk.

COLIN. Mind you, that's true. They canna thole folk. They're aye hunting oot a bit o' the train where there's no folk, or a bit o' the country where there's no folk. And they're aye pitting up fences and wa's and notice-boards and gamies to keep the folk awa fra them. They rail off wee bits o' the House of God so that folk 'll keep their distance while they're worshipping Him. I've noticed it. It's a queer thing.

JEAN. Aye, it's queer. But you see it better when you're in service. If you say anything else to them but " Yes, Mem," and " No, Mem," they look at you whiles as if you were Balaam's Ass. It's no' that they don't like letting on now and again to theirselves that you're sort of human. I've heard Mrs. Gobie talking to a Persian cat just the way she does to me. But that's only a game. They'd get an awful fright if they thought you were really human.

COLIN. It's God's truth. They would.

JEAN. And it's no' only the gentry. If a scavenger gets a wee pickle o' siller in the bank, he's just the same.

COLIN. Aye. My faither's gone that way. I think he's feart they'll ask him for his money. . . . Jean, ye're a kind of mensefu' bit hizzie too.

JEAN. Ugh, no! But I keep my eyes open.

COLIN. It's funny. . . . There's more tae 't nor that. . . . When you came in the wee door, honest, Jean, I felt that bad I think I would hae doen myself a mischief.

JEAN. Aye. I thought you lookit kind o' stauchered.

COLIN. Stauchered! I was at the end o' my tether. I was tumbling to bits. And now, some way, I feel more like a man. And kind of cosy inside me. I wunner . . .

JEAN. Och! it'll be yon rain-cloud that's just blown over. It was naething we were talking aboot.

COLIN. No. It was naething we were talking aboot. And it's naething to do wi' the weather, forbye. . . . Jean!

JEAN. Colin?

COLIN. It's half-past one. There's a charabanc leaves Duthie for Glasgow at this very minute. It'll be going by here in three minutes.

JEAN. What are you talking about, Colin Kilgour?

COLIN. We'll awa to Glasgow and get marriet in a Registry's office.

JEAN. Now, don't be silly. There'd be an awful

to-do. You're going to stay here and get married into the gentry to-morrow.

COLIN.   Am I hell!   Look at this.

[*He throws his silk hat over the wall.*]

JEAN.   Oh, Colin! The Murdochs 'll not think that's very honourable.

COLIN.   Who's the best judge of honour—a Scots poet or a cleckan of Glasgow profiteers? Come on, Jean.

JEAN.   Colin, I'm feart!

COLIN.   Of course you're feart. So am I feart. There's not a thing worth doing in the whole world that doesna half terrify the soul out of ye!

JEAN.   But what about Miss Murdoch?

COLIN.   I'll write her a letter she and her children 'll hand down from generation to generation. Come on. We'll miss the 'bus.

JEAN.   Colin, you're an awful one!

[*They kiss each other.*]
[*The horn of the charabanc is heard.*]

JEAN.   Mercy! They're roond the corner. We'll have to run!

[*The lovers hasten out by the wicket.*
The sun blazes out gloriously. The blackbird sings. So do the folk on the charabanc. Their voices fade in the distance, but the stage is full of bird-song and sunshine. After a pause, an angry voice is heard.
Enter KITTY *in a flaming rage, followed by* BETTS.]

KITTY.   You can all go and blooming well drown yourselves!

BETTS.   Kitty, Kitty, do have a bit of common!

KITTY.   What do you mean by following me? It's all your fault. I don't want you. I don't want anybody!

BETTS.   I say, Kitty, don't be a hysterical idiot.

KITTY.   Why can't you and that beastly cat, Connie

R   [245]

Baigrie, leave Colin's poetry alone? Going and learning all that rot, guying it all through lunch!

BETTS. I thought you admired his poetry.

KITTY. You did nothing of the sort. And some of it's jolly good when you consider the life he's had. And he's a far better man than you. And Connie and you think you're so unutterably funny, and you're not.

BETTS. But look here, Kitty . . .

KITTY. Don't Kitty me! You're in love with her. That's what you are!

BETTS. Don't be a fool.

KITTY. You are, you are, you are! If you can call it love. She's—she's got the soul of a movie star and the looks of a charwoman. Men run after anything that's shameless enough. But I may as well tell you, you're making a fool of yourself, as you'll find out when you marry her.

BETTS. But I'm not going to marry her. Besides . . .

KITTY. Besides, it's none of my business? I know, I know. And a few months ago you said I meant everything in the world to you.

BETTS. Look here, you know, if it comes to that . . .

KITTY. Yes, I know what you're going to say. That I jilted you. Only a cad would say it.

BETTS. But I didn't . . .

KITTY. Only an unutterable, beastly cad!

BETTS. Listen, Kitty. You mustn't speak to me like that.

KITTY. Oh, I mustn't, mustn't I?

BETTS. No, you mustn't. I as near as a touch hit you a good sounding smack on the chops, just now.

KITTY. You'd hit me, would you, you cowardly rotter!

BETTS. See here, you're asking for it. I warn you!

[*Old* KILGOUR *appears at the wicket.*]

KITTY. You haven't got the guts.

[246]

BETTS. Oh, haven't I ?

KITTY. No, you haven't. If you had had the guts, we'd have been married ages ago. Only you're nothing but a wabbit-looking whatshisname, and . . .

BETTS. Right. That settles it. Take that. (*He gives her a sharp smack on the cheek.*) And that, and that, and that ! (*He kisses her enthusiastically.*)

KITTY. Oh, Ronnie !

KILGOUR. Hey, hey ! What's this, what's this ?

BETTS (*full of fight*). What the devil do you want ?

KILGOUR. Whaur's my Colin ?

BETTS. I haven't got your damned Colin. Go and get him yourself. And you can tell him that his part of to-morrow's jamboree is off, do you hear ? Off ! Tell him he's a—a crult. With Mr. Betts' compliments.

KITTY. No, no !

KILGOUR. I canna just get my bearings on this business. There's a hantle here needs redding up.

BETTS. Sorry. No speak Esperanto. Miss Murdoch and I are making a bee-line for my Buick. You can tell your son that letters to C/o the Smiddy, Gretna Green, will be forewarded. Cheer-oh !

KITTY. Oh, Mr. Kilgour, I'll write to Colin.

BETTS. " They'll be fleet steeds that follow," said young Lochinvar !——

> [BETTS *and* KITTY *go.*]
> [MRS. MURDOCH *comes in.*]

MRS. MUR. Oh, hello, Mr. Kilgour. Did you see Kitty and Mr. Betts ?

KILGOUR. I did, Mem.

MRS. MUR. Their coffee's getting cold.

KILGOUR. Indeed, Mem ? Do you tell me that ? That's a bad business that their coffee's getting cold ! Ho ! ho !

> [*Enter* MURDOCH, PRINGLE *and* MISS BAIGRIE.]

MURDOCH. Where's Kitty ?

MRS. MUR.   Nobody seems to know.   What a tiravee about nothing!   And here Mr. Kilgour seems to be having a bit of a joke to himself.

MURDOCH.   Hey?   Why are we honoured by a visit from the great Mr. Kilgour?

KILGOUR.   Ye'll ken shuin eneuch.   Eh! hey, hey, hey!

MURDOCH.   You're damned joco!   See here, Kilgour, mebbe you'll explain what the hell you're doing in my garden!

KILGOUR.   I'll explain all richt.   Oo aye, I'll explain. He's awa.

MURDOCH.   Who's awa—away?

KILGOUR.   Colin's awa.   He gied me a wave from the Glesgie 'bus when it passed me at the road-end. He's awa wi' Jean McLeish.

MURDOCH.   Jean who?

MRS. MUR.   Jean McLeish.   My old table-maid! Oh, what a like thing!

[MISS SOULIS *appears at window.*]

MISS SOULIS.   Whatever's the matter?

KILGOUR.   He's awa, miss.

MISS SOULIS.   Who?   Professor Nish?

MURDOCH.   Professor Nish my Auntie Kate!

MRS. MUR.   My poor lassie!   What'll she do?   What-ever'll she do?

KILGOUR.   I wouldna fash about her, Mem.   She's awa tae.

MURDOCH.   What?

KILGOUR.   She's awa tae Gretna wi' yon cratur Betts.

MURDOCH.   You're lying, man!

[*Enter* MRS. WATSON-DICKSON *by the wicket. She senses the atmosphere and bounces out again in some confusion.*]

MISS SOULIS.   Oh, how perfectly dreadful!

KILGOUR.   He doesna ken she's awa!   She doesna ken he's awa!   They've jumpit awa tae the opposite airts like a pair o' Hallowe'en nuts! And good luck to them!

PRINGLE. Mr. Murdoch, look here, we'll stop them yet!

MISS SOULIS. The car's just leaving the garage. Run, run!

> [*A motor-horn plays a bar from the Wedding March from* Lohengrin.
> *A short silence.*
> *The blackbird is heard again.*]

KILGOUR. Ye're owre late, I'm thinking.

CURTAIN

THE GIRL WHO DID NOT WANT
TO GO TO KUALA LUMPUR

PERSONS

MARY
HARRY
MARGARET
OLD TOM
MAJOR UNTHANK
MRS. UNTHANK
ELLEN
MRS. SYME
SMELLIE
THE POSTMAN

DEDICATED TO
SAM MAVOR

This play was first presented by the Scottish National Players in the Lyric Theatre, Glasgow, in November 1930, with the following Cast:

THE LADY ARTIST	.	.	. Madeleine Christie.
THE BOY	.	.	. Ian Sadler.
THE GIRL	.	.	. Jean Taylor Smith.
THE OLD ARTIST	.	.	. James Sloan.
THE UNCLE	.	.	. Douglas Lamond.
THE AUNT	.	.	. Meg Buchanan.
THE POSTMAN	.	.	. George Yuill.
THE DRUNKEN MAN	.	.	. Alan MacKill.
THE LANDLADY	.	.	. Catherine Fletcher.

The play was produced by Elliot Mason.

THE GIRL WHO DID NOT WANT
TO GO TO KUALA LUMPUR

ACT I

Mary's studio.

[HARRY *is idling restlessly. He finds some chocolates and eats one; fingers a bit of brocade; turns sharply as* MARY *enters.*]

HARRY. Oh, hello, Mary.

MARY. Hello, Harry.

HARRY. So there you are. I say, Mary, you shouldn't leave your studio door unlocked. I might have been a burglar.

MARY. Well, you aren't a burglar. You don't look like one.

HARRY. I don't know. Burglars are often quite well-turned out nowadays. They are nearly all public-school boys who have gone wrong. I hardly blame them, either, poor things.

MARY. Why not?

HARRY. I know a fellow who had been to a public school. He was so strong he could hardly walk and such good form he could hardly speak. He wasn't nearly so clever nor so ornamental as I am, and much, much more expensive. Thank God, Mother educated me herself. What have you got there, Mary?

MARY. Cakes for tea. Get out the kettle, like a good boy, and put it on the hob.

HARRY. Oh, do let me see. Now, why did you buy macaroons? They aren't pretty, and they taste beastly. Why no éclairs? You know how I love éclairs.

MARY. I didn't ask *you* to tea. Get that kettle.

[255]

HARRY. Are you having a party? How thrilling.

MARY. No. Not exactly a party. Margaret and her aunt are coming round to say good-bye.

HARRY. Margaret? Margaret who?

MARY. Margaret Unthank. Don't you know her?

HARRY. No. Everybody I know is called Joan or Betty. Is she nice?

MARY. Yes. Very nice.

HARRY. Why is she going away, then? Why is she going?

MARY. Her uncle has got a job in the Malay Straits somewhere. Unthank is his name. He's gone bankrupt three times, and drinks like a fish. I suppose that is why everybody seems to like him.

HARRY. I know I am very dense, but I don't understand. Why should a nice girl go to the Malay Straits? There is nothing but serangs and krises and head-hunters and things out there. She'll be horribly unhappy.

MARY. Oh, I don't know.

HARRY. Of course you don't know. You don't understand women.

MARY. I suppose not.

HARRY. I think you understand me, because I've been at a great deal of trouble to explain myself to you; but for a girl who pretends to interpret nature on canvas, you are the most ignorant and unsympathetic person I could imagine.

MARY. Umph.

HARRY. Now, here is this poor little wistful, blue-eyed thing, longing for life and gaiety and sympathy, making her first tremulous entry into womanhood, and you send her out among a gang of savages, to ruin her complexion and her liver and everything in that filthy climate.

MARY. I'm not sending her out. I told you she is going with her uncle.

HARRY. I beg your pardon. You are such a responsible woman, I imagined you responsible for this among other things. You may consider yourself cleared. I take your word for it. I am at least a gentleman.

MARY. You are at least a blether. Have you filled the kettle? You don't mean to say you've put it on the hob without filling it? Tuts! Take it to the sink at once. It is a mercy you haven't burned the bottom out of it.

HARRY (*filling the kettle* OFF, *and returning, but talking all the time*). Mary . . . I am lonely and unhappy . . . I have an inferiority complex . . . I feel thoroughly out of sorts. . . . Please, soothe me a little instead of cursing and swearing at me. That story of poor Margaret made me feel quite ill.

MARY. Well, go away. Don't be sick here.

HARRY. How dreadfully vulgar! I like these gladiolas. (*Looking at picture.*)

MARY. They are not gladiolas. They are supposed to be phloxes. Look here, have you nothing else to do but messing about here? You're in the way, you know.

HARRY. Do be careful, Mary. To a sensitive man like me that might sound like a hint that he was not wanted.

MARY. Neither you are. To-day. Haven't you any work to do?

HARRY. I told you last Friday that ALL my work is to do. I come here for inspiration. You're so virile, Mary. I say, where did you pick up that tea-cloth?

MARY. It's Czecho-Slovak work. My cousin sent it to me.

HARRY. Which cousin?

MARY. My cousin Herbert.

HARRY. You make me jealous now. You seem bent on raising all my stormiest passions this afternoon. When is Margaret coming?

MARY. Any moment now. Oh, for heaven's sake, get out!

[*Enter* MARGARET.]

MARGARET. Oh, I beg your pardon.

HARRY. Are you Margaret? But of course you are.

[257]

I was just telling Mary exactly what you looked
like—the colour of your eyes, the way you do your
hair . . .

MARY. Something about her liver too, I think.

HARRY. . . . And I was correct in every detail. I
quite frighten myself sometimes. It is an extraordinary
faculty. Like being able to tell if there are mice in the
basement. Shy, temperamental people often have it.
It's such an adventure meeting quite new people that I
keep dreaming what they will be like until quite often I
dream true. Ever since I was a tiny little kid, Mother
tells me, I have been different from other boys. Temperamental. I was delicate as a baby. Our doctor had
just taken shares in a sort of artificial infant food,
and he insisted on Mother giving it to me instead
of . . .

MARY. Harry, will you kindly let go Margaret's
hand and stop these reminiscences of the crèche. Don't
mind that fool, Margaret. He's mad. He's going
presently. I'm so glad you haven't brought the old
people. We'll have a nice quiet talk.

HARRY. Why didn't you say "a nice cosy chat"?
How that would have annoyed me!

MARGARET (vaguely). Yes? (To MARY) They're
coming up afterwards. There was a sort of last-minute
hitch about the cabins for to-morrow. They have gone
to see about it.

HARRY. Oh, I hope it's serious.

MARGARET. Oh, I hope not! Why?

MARY. Margaret, this is a drivelling idiot called
Harry. He escaped from the Asylum last year. He
was such a bad influence in the Asylum, and the other
patients were so fed up with him, that the warders made
no attempt to catch him, and here he is.

HARRY. Isn't she a refreshing old dear? Margaret
was just asking me a very pertinent question, to which I
shall now reply, if you have quite finished amusing us

all with your ready woman's wit. . . . I hope it is
serious, because I hope you don't go.

MARGARET.   Oh, why not? I mean—you . . .
You've only just met me.

HARRY.   It is because I have only just met you.   I
feel I should like you awfully if we had time to be friends.
I take such a long time to make friends.   Real friends,
I mean.   Especially women friends.   I think we're all
so afraid of each other, don't you?   I mean, people who
are really worth knowing are always so afraid.   I simply
hate jazz flappers.   They are always expressing themselves—like motor-bicycles with no cut-out.   They are
so obsessed with their own personalities.   And I loathe
their personalities.   You are much more my type.   Do
you play croquet?

MARGARET.   No, I don't think so.   I don't know
many card-games.   Auntie and I play a little bézique
sometimes in the evening.

HARRY.   There you are, now!   How many girls play
bézique with their aunts nowadays?   But you don't
mind being démodé.   You have a strong character.
Mine is very weak.

MARGARET.   I don't think so at all.   No, Harry.   I
mean, I don't think it can be.   Your character, I mean.
Weak, and so on.

HARRY.   Don't you really think so?   Well, in a
way you are right.   I can be as obstinate as a mule in
some things.   Little things, you know.   For instance,
I never wear braces.   Mother bought me a pair, but I
threw them out of the window.   They are probably
holding up some unspeakable person's perfectly repellent
trousers at this very instant.   A solemn thought.

MARY.   Harry, if you are determined to stay where
you are not wanted, will you kindly step across the landing to Mr. Garscadden's studio and ask him for the loan
of another teacup?   With my compliments.

HARRY.   No.   With my own compliments.   I would

[259]

rather have a poke in the eye from a wet haddock than the most beautiful of your compliments.

[Goes out.]

MARGARET.   Is he really . . . I mean . . . what you said just now ?

MARY.   A loony ?   Oh, no.   He's a quaint thing. Quite nice.   You can say anything in front of him. He is rather clever.   He makes wooden jewellery and paints it, and that sort of thing.   He is supposed to be studying Law.

MARGARET.   He's not my idea of a lawyer.

MARY.   What *is* your idea of a lawyer ?

MARGARET.   Oh, I don't know.   Sort of legal-looking.   Are you painting much just now ?

MARY.   Lots.   What are you really thinking about ?

MARGARET.   Lots of things. . . . I don't know . . . Miss O'Hanlon, I'm nearly desperate.   I don't know why I should speak to you like this, but you were awfully good to me at school.

MARY.   Are you in love ?

MARGARET.   No, no, no.   It's just going away like this.   And I've never had a chance.   I've never made any friends, because I don't see a soul, and you know what Uncle Dick is—one week swell dinners to horrible persons who come to be cheated by Uncle Dick, and the next week retiring to what he calls his Highland fastness —in Hull, though I'm not supposed to tell anyone—his creditors might get to know—jumping whenever we hear the door-bell.   And bézique with Aunt Annie.   And now I'm going to a place all over black men and mosquitoes, to—to—to wither on my stem.

MARY.   Oh, do cheer up.   You'll probably meet somebody on the way out.

MARGARET.   No.   We're going on the cheap. There'll be absolutely nobody on board.   But sailors, of course.

[*Enter* HARRY *and* TOM GARSCADDEN. TOM *is eighty-five.*
He has a white beard.]

HARRY.   Margaret, I have brought Mr. Garscadden
to see you.   He is very wise.   He is eighty-five.   I told
him all about you.

TOM.   The half hath not been told.   (*Bows in a
courtly fashion.*)

MARGARET.   How do you do.

TOM.   Thank you, I am well.   My kidneys troubled
me this summer, but God bless you, they are now as right
as a trivet.

HARRY (*ecstatically*).   How nice to be old enough to
talk about kidneys!   And, please, what is a trivet?

TOM.   Will you shut your mouth?   Miss O'Hanlon,
my dear, I don't like your friends.   Not *all* of them.
Some of them.   Eh?   Ha, ha?   Eh?   I think, Miss
Margaret, that there is no lovelier thing in nature than a
fresh young girl.

HARRY.   He talks as if she were the fish course.

MARGARET.   Yes?   I mean, no.   At least . . .

TOM.   Come, come.   You're in trouble.   What's
ado?   God bless me, I'm an old man.   You can tell
Old Tom, can't you?

MARY.   There's really nothing wrong at all, Tom.
It's Harry's nonsense.   It was very kind of you to come
in; but we only wanted a teacup.

TOM.   A teacup!   How the hell can I paint master-
pieces if I'm to be jiggered up every five minutes for
teacups!   Fetch your ain bloody teacups!

[*Enter* RICHARD UNTHANK *and* MRS. UNTHANK. RICHARD *is a*
very handsome man of fifty-four. MRS. UNTHANK *is a*
walking cold in the head.]

MRS. UNTHANK.   Miss O'Hanlon, is it not?   *So*
pleased.   This is my husband, dear Margaret's Uncle
Dick.

MARY.   How do.

MRS. UNTHANK.   Did I hear the old gentleman mention "hiccup"? I have been a martyr to hiccup for the last ten years. No martyr could have suffered as I have suffered. Do tell me, sir . . .

TOM. Not hiccup, madam, teacup.

[Goes out in a rage.]

MRS. UNTHANK. How eccentric. How charming. Who is he, Miss O'Hanlon?

MARY. Tom Garscadden, the painter. I should have introduced you. By the way, have you met Harry Fiddes? Mrs. Unthank, Major Unthank.

MRS. UNTHANK. How do you do.

UNTHANK. How do. (*He takes no further notice of* HARRY, *but screws his eyeglass at a picture.*) Pooty thing this, Miss O'Hanlon. Quite good. The yellows are well stated.

MARY. Stated?

UNTHANK. Yes, I said "stated." There's a feeling about them. Representational a bit, but, of its class, admirable. Tentative. Perhaps later, when you have learnt to distort the figure, your patterns will be most interesting.

MARY. I thought I had distorted it rather well. The left leg is quite out of drawing.

UNTHANK. Not enough, my dear, not enough. *L'audace. L'audace. Toujours l'audace.*

MARY. But don't you think the restrained line work gives a sort of—a sort of a contained sort of an effect? What I mean to say . . .

[Re-enter TOM, with a teacup.]

UNTHANK. Look at Zuzubagio. Look at Mentz. They are restrained only by the frame. Contained effect? Possibly. Yes, possibly. But see what you lose in *brio*!

TOM. Good day to you.

UNTHANK. Ah, Mr. Garscadden, isn't it? I can hardly expect the old warrior to agree with my views. I was saying how charming I find this little bit of *décor*.

[262]

TOM. No' bad for a lassie. Here's your teacup, woman. No, sir, there was never a woman who could achieve a nobler work of art than hemming hankies.

UNTHANK. Indeed? Well, Margaret, my dear, the world goes on wagging. Time, my dear, time is on its way. Inexorable. We must tear you away from your Bohemians.

MRS. UNTHANK. Are you a Bohemian, Mr. Gaspulton? I used to know a delightful Bohemian family before the dreadful War. We went there. To Baden-Baden. Every spring.

TOM. Did you?

MRS. UNTHANK. Yes, we did, we did. To take the waters. Such a lovely Kursaal. The music was so nice. We listened to it every day. But we lost everything in this dreadful War.

UNTHANK. Annie, my darling!

MRS. UNTHANK. Yes, dicky-bird?

UNTHANK. Perhaps, Mr. Garscadden, you will call on me at my club if you are ever in town.

TOM. What town?

MRS. UNTHANK. He means London, Mr. Rasputin. Poor Dicky, he can never remember he is living in the Provinces and that they hardly quite understand. We are so sorry, Miss O'Hanlon, to make such a short visit. We go off to-morrow, or we should have loved to come again and see your quite ravishing pictures. Good-bye, good-bye.

UNTHANK. Come along, Margaret. Good-bye, Miss O'Hanlon. It has been a short acquaintance, but, perhaps, not without meaning. One never can tell, can one?

MARY. No, I suppose not. Good-bye. Good-bye, Margaret. The ten o'clock, isn't it? If I'm up, I'll see you off.

HARRY. And so shall I.

MARGARET.   Oh, that will be awfully good of you. But perhaps . . .

UNTHANK.   Come along, come along. Good-bye, good-bye.

> [*Exeunt* MARGARET *and* MAJOR *and* MRS. UNTHANK.
> MARY *sees them to the stair-head and returns in a moment.*
> HARRY *stabs a cushion with a palette-knife.*
> TOM *stands holding his teacup.*]

MARY.   What a damned shame!

TOM.   Who were those?

MARY.   I told you, Tom.   Major and Mrs. Unthank.

TOM.   Not Dick Unthank, who did two years for some bucket-shop business or other?

MARY.   There was something like that, I think. He's had a lot of trouble.

TOM.   He's just missed another bit of trouble, and that's my boot on his hinterlands.   Who was the young lassie?

MARY.   His niece.

TOM.   Whose niece?

MARY.   Dick Unthank's niece.

TOM.   She was? I don't believe it. It's not in Nature.   And old Mop-Nose, was she her aunt?

MARY.   Yes, yes.

TOM.   And Dick's clearing out again?

MARY.   Yes, he's got a job as a representative of something.

TOM.   And he's taking her with him?

MARY.   Yes, yes, yes, yes, yes.   You've got it *quite* right.

TOM.   My God! That's all I say. My God! But he's a damned rogue, and the old girl's a disgusting fool. Slopping and sniftering and dribbling about like that!   Where are they going?

MARY.   Oh, you tell him, Harry.   It's bad enough that it should happen without having to go over it twenty times.

HARRY. I won't tell him anything of the sort. My heart is broken. I'll begin to snivel in a minute.

MARY. Couldn't we stop them?

HARRY. What can we do? A weak woman, a doting old man, and a mere child?

TOM. Hold on a bit. I'm kind o' getting the hang of this business. I follow. Mary, this can't be. The wee lassie cannot go. We'll stop her. What can we do? Dick Unthank. He's aye dancing near the door of the jail. Couldn't we put the police on him?

MARY. The police know all that is to be known about Major Unthank.

HARRY. Couldn't we poison the aunt's medicine and get Dick hanged for it?

TOM. You couldn't poison yon.

MARY. If I were a man I'd elope with Margaret. Right away. To-night.

TOM. If I were ten years younger . . .

HARRY. You'd be about ninety. Don't be silly. Think. Think. What's the good of a hundred years' experience of life if you can't help in a simple thing like this?

TOM. It would be near as bad as the Malay Peninsula, but why don't you marry her?

HARRY. Mamma would give me hell. I daren't. Think of somebody, Mary.

MARY. I've lived in Glasgow for twenty years, and I don't know a decent man who isn't married—except old Tom.

[*A knock.*]

HARRY. Hush. Perhaps it's the Fairy Prince.

[*He opens the door.*]

Come in. Come in, come in, come in.

[*Enter a* POSTMAN.]

Yes. Miss O'Hanlon. Here she is.

POSTMAN. Excuse me, miss, but I have a letter here

for a Miss O'Halloran, at this address, 19ª Hope Street.
Will it maybe be for you, now?

MARY.   From Belfast?   Yes, that's for me.   Thank
you.

POSTMAN.   I am very pleased.   Not at all.   Good
day to you.

TOM.   Stop.   Where do you come from?

POSTMAN.   I come from Salen.

TOM.   What's your name?

POSTMAN.   John Sobieski Stewart.

TOM.   It's a royal name.

POSTMAN.   That is true.

TOM.   Can you fight?

POSTMAN (*laughs*).   Excuse me.   I am the Amateur
Cruiser Weight Champion of Scotland.

TOM.   That'll do.   Are you a poet?

POSTMAN.   My verses on Fionn won the first prize
at the Argyllshire Mod.   I have tried the poetry in the
English too, but I have not yet been so successful whatever.

TOM.   Sit down.

MARY.   But the poor man has his rounds to do.   He
will get into trouble.

POSTMAN.   I have finished for the day, I thank you.
I am in Government employ.   I am on my way home.

MARY.   Are you married?

HARRY.   I see, I see!   Oh, I see it!

POSTMAN.   No, ma'am, I am not married yet.

MARY.   You're not engaged or anything?

POSTMAN.   Up to the present no young lady has had
any success with me at all, at all.

MARY.   Oh, good!   Oh, good!   Do you like pictures?

POSTMAN.   Some pictures I find very pleasant to look
at.   (*He looks with some misgivings at the modern works
on the wall.*)   I assume you do not mean the moving
pictures?   I go to them with my Auntie.   There is

great impossibility in the moving pictures. If you would have an instance, surely it is not possible for one man to beat fifteen and him with no gun or bullet, and them hanging round his waist. Six I could beat if they were not very strong, but no, no, not fifteen.

MARY.   No, I don't mean movies.   ^

[*She rakes behind a curtain at back and produces a portrait of* MARGARET.]

Do you like this?

[TOM *grunts : ! ! !*]

POSTMAN.   Well, I do not think as a picture that it is a very good picture, but, as a girl, I think that is the most beautiful girl I have ever beheld.

HARRY.   Oh, isn't she?   Isn't she?

POSTMAN.   Her hair is like the golden web that is the canopy of a fairy's barge; and her eyes are like two of the Pleiades reflected in the dark waters. Her little mouth is full of loving. To look on her makes me think of my own glen in a day of sunshine with a far-off piper on the sea-shore playing faint songs of loves long ago.

TOM.   God bless my socks!

MARY.   Oh, how lovely!

POSTMAN.   It is quite good. But I could do better before I became a teetotaller. It is not worthy of her, so gentle as she is. (*He gazes, enraptured. Pause.*) But I will be late for my tea. (*He sighs.*)

HARRY.   Mr. Stewart, do you think that the day of Romance is over?

MARY.   Don't ask him such a silly question.

POSTMAN.   No, sir, I do not.

ALL (*speaking at once*).
{ Well, look here . . .
{ This young lady in the picture . . .
{ Do you possibly think you could . . .

HARRY.   I beg your pardon, everybody.

TOM.   Granted.   Now let me speak.

MARY. You'll only make a mess of it. No doubt you make topping speeches at the Art Club at half-past eleven. . . .

HARRY. But this is a delicate situation. It wants tact.

TOM. Tact! Tact is skill in the management of fools. Mr. Stewart, here's a maniac, but he's no fool. Look here, Postie, to put it plump and plain . . .

HARRY. No, no, no, no!

MARY. A very particular friend of mine . . .

TOM. Oh, damn the lot of you!

CURTAIN

ACT II

The UNTHANKS' *Flat. The living-room. It isn't really a flat
but one floor of a big house, and it is farmed out by a widow
called* MRS. SYME.

> MRS. UNTHANK *and* MARGARET *are packing cabin trunks
> and things. At least,* MARGARET *is packing mournfully
> and* MRS. UNTHANK *is trying on a solar topi before a
> mirror.*
> *The room is in a devil of a mess, and both the women have
> been in tears.*

MRS. UNTHANK (*drying her eyes*). I expect they will
call me the Mem-Sahib and you will be the Missy-Baba,
although you are quite grown up. That's how they do,
you know, in the East. There are no Ten Command-
ments there, the poet says. . . . I do hope Dick will be
able to keep up the position we are accustomed to on the
wretched, wretched salary they are giving him.

MARGARET (*goaded*). The position we are accustomed
to!

MRS. UNTHANK. Yes. Some of those people who
retire and come home from the East are quite dreadful.
It would be abominable to be expected to know them.
After all, your uncle is a gentleman.

[MARGARET *sniffs.*]

Now, Margaret, I think I heard you sniff. If you
have caught a cold, you might at least use your pocket-
handkerchief. I will never make a lady of you. Never.
There's one good thing about the East—the sun shines
all the time, and I may get rid of this repulsive nasal
catarrh. It makes me such an invalid. What was I

[269]

saying ? I mean what was I talking about, the remark before last ?

MARGARET. You were saying that Uncle Dick was a gentleman.

MRS. UNTHANK. So I was, so I was. What culture. What refinement. Nothing bourgeois or banal. The sort of man who would spell Oxo, OCKSO.

[*Enter* ELLEN.]

Well, Ellen ? Can't you see we're busy ? If you won't help, perhaps you will refrain from hindering.

ELLEN. Please 'm, Mrs. Syme wants to know if the Major has come home yet.

MRS. UNTHANK. My compliments to Mrs. Syme, and tell her to mind her own business.

ELLEN. Thank you, m'm.

MRS. UNTHANK. There is no necessity to be pert, Ellen. No necessity at all.

ELLEN. I have neffer been accused before of not knowing my place, Mrs. Unthank.

MRS. UNTHANK. I myself accused you of that very thing on Friday, no fewer than four times. Close the door softly when you go out.

[ELLEN *bangs the door.*]

The idea ! Impertinence !

MARGARET. Where is Uncle Dick, Aunt Annie ?

MRS. UNTHANK. He was detained at his Club on very important business. He said he would be home early to help us with the packing. I wish I could get him out of the habit of leaving everything till the last moment. He is so unmethodical.

[ELLEN *appears at the door.*]

ELLEN. Mrs. Syme to see you, m'm.

[MRS. SYME *enters.*
ELLEN *stays to enjoy the fun.*]

MRS. SYME. Well, Mrs. Unthank.

MRS. UNTHANK. Well, madam ?

MRS. SYME. Maybe you'll explain the message you've just sent me by Ellen.

MRS. UNTHANK. What message?

MRS. SYME. To mind my own business.

MRS. UNTHANK. Ho! Very good. Very nice. I hope you will mind it, madam. I hope you will.

MRS. SYME. My husband left me this muckle white elephant of a house, and since then it has been my business to let it out by flats to respectable parties.

MRS. UNTHANK. Ah; well, I can't congratulate you on the way you conduct your business. We have been most uncomfortable, and I shall tell all my friends.

MRS. SYME. I canna congratulate *myself*. It was a blank day I let you and your jail-bird of a man ever darken my door.

MRS. UNTHANK. Jail-bird! Jail-bird!

MRS. SYME. Yes, jail-bird. Can you stand before my face and deny that he has done time?

MRS. UNTHANK. Yes; but for nothing disgraceful or low. It was for fraudulent company-promotion, and you know it.

MRS. SYME. It seems to me that's as bad as picking pockets.

MRS. UNTHANK. You cannot be expected to know how gentlefolk feel about a thing like that. It is quite a different thing. And now, will you kindly leave the room? My niece and I are much too busy to entertain you.

MRS. SYME. NO.

MRS. UNTHANK. No what?

MRS. SYME. No, thank you. I won't leave the room.

MRS. UNTHANK. Will you be good enough to tell me why not?

MRS. SYME. I'll take you at your word. Mind my ain business. I'll mind it. (*She sits down.*)

MRS. UNTHANK. May I ask what you mean?

MRS. SYME. I mean this, that I've heard enough of
you, and seen enough of you, to make gey sure that not
one of your boxes leaves my house till I've seen my rent.
Aye, and that none of my bits of valuables goes in they
boxes!

MRS. UNTHANK. You woman!

MRS. SYME. I'll thank you not to curse and to swear
at me. I'm not used to your high society ways.

[*Words fail* MRS. UNTHANK, *and she walks out like a
tragedy-queen by bedroom door* R.]

[*Silence.*]

MRS. SYME. I've nothing against you, Miss Unthank,
but you have to stick up for yourself in this world. Ellen,
get away to your kitchen, this minute.

[*Exit* ELLEN.]

MARGARET. Yes. I quite see that it must be rather
difficult. With all sorts of people, I mean, coming in
and going out, and so on.

MRS. SYME. You wouldnae believe all I have to put
up with. Where are you going?

MARGARET. Oh, nowhere. I've all the packing to do.

MRS. SYME. No. I mean after you leave here.

MARGARET. Oh, that! I can never get the name of
the place right. But I'll show you it on the Atlas.
(*She fetches an atlas.*) You see, there are the Malay
Straits . . .

MRS. SYME. Straits! They look all twisty ways!

MARGARET. We're going to that yellow place, there.
Kuala Lumpur; that's the name; and then up-country
a bit.

MRS. SYME. Hold on till I get my specs. Certy!
yon's an awful like place.

MARGARET. Oh, I don't know. It does look a bit
dull on the map, but then everywhere looks dull on a
map, don't you think?

MRS. SYME. And what will a bonny bit lassie like you
do in a place like yon?

MARGARET. Oh, I expect I'll read a bit. And go for walks, if there are no snakes. And try to learn the language. (*She begins to cry.*)

MRS. SYME. There now, there now, my wee doo! Come to old Granny Syme. Did they, then, my precious.

MARGARET. I don't want to go. I don't want to go.

MRS. SYME. Dearie me, then, why are you going? You never see me doing anything I don't want, and I'm only a lone old body.

MARGARET. They've been so kind. Keeping me and all that, after they had spent all the money that Father left me. And, besides, what could I do? I'm absolutely useless. I couldn't do a thing. I could teach, of course, but then I don't know what to teach.

MRS. SYME. You'll have to get marrit.

MARGARET. Oh, don't be silly! How can I get married when we take the ten o'clock for Southampton to-morrow morning? There's only twelve hours. No, eleven.

MRS. SYME. If I were you I'd marry the policeman on the beat—or the postman.

MARGARET. Oh, I would, I would! Anybody!

[*Enter* UNTHANK *and* SMELLIE. *They are in dinner-jackets.* SMELLIE *is forty-seven, very ugly and a little drunk. They have been dining together.*]

UNTHANK. Well, well, well. Come along, Mr. Smellie. Come along. We are in rather a mess, but we are on the move to-morrow afternoon to Aberdeen. Starting a branch there. This is my niece, Margaret, Mr. Smellie. No, no. Not that one. This one. Sit down. Sit down.

[SMELLIE *has advanced ingratiatingly to* MRS. SYME. MARGARET *has retired* R. *on their entrance.*]

SMELLIE. Nice night, Miss Margaret.

MARGARET. Very nice.

[273]

UNTHANK (*ignoring* MRS. SYME).   Where is your auntie,
Madgie?

MARGARET.   I think she's lying down.

UNTHANK.   Have a cigar, Smellie.   And wait a bit.
There used to be a small pot . . . Ah, yes.   Splendid.

[*He unearths a decanter and a syphon.*]

Say when . . .

SMELLIE.   Well, happy days.

UNTHANK.   Forgive me a minute, old boy.   I'll look
in and see if my wife's all right.   She has *migraine.*
Most frightfully awkward to-night, of all nights!

[*Exit* R.]

[SMELLIE *beams on* MARGARET *with a watery beam.*
    MRS. SYME, *in a chair against the wall, at back, does not
    beam.*]

SMELLIE.   Look'n't a picture-book?   Phottygrafts?

MARGARET.   No.   It's a map.

SMELLIE.   Oh, map!   Thought it was phottygrafts.
I beg your pardon.

MARGARET   Oh, it doesn't matter, really.

SMELLIE.   No.   Does matter.   'f I'm in the wrong.
Always apologise.   Great boy your uncle.

MARGARET.   Yes.   He is very nice.

SMELLIE.   Tell you what he is.   Sportsman.   Great
respeck for your husband, Mrs. Unthank.

MRS. SYME.   He is not my husband.

SMELLIE.   Well, your son.   Great credit to you.
Must be proud of him.   Sharper than serpent's tooth to
have an Unthank child.   Which nobody can deny.   So
we'll all sit down together and wait for his reply.   Eh?
Haha!   What?

MRS. SYME.   I didn't speak.

SMELLIE.   No.   I just said "What?" as a sort of
thing to say.   Was'n' askin' question, really.   Just
rhetorical question.   You play piano, Miss Unthank?

MARGARET.   No.   I'm afraid not.

[274]

SMELLIE. Oh, yes, you do. Play some'ng for me. I
like music. Subscribe Cho'al and 'rchestr'l Union. Ten
quid of the best. Mos' 'mjoyable. Do play some'n'.

MARGARET. I really don't play. Honestly, Mr.
Smellie.

SMELLIE. No, now, now! 'Low me c'nduct you to
th' piano.

> [*He rises unsteadily.*
> MARGARET *shrinks towards door.*
> *Re-enter* UNTHANK.]

UNTHANK. Margaret dear, will you go to your aunt?

> [*Exit* MARGARET.]

Sit down, old boy. Hello! You haven't got a drink.
To think Scotch hospitality should come to this pass!
(*Provides another drink for* SMELLIE.) Well, Mrs. Syme,
it is a pleasant evening. Shall we go upstairs and discuss
the little matter of the . . .

MRS. SYME. No.

UNTHANK. Very well. As you wish it. Well, old
boy, what would you like to do? I say, look here—will
you let me have a couple of tenners till to-morrow morning? I've been paying things in cash and run myself
short. I'll give you a cheque.

SMELLIE. How much do you want? (*He fumbles
with his note-case.*)

UNTHANK. Oh, fifty will do very well. See. I'll
sort 'em out for you. I'll let you have the cheque. . . .
Ah, here is my cheque-book. (*He writes a cheque.*)
Now, Mrs. Syme, will you have the goodness to come
this way?

MRS. SYME. I'll have the goodness, all right.

> [MRS. SYME *and* UNTHANK *go out* L.]

UNTHANK (*passing* SMELLIE). Eccentric old bird. Old
friend of the family. Old nurse.

> [*Exit.*]

SMELLIE (*counts his notes*). Funny feeling. Been in

this sorrow situation before. When, now? Queer. Like a dream. (*He sees the solar topi where* AUNT ANNIE *has left it.*) The topi, now. Tha's not it. No. But stop a bit. Stopabit. Unthank told me—family—moving—to Aberdeen. Don' wear sun-helmets in Aberdeen. Aha! Dr. Watson! Stopabit. (*He fumbles with note-case.*)

> [MARGARET *enters down-stage ; finds a hat and coat she has left lying over the chair and puts them on quickly. She registers determination to be gone—out of it all. She casts a glance at* SMELLIE, *and then stops, with her hand to her mouth. An idea has struck her.*]

Now I've told myself 'gain and again, mus'n' carry so mush—much money about with me. Well, it's nos so much now. Whassee say? Coupla tenners? Couple! Oh, deary, deary me! I mus' sober up. (*He wets his handkerchief at the syphon and dabs his ears, staring the while at his note-case.*) I know! I've been bilked. Thass what I've been. Bilked. Oh, no! Poor old soft Bob Smellie, poor old chap, nossusha—not such a fool as that; nosso green. Hey, Major!

MARGARET. Mr. Smellie. Do sit down again.

SMELLIE. D'you hear all I said jussnow?

MARGARET. I heard you talking to yourself, but I couldn't make out quite . . .

SMELLIE. Thassall right. Mussn' mind me. I'm not susha bad sort of chap. Honest.

MARGARET. I'm sure you're not, really. But may I speak to you a minute? Before my uncle comes back.

SMELLIE. Go right ahead. I'm lis'n'n.

MARGARET. I hardly know how to begin.

SMELLIE. There's that funny feeling again. All this's happened to me before.

MARGARET. Mr. Smellie, I must have some money.

SMELLIE. Eh? Oho! You must, must you? Well, look here, missy; you just liss'n t'me. I am not so—so inebriated as I look. And I wasn' born yessday.

MARGARET. I knew you'd misunderstand me. I never asked for money before. I'm not like Uncle Dick, honestly. I really need it. Of course he really needs it too. But you know what I mean.

SMELLIE. See here. Liss'n t'me. I am older than you, and I'm wiser than you. Mush, mush wiser than you. I've seen life. And you can take it from me this game's not worth the candle. I like you. Thass why I'm telling you. You seem a decent sort of kid.

MARGARET. Oh, Mr. Smellie, I must have the money! I don't want to go to Kuala Lumpur!

SMELLIE. Who's he?

MARGARET. It isn't a he. It's a place. Out East, you know. Aunt and Uncle are going, and they want me to go with them; they take everything for granted; and I won't go, I won't go! I'm running away. I'm going to take rooms in a hotel. We start to-morrow by the ten o'clock from Central . . .

SMELLIE. Not going to Aberdeen?

MARGARET. No, no, no!

SMELLIE (*looking at cheque*). Hey! Going before the bank's open, eh? (*Rises unsteadily and takes off his coat.*) You see this cheque. I'm going to—I-am-going-to-make Major Unthank bloomin' well EAT it.

> [*He makes for door* L.
> MARGARET *tries to stop him.*]

MARGARET. Oh, what are you going to do?

SMELLIE. Lemme go, missy. You're not on in this act.

> [*There is a slight scuffle.*
> *Enter* UNTHANK. *He takes in the situation and its possibilities at a glance.*]

UNTHANK. Well, Mr. Smellie! Stand back, you infernal rascal! No, don't you dare to speak to me! Margaret, my dear, go to your aunt. I shall settle accounts with this ruffian.

SMELLIE. Look here! I never touched her. . . .

T   [277]

UNTHANK. You may tell that story to the Jury, if you survive the thrashing I am about to give you. Go away, Margaret.

MARGARET. But, Uncle Dick . . .

UNTHANK. Do you hear me ? Do as I tell you.

[*Exit* MARGARET, R.]

Sit down, sir. SIT DOWN, SIR! I asked you to my house because I believed you to be a gentleman. I was wrong. I leave the room for a few minutes, and you take advantage of my absence to insult my niece. I shall not soil my fingers nor my horse-whip upon you. I shall hand you over to the police.

SMELLIE. Look here . . .

UNTHANK. Not another word. (*Goes to the telephone.*)

SMELLIE. Look here. I'm very sorry . . .

UNTHANK. Sorry! Sorry, by thunder! If I had been a younger man, or in decent health, you'd have been a dead man. What is your sorrow worth ? . . . I say, what is your sorrow worth ?

SMELLIE. Eh ? I beg your pardon. I thought it was a rhet—a rhetorical question. . . . I don't know.

UNTHANK. Look here. I'll be quite frank with you. I don't wish my niece's name to be mixed up in a scandal. To have her name bracketed with yours in the Sunday papers would be a profanation, a profanation, sir. See here. I am willing to make allowances for you. You are one of those men who should never touch alcohol. As one business man to another, how much is it worth to you to keep this disgusting affair dark ?

SMELLIE. What would you suggest ?

[*A bell rings faintly.*]

UNTHANK. Oh, as between gentlemen . . . What about five thousand ?

SMELLIE. Five thousand what ?

UNTHANK. Guineas. You'd better cough up, my

friend. And quickly, too. I'm not a patient man. Come along.

SMELLIE. Aye. Yes. Imphm. Cough up? This is a fine antidote to whisky, I can tell you. I'm as clear as a whistle now. See here. D'you know who I am? I'm Smellie.

UNTHANK. I can't help your infirmities.

SMELLIE. No back chat. . . . I know what this is. It's a frame-up, you blooming blackmailing hound!

UNTHANK. You be careful. You be very careful.

[VOICES *are heard outside.*]

MRS. SYME (*without*). Away to your bed, Ellen. I'll open the door.

ELLEN (*without*). It's all right, mem, really.

MRS. SYME (*without*). Away to your bed. It's the pollis, as like as not.

[*Pause. Then—*
Enter MARY O'HANLON, GARSCADDEN, HARRY *and* STEWART,
still in his Postman's uniform, followed by MRS. SYME.]

Here's half Glasgow in to see you, and it the back end of midnight. It's a mercy you're away to-morrow.

TOM. Good evening to you. Is Miss Unthank at home?

UNTHANK. She is most emphatically not at home— to anyone—at this hour of the night. I am surprised at you!

TOM. Our business with Miss Unthank is very urgent and private.

UNTHANK. Get out of here.

TOM. Don't shout at me.

MARY. Please, Major Unthank, it's really awfully important. We simply can't go until we've seen Margaret.

UNTHANK. You simply must go, the whole pack of you. I have had pretty nearly more than I can bear to-night.

TOM. You listen to me . . .

MARY. Oh, Tom, do shut up. Harry, you speak to him. Major Unthank, we will not leave this house till we have seen Margaret. There now.

UNTHANK. Then I shall call up the police and have you removed.

SMELLIE. Fine. That's fine. I want a word or two wi' the police myself. Call up the police, Unthank. You were in an awful hurry to do it a minute ago.

[ELLEN, *in a dressing-gown, peers in at the door.*]

UNTHANK. Miss O'Hanlon, do be reasonable. My niece has gone to bed. She has a long journey before her. I shall give her any message you would like to leave. Now, do please go away. I am very tired and harassed.

MRS. SYME. You stick to your p'int, my lady. Never you mind his wheedling.

SMELLIE. And I'll tell you another thing. She's not gone to bed. She was going out a minute ago.

TOM (*in a bull-like bellow*). Miss Margaret!

MARY and HARRY (*more self-consciously*). Margaret!

[*They repeat this, like the Forsaken Merman's Children, once or twice.*]

SMELLIE. Margaret!

[MARGARET *shoots from the door* L. *like a stone from a catapult. Someone has obviously been detaining her.* MRS. UNTHANK *follows.*]

MRS. UNTHANK. Margaret! Richard, she struck me!

UNTHANK. Oh, shut up!

MARGARET. What do you want?

TOM. Calm yourself, Miss Margaret. It's all right now. It's all right now.

MARGARET. Please don't say "It's all right," as if I had had a fit in a tram-car. Mary, tell me. What are you doing here?

MARY. My mother used to say . . .

[280]

MARGARET. I never knew you had a mother.

MARY. Oh, yes, I had.

MARGARET. How funny! I didn't know.

MARY. Well, you might have known. But that isn't the point. You see, dear, we've come to rescue you.

MARGARET. Oh, thank you very much—but how?

HARRY. I knew it would be very difficult to explain.

UNTHANK. Exceedingly difficult. Nobody appreciates a good rag more than I do, but this is going too far. One doesn't expect too much from artistic people, but there are boundaries between civilisation and savagery. You (to HARRY) are uncivilised, sir.

HARRY. Oh, no, no, Major Unthank. I am very, very civilised.

TOM. Nobody gives a docken whether you're civilised or not.

MARGARET. I think I'll laugh or faint or squeal or do something desperate in a minute. Mary, for God's sake!

MRS. SYME. One, two, three, four, five, six, seven, eight. There's seats enough for all of you. Sit down. Ellen, you besom, awa' to your bed.

> [All sit down. Exit ELLEN. There is a good deal of difficulty about sitting down, as there aren't really eight seats. SMELLIE, who is not yet sober, though a long way in that direction, is the pink of embarrassing politeness.]

(To TOM, on her right). It's been a nice evening for the time of year.

TOM. Yes, but cold. Perishing cold.

MRS. SYME. At your time of life you should wear a newspaper in the back of your waistcoat. It protects the kidneys.

TOM. Oh, leave my kidneys alone, ma'am. Let's get to the point.

MRS. SYME. I never touched your kidneys, and am

[281]

hotching to hear what the point is. It looks to me like you're a' daft.

TOM (*rising*). Madam, I am Thomas Garscadden, a poor painter, but not ill-spoken of in this town. I take leave to tell you . . .

MRS. SYME. You would ken my Alec, Mr. Syme. He was a painter, and a decorator too.

TOM. Madam, I am a painter but not a decorator.

UNTHANK. This is the most farcical situation I ever took part in! (*To* HARRY) Yes, sir. God knows you don't look a gentleman, but you look almost intelligent. What the devil do you mean by bringing your lady artists and plumbers and postmen into my house at this time of night?

HARRY. Ah, postmen! That's it. Mary, I really think you'd better let me speak. You have no tact. Major Unthank, this is Mr. Stewart. We have brought him here to introduce him to Margaret. When we have introduced him to Margaret we want a little private and intimate conversation—just Mr. Stewart and Margaret and Mary O'Hanlon and Mr. Garscadden and me—and, of course, you and Mrs. Unthank, if you like. And —and—any of your friends who like to join in. Margaret, may I introduce Mr. Stewart.

STEWART. How do you do, Miss Unthank. I hope you are very well.

MARGARET. Yes. Quite well, thank you.

STEWART. I am very glad to hear it.

MRS. UNTHANK. I may be very stupid, but if this is supposed to be funny, I must say I fail to appreciate it.

UNTHANK. Well, my man, will you say what you have got to say; give your message, whatever it is, and clear out?

STEWART. I will, sir. I have the great privilege to ask for permission to pay my respectful addresses to your niece, Miss Unthank.

MRS. UNTHANK. Oh, how terrible! He has been drinking.

UNTHANK.   I shall make a point of seeing the Postmaster first thing to-morrow.   First thing.   Now, take yourself off.

STEWART.   Madam, I have not been drinking.   I am a teetotaller.

UNTHANK.   There is the door.   Get out at once, if you don't want to be thrown downstairs.

STEWART.   I have never been thrown downstairs.   I do not know whether I should be liking it or not.   But you, sir, would not find it easy to throw me downstairs, whatever.

UNTHANK.   You are an impudent blackguard!

STEWART (*taking off his coat*).   Oh, dear me!   That was a very foolish thing to be calling the Amateur Cruiser Weight Champion of Scotland.   Indeed, very foolish. (*To his coat*) Lie there, servant of the General Post Office.   Now, sir.   Will you most kindly take back that word?

UNTHANK.   !!!!!!

MARGARET.   Mr. Stewart, you mustn't hit my uncle.

STEWART.   I did not intend to hit him in your presence, Miss Unthank.   I am going to carry him into the street, and there I will hit him.   I will not hit him very hard, because he is your uncle.

UNTHANK.   Call that madman off, somebody!

MRS. SYME.   Come, come now.   There's to be no fighting in my house.

STEWART.   There will be no bloodshed in the presence of delicately-nurtured ladies.   I have already said that I will transport him into the street.

TOM.   Now, now, Stewart.   You'll lose your job.

STEWART.   My job!   What care I for my job!

MRS. SYME.   Oh, hold your tongue, you daft Heilanman!   Sit down, do you hear me?   If you've something to say to the man, can you not say it without hitting him in the eye first?

STEWART.   With all respect to you, ma'am, I have no

[283]

wish to converse with the gentleman but with a pair of fists. He has put an insult on me. (*Sits down.*)

MRS. SYME. Aweel, you can just tell me what you want, for it's time we were a' in oor beds.

STEWART (*standing up again*). I have no gift of language to explain what I mean. But I will try whatever. In the old days a humble wooer could come at his lady's love by a little here and a little there over days and nights and weeks and months, till she said, " I'll have you." And he would then lift her from under the dirks of her kinsmen and away they would go. But in these days there is no time. I must lift her from under the dirks of her kinsmen, and later, if it is in the bountifulness of Heaven, come at her love. There is not time to be delicate nor to hint nor to advance and to retire nor to set to partners. . . . Miss Unthank, I have the greatest pleasure in asking you to accept the hospitality of my auntie. My auntie is a Macintosh of Kinrara. If you do not wish to accept that, this lady, Miss O'Hanlon, will give you shelter. You will be so very kind as to pay no attention to what your uncle says or to what your aunt says. You will follow, if you please, your own judgments and desires. I will take the liberty of seeing that no one prevents you from doing whatever it is that you wish. If after you have left this house of captivity, you wish that you should never see me again, you will never see me again—neither you nor the Postmaster nor nobody else. That is all I have to say.

MARGARET. Well. Thank you very much, Mr.— Mr.——

STEWART. Mister Stewart, ma'am.

MARGARET. Thank you very much, Mr. Stewart. I appreciate your kindness very much indeed.

MRS. UNTHANK. I really haven't the slightest idea what Government employees will do next. Do you seriously propose that my niece should go to-night to the slum-dwelling of your frightful aunt——

STEWART. She is one of the Macintoshes of Kinrara.

MRS. UNTHANK. I don't care if she is one of the Burberries of Dunhills. The thing is out of the question. I had no idea Margaret had such common tastes.

STEWART. If you are suggesting, ma'am, that your niece has ever condescended to address a word to me in her life before this night, you are wrong. She has not seen me before, nor I have not seen her. Only her picture, and that was by a lady artist.

MRS. UNTHANK. That is quite enough. Margaret, go to your room.

MARGARET. But, Aunt Annie . . .

MRS. UNTHANK. I have borne quite enough.

TOM. Miss Margaret . . .

MARY. Margaret . . .

MRS. UNTHANK. Come, Margaret. Not another word.

MARGARET. Mary, I know it's feeble of me. But I can't.

MRS. UNTHANK. Come.

[*Exeunt* MARGARET *and* MRS. UNTHANK. *Silence.*]

MRS. SYME. Aweel. I'll away to bed. I'm getting an old woman.

[*She opens the door, and finds* ELLEN *listening behind it.*]

Out o' this house you go to-morrow, you impudent besom!

[*Exit, scolding.*]

TOM. There doesn't seem to be anything more to say. I wish you a very good night, sir.

[*He stamps out.*]

MARY. Major Unthank, if you knew what I think of you . . .

[285]

HARRY. I'm sure he knows, Mary. Don't let's wait.

[*They go.*

STEWART *heaves a monstrous sigh, and slowly resumes his coat. He looks at* SMELLIE, *who has fallen asleep, and then bends on* UNTHANK *a majestic eye.* UNTHANK *cringes. After a rapid glance at* MARGARET'S *door,* STEWART *goes.*

UNTHANK *is irresolute as to what to do with* SMELLIE. *He decides to leave him alone, and turns out the lights.*]

CURTAIN

ACT III

*Same as Act II. Four or five hours later. A grey light is filter-
ing through the window. A milk-boy outside whistles in a
piercing fashion and clatters his cans.*

[SMELLIE *awakes; staggers to the window; pulls up the
blind; finds it is not yet daylight; helps himself to
some soda-water.*]

SMELLIE. Well. Well. Well. Well. Well. Well. Ha!
My note-case! One, two, three. An expensive kind of
an evening for you, Bob. Well, it'll be a lesson. Oh,
mother, my head, my head! (*Sits down in an attitude of
dejection.*)

[*To him* MARGARET, *dressed for going out. She carries an
attaché-case. She switches on the light.*]

MARGARET. Oh!

SMELLIE. Good morning.

MARGARET. What a fright you gave me! Good
morning.

SMELLIE. Don't mind me. I'm just going. What
time is it?

MARGARET. About half-past five.

SMELLIE. A.m. or p.m.?

MARGARET. A.m.

SMELLIE. Bed-time. I'd better be getting home.

MARGARET. Yes. I—we thought you had gone long
ago.

SMELLIE. Once you'd skinned me, I thought you
didn't give me a thought.

MARGARET. Skinned you?

SMELLIE. Yes. Mademoiselle from Armenteers.

[287]

Skinned me. Of course it was all a plant, but the funniest plant that ever grew. I've half a mind not to go to the Procurator Fiscal after all.

MARGARET. The Procurator Fiscal?

SMELLIE. Never heard of him, I suppose? He's the little fellow who puts blackmailers and conspirators and other crooks, however charming, into the nick, quod or chink.

MARGARET. Oh!

SMELLIE. Yes. Oh! (*He goes to the window and pulls up the blind.*) Hello! It looks as if I'd be saved the trouble.

MARGARET. What do you mean?

SMELLIE. There's a man watching the house.

MARGARET. Oh! (*Goes to the window.*) It's the Postman.

SMELLIE (*rubbing his eyes*). By Gemini, so it is! The Postman. Let me think. My head! My head!

MARGARET. Now, I really *must* go!

SMELLIE (*seizing her wrist*). Stop a bit. What was put in my drinks last night?

MARGARET. Oh, *do* let me go. You'll wake everybody up.

STEWART (*from the street*). Let go that lady!

SMELLIE. Hello! Jolly Jack the Sailor!

[STEWART's *head and shoulders appear over the sill. He scrambles into the room.*

SMELLIE *has not released* MARGARET's *wrist, so* STEWART *twists his arm behind him and pushes him across the room. He then folds* MARGARET *to his bosom.*]

STEWART. What is it now, then, what is it, my lovely?

MARGARET. Well. I couldn't sleep . . .

STEWART. Have you tried a hot mustard foot-bath? My Auntie says it's fine.

MARGARET. Oh, is it? I must try it. I often can't sleep.

STEWART. Well, you try it. But I was interrupting you.

MARGARET. And then, all of a sudden, I felt I couldn't stand it. Going to Kuala Lumpur, I mean.

STEWART. Of course you couldn't, my little white love.

MARGARET. Oh, but look here, you mustn't call me that. (*She breaks away.*) Do sit down, Mr. Stewart.

STEWART. One moment, please, till I put this gentleman out. Or is it your wish that I should first give him a sound beating?

MARGARET. No. No. No. The poor gentleman has suffered enough already. Please go away, Mr.— Mr.——

SMELLIE. Smellie.

MARGARET. Mr. Smellie. Call again, would you? I'm quite sure my uncle will be able to explain the misunderstanding.

SMELLIE. I should think explaining is your uncle's strong card.

STEWART. Will you have the kindness to keep your tongue off this lady's uncle, or any of her other relatives, and take yourself off.

SMELLIE. All right, all right, Postie. Good morning, miss. I can't make any promise. I can hardly speak, much less think. Don't touch me, damn you!

[*Exit.*]
[*A pause.*]

STEWART. Where were you going, so early in the morning?

MARGARET. Were you standing out there all night?

STEWART. I was. Where were you going so early in the morning?

MARGARET. Oh, why did you stand there all night?

STEWART. Because my heart is full of you. Where were you going so early in the morning?

[289]

MARGARET. I don't know. Over the edge of the world, I think.

STEWART. It is dark and lonely over the edge of the world.

MARGARET. Is it? Oh, is it?

STEWART. Yes.

[*A pause.*]

Margaret, would you be thinking . . . maybe—I'm a postman and you are a bright lady. But—I thought— if . . .

MARGARET. I don't know what you mean.

STEWART (*laughing*). Fine you know what I mean, though I wish I could find more facility in expressing it. For my own sake, whatever.

MARGARET. You are one of the queerest ever I saw.

STEWART. Yes. I'm queer. They say up in Salen that I'm a fairy.

MARGARET. A what?

STEWART. A fairy.

MARGARET. But I thought fairies were all—I mean, that they were all ladies, to begin with.

STEWART. Maybe, it is so. I never pay any attention to old wives' stories, whatever. But they say one autumn night the wee folk walked round and round my father's croft, widdershins, crying like grasshoppers, and in the morning there was a bairn that was the image of the bairn that was there before; but it was not the bairn. There was something queer and clever in its eyes.

MARGARET. I'm afraid of you.

STEWART. Och, it was all clashmaclaver. Look You see nothing queer and clever in my eyes now?

MARGARET. No.

STEWART. What do you see in my eyes now?

MARGARET. I don't know.

STEWART. Does it make you feared or glad?

MARGARET. Both feared and glad.

[*They embrace.*
Enter ELLEN, *with a pail and brushes for the fireplace.*
She lets them fall.
STEWART *speaks to her angrily in the Gaelic.*
ELLEN *replies in the Gaelic, with a kind of pert humility.*
STEWART *laughs, and speaks jovial Gaelic.*
ELLEN *laughs too, and speaks coy Gaelic.*]

STEWART. I ask your pardon, Margaret. I forgot you had no Gaelic. Miss Robertson is from our part of the country.

ELLEN. I sought you were going for to be a minister in Glasgow. And here you are a Postie. Well, well. I did not recognise you when first you came, forbye I was chust a wee girl when you left Salen.

STEWART. Oh, dear me, they wouldn't make a minister of a fairy, whatever.

ELLEN. It is a great pity you were not a minister, so prettily you talk.

STEWART. Well, now, I can tell you no lie, but a minister I will be, come March.

ELLEN. Your auntie will be very glad. No indeed, yes.

STEWART. It is true I will be a minister. It will be all right then for you to marry a minister, Margaret?

MARGARET. But I thought you were a postman.

STEWART. I greatly fear I will not be a postman much longer after to-day. But och! I am not caring, whatever.

MARGARET. But why are you a postman?

STEWART. We were aye ones to be independent, our family. My father was the schoolmaster at Salen, and he walked himself through the college as a surfaceman. And I tell you there are some surfacemen on the railway are a gey rough lot. And you will not find a rough postman in all the length and breadth of Scotland, no indeed.

ELLEN. And that is a true word, indeed, Miss

[291]

Margaret. Posties was aye the most gentle of all the
callings.   It is not like tramwaymen or pollis.   Coarse,
coarse, but kind-hearted if you know them.

MARGARET.   Yes, now, that's very true, Ellen.   I
never thought of that before.   It must be handling all
that correspondence.   And yet it can't be.   Look at
post-office girls.

ELLEN.   Very haughty and proud are post-office girls.

MARGARET.   Oh, they are, aren't they?   And those.
leather things they wear on their arms!

ELLEN.   I think it will be that in every walk of life the
men are aye the nicest.

MARGARET.   Now, I hardly think that.   Oh, no,
that's not quite true.   If you take actors and actresses,
now . . .

ELLEN.   I have, very little acquaintance with the
theatricals.

MARGARET.   We used to meet quite a lot in Hull.
Uncle knew lots of all sorts of people.   But I say, it
seems so funny talking like this at half-past five in the
morning.

ELLEN.   It's the fairy's fault.

MARGARET.   The fairy?

ELLEN.   Aye.   Him.   (*She indicates* STEWART.)
Wherever he went in Salen, all the folk grew queer-like
when the fairy tinker made the minister and the kirk
session all dance to his fiddle.

STEWART.   Now don't you be telling Miss Unthank
these immoral old bawrs.

ELLEN.   It is no bawr, whatever.   Hoo, hoo.   It is
the bonny minister you will make in your gown and your
bands.

STEWART.   I will make a very good minister.   I am
very eloquent.

ELLEN.   I do not know what is " elephant," but do not
birse up at me, whatever.   I know you, John Stewart.

STEWART.   I wish that you a little better knew your

[292]

place.　She is a decent girl, Miss Unthank, but foolish, foolish.

MARGARET.　Oh, I don't think so at all.

ELLEN.　Foolish!　Listen at him, who comes blusting and fighting into a strange house in the evening, and then creepy-creeping in at the window in the dawning!　That is foolish, I promise you.

STEWART.　And it is very foolish to stand here havering and waking up all the household.　Here is the light of day coming shyly up the terrace.　Madame, will you come with me?

MARGARET.　Oh, yes.　I will.　I will.

STEWART.　Very well, then.　(*To* ELLEN) Will you make a noise like the hammers of Hell with your mop and pail, that they may not hear us open the front door?

ELLEN.　Indeed and I will.

STEWART.　Oh, God, I cannot say what is in my heart!

MARGARET.　Can't you?

STEWART.　Would it do if I were to rouse your uncle and give him a beating?

MARGARET.　No.　No.　No.

STEWART.　Or just to talk to him?　I could find words for him.

MARGARET.　I'm sure you could. . . . Oh!

STEWART.　What is it, O my white darling?

MARGARET.　It's just . . . I was going to . . . I was going to say your Christian name, and I suddenly remembered I didn't know it.

STEWART.　It is John, Margaret.

MARGARET.　Not Ian, or anything of that sort?

STEWART.　It is not Ian, but John.　The sons of grocers are called Ian.　I am Ian in the Gaelic but John in the English.

ELLEN.　Body of me, are you two going to stay here for breakfast?

STEWART.　You are quite right, Ellen.　Come, Margaret.

U　　　　　　　[293]

[*He takes her respectfully by the arm, but she clings,
  stumbles, and the thing becomes an embrace.*
Enter UNTHANK, *in pyjamas, carrying a revolver.*
ELLEN *screams and runs out.*]

UNTHANK. Well?

[*They face him.*]

Is this your idea, Margaret, of how a nice girl should
behave?

MARGARET. Yes, it is.

UNTHANK. Well, it isn't mine. By gum, it isn't
mine!

MARGARET. I think your ideas are rotten. What do
you know about nice girls or nice anyone else? I'm
going to marry Mr. Stewart.

UNTHANK. The postman?

MARGARET. Well, he's a clergyman, really.

UNTHANK. Oh, is he?

STEWART. I will be ordained, sir, in a very short
while.

UNTHANK. Then God help your parish!

STEWART. I shall incessantly ask Him to do so.

MARGARET. And you stop sneering at Ian—I mean
John—because I won't have it.

UNTHANK. Oh, you won't, won't you?

MARGARET. No, I won't. He's far, far better than
you are. He lives by working and you live by cheating.

UNTHANK. I say, you are brightening up, Madge!
However, joking apart and fun's fun and all that sort of
thing, your clerical-postal friend had better clear out,
if he doesn't want a bullet in him.

STEWART. I am afraid of no bullets.

UNTHANK. How brave of you. Now we know that,
be good enough to go away.

STEWART. If you had a battery of howitzers and a
regiment of cavalry at your back I would kill you with
my two hands rather than you should keep Margaret.

UNTHANK. Buzz off, Ian.

STEWART. You are just a silly old man.

MARGARET. Darling, he'll shoot at you! He's killed a man before.

[*With a rapid movement,* STEWART *lets fly a vase at* MAJOR UNTHANK. *It hits him amidships. The revolver goes off.* UNTHANK *falls.* STEWART *makes a Douglas Fairbanks leap at him, turns him over and puts on a half-Nelson.*]

STEWART. You would shoot, would you?

UNTHANK. Damn you, let go! Damn you, you've half killed me!

[*Enter severally* MRS. UNTHANK, MRS. SYME *and* ELLEN.]

MRS. SYME. In the name of goodness, what is all this?

MRS. UNTHANK (*rushing at* STEWART *and pulling his hair*). Let go at once, will you!

STEWART. Ouch!

MARGARET. Oh, darling, please let him up. He'll promise not to shoot again. Do promise, Uncle darling!

UNTHANK. Of course, I promise.

[*The parties disengage.*]

MRS. UNTHANK. What is all this?

STEWART. It was to be a swift and silent elopement. Two lovers stealing away at dawn. It was nearly a horrible murder.

UNTHANK. Oh, don't be frightened. I never meant to hit you.

STEWART. It was you who was nearly murdered.

UNTHANK. By gum! I believe you're right.

STEWART. I am very seldom wrong. Sir, I have the honour to ask you for the hand of your niece.

UNTHANK. Wait a minute. You half throttled me. That's better. Are you, then, able to support my niece in the position to which she has been accustomed?

STEWART. Sir, I lack the elasticity of conscience to do so. But if she is willing to become the wife of a parish minister, she will be supported in that very respectable position.

MRS. UNTHANK.   Of the Church of Scotland?

STEWART.   Of the Church of Scotland.

MRS. UNTHANK.   Well, that's something, anyhow.

MARGARET.   Oh, Uncle, he's been so lovely about it. Asking you, and all that.

UNTHANK.   He has.

MARGARET.   It'd be so much nicer if you said "Yes."

UNTHANK.   Sir, I have a proposition to make to you.

STEWART.   Sir, I am prepared to listen.

UNTHANK.   Sir, you would be wasted on the Church.

STEWART.   I do not think so.   Even as a student I have been highly appreciated.

UNTHANK.   I have no doubt of that.

STEWART.   I thank you.   What is your proposition?

UNTHANK.   Sir, if you will permit me to be your agent, I shall feel very proud.   You have a career in front of you.

STEWART.   Well?

UNTHANK.   Look at yourself.   At your face.   Your features.   Your way of tossing a vase.   Your leap on a prostrate foe.   In the Talkies.   I have some influence there.   Are you willing?

STEWART.   You'll pardon me asking, but what is your own profession?

UNTHANK.   I am an undischarged bankrupt.   And a damned good profession too.

STEWART (*with a laugh*).   Well, one thing or another. It is all one to me.   I will be what my lady here wishes me to be.   No more nor no less.

MARGARET.   But Movie stars divorce each other.

STEWART.   I do not blame you for being indecent. It is the fault of your upbringing and associations.   But after a little while with me and my auntie you will be more circumspect in your talk. . . . Sir, we will talk of this later. But I forget. You are going to Kuala Lumpur.

UNTHANK. Not necessarily. Oh, by Jove, not necessarily. Look here, lunch with me, will you ? At the Central. But—if you don't mind—not in uniform. At one o'clock.

STEWART. At one o'clock. Now, Margaret, we shall go.

UNTHANK. But that isn't necessary.

MRS. UNTHANK. I can't consent to it for a moment.

MRS. SYME. Ach, haud your tongue.

UNTHANK. Mr. Stewart will do whatever he likes, Annie. You don't understand him yet. He hasn't half-strangled you.

MRS. UNTHANK. I should like to see him try !

MRS. SYME. Nae doubt ye would, but your days for that kin' o' thing is past.

MRS. UNTHANK. Hold your tongue, woman.

MRS. SYME. The same to you, and many of them.

UNTHANK. Be quiet, both of you. One o'clock at the Central ? Good morning, then. Bring Margaret.

STEWART. Good morning to you. I will.

MARGARET. Listen. I'll wait. I'm not afraid of them now.

[*The young couple go to the door. They embrace.* UNTHANK *pulls the window-curtains apart.*]

UNTHANK. Came the dawn.

[*Picture.*]
[*A pause.*]

Good lord ! who's this ? (*He is looking out of the window.*)

[*The door-bell rings.*]

Margaret, here is one of your friends. Upon my Sam, who do they think you are ? Coming to your levée at six o'clock in the morning ! Madame du Barry, or what ?

[*Enter* ELLEN, *followed by* TOM.]

[297]

ELLEN. Mr. Gamstooken.

TOM. Good morning. Your servant, **madam**.

MRS. UNTHANK. You are an early riser, Mr. Garscadden.

TOM. I couldn't sleep. You'll maybe think it odd of me to call at this hour of the morning, but I've always been a sort of chap like that. When I make up my mind . . .

UNTHANK. Do you often pop in at six to recite bits of your autobiography, Mr. Garscadden ?

TOM. No. And you may as well have it plump and plain—Miss Unthank is not to go to Kuala Lumpur.

UNTHANK. And why not ?

TOM. Because, if she will have me, I'd like to marry her.

MRS. UNTHANK. When I was a girl I once had two proposals within half-an-hour, but *not* at this hour of the morning.

MRS. SYME. No, they'd have time to sober up.

MRS. UNTHANK. You are an incredibly vulgar old woman.

MRS. SYME. You're a story-telling besom.

MRS. UNTHANK. Will you kindly be quiet ?

MRS. SYME. I'll be quiet when I like in my ain hoose.

MRS. UNTHANK. This may be your " ain hoose," but that gives you no right to interfere in private matters . . .

MRS. SYME. Private ! Ho !

MARGARET. Do shut up, Auntie. Well, Mr. Garscadden ?

TOM. Margaret. Will you—could you marry an old boy like me ? I can still walk my twenty miles a day.

UNTHANK. You've been forestalled, I think, even in pedestrianism. The postman !

TOM (*noticing* STEWART *for the first time*). Oh, you're here, are you ? I thought you'd turned tail.

STEWART. No, sir, I have not turned tail.

[298]

TOM. Weel. My offer still stands. I'm not a bad painter. I was a big man in the Glasgow School before half the young pups you hear of nowadays were out of their hippens. I sell a picture now and again to a blasted profiteer who wants to make money on it when I'm dead. Lassie, will ye have me ?

MARGARET. I'm very sorry, Mr. Garscadden. It's awfully sweet of you. But it's really out of pity for me, isn't it, and so on ?

[Bell rings.]

TOM. No. Honest to God, it isn't. I've been thinking about you all night, and you'd suit me fine. And, believe me, it's the old boys that make the best husbands.

MARGARET. Well, I mean to say . . . As I say, it's awfully nice of you. But really . . . Anyhow, I'm afraid I'm fixed up already.

[Enter ELLEN, with HARRY.]

ELLEN. A gentleman to see you, Miss Margaret.

HARRY. Margaret, I couldn't sleep . . .

UNTHANK. This wave of insomnia has swept the city.

HARRY. Margaret, I love you.

MARGARET. Oh ! . . . Do you ?

HARRY. Yes, I do. Don't interrupt. . . . Margaret, I've been through Hell. It's worried me so much that it's made me pull up my socks for once—do something definite. It shows what a good influence you'd be in my life. I mean, what does anything matter ? Will you marry me ?

MARGARET. No.

HARRY. Oh ! . . . But we understand each other so well, don't you think ? You're such a sympathetic type. And so am I really, though you'd think I was a bit egocentric.

MARGARET. Oh, I'm sure you're not egocentric.

HARRY. Well, all this shows I'm not, doesn't it ?

[299]

You can't be romantic and egocentric, can you? I say, isn't there any hope? I mean, you understand me so well. You penetrate right into the heart of things.

[*Bell rings.*]

There's the morning milk. Doesn't that fill you with immortal longings?

MRS. SYME.   You can keep your breath to cool your porridge. The postie's got her.

HARRY.   Oh, has he? Well, I do honestly congratulate you, Mister, if she doesn't change her mind at the last minute. I wish I had been quicker in making up mine.

[*Enter* ELLEN, *almost hysterical, with* SMELLIE. *He still wears his dinner-jacket.*]

ELLEN.   Here's another, Miss Margaret.

UNTHANK.   Well, what do you want?

SMELLIE.   I've got nothing to say to you. I know your sort.

MRS. UNTHANK.   Why have you come here?

SMELLIE.   I have come to rescue this decent young girl from worse than death.

MARGARET.   But nobody said Kuala Lumpur was worse than death, Mr.——

SMELLIE.   Smellie.

MARGARET.   Mr. Smellie.

SMELLIE.   I was not referring to Kuala Lumpur. As a matter of fact, I think Kuala Lumpur was a plant.

TOM.   It's a place.

SMELLIE.   Damn it, I know that.

TOM.   Don't swear at me.

HARRY.   He isn't swearing at you, Mr. Garscadden.

MARGARET.   John.

STEWART.   What is it, my white love?

MARGARET.   Let's go and have breakfast somewhere.

STEWART.   And where, now, will we go for that same

breakfast, the two of us? For there is not a hotel in all the regions of the whole world that I can see fine enough for yourself. Unless it would be in Oban.

MARGARET. But listen. We can't possibly be in Oban in time for breakfast. Can't they give us a decent breakfast in Argyll Street, somewhere?

STEWART. They will have to, whatever.

[*They go out, gazing into each other's eyes, oblivious of aunts, uncles, Bohemians and busybodies.*]

CURTAIN